DYNAMIC PROTOTYPING WITH SKETCHFLOW IN EXPRESSION BLEND

*SKETCH YOUR IDEAS...
AND BRING THEM TO LIFE!*

Chris Bernard and Sara Summers

800 East 96th Street, Indianapolis, Indiana 46240 USA

Dynamic Prototyping with SketchFlow in Expression Blend

Copyright © 2010 by Pearson Education, Inc.

ISBN-13: 978-0-7897-4279-7
ISBN-10: 0-7897-4279-9

Library of Congress Cataloging-in-Publication Data:

Bernard, Chris (Christopher M.)

  Dynamic prototyping with SketchFlow in Expression blend : sketch your ideas--and bring them to life / Chris Bernard and Sara Summers.

     p. cm.

  ISBN 978-0-7897-4279-7

1. Microsoft Expression blend. 2. Graphical user interfaces (Computer systems) 3. Web sites--Authoring programs. 4. Web sites--Design. I. Summers, Sara. II. Title.

  QA76.9.U83B485 2010

  005.4'376--dc22

                    2010001973

Printed in the United States of America

Second Printing: April 2010

Associate Publisher
Greg Wiegand

Acquisitions Editor
Loretta Yates

Development Editor
Kevin Howard

Technical Editor
Branden Hall

Managing Editor
Kristy Hart

Project Editor
Jovana San Nicolas-Shirley

Copy Editor
Water Crest Publishing

Indexer
Erika Millen

Proofreader
Kathy Ruiz

Publishing Coordinator
Cindy Teeters

Interior Designers
Sara Summers
Chris Bernard

Cover Designer
Sara Summers

Cover Coordinator
Ann Jones

Compositor
Gloria Schurick

Trademarks

Warning and Disclaimer

Bulk Sales

Que Publishing offers excellent discounts on this book when ordered in quantity for bulk purchases or special sales. For more information, please contact

  U.S. Corporate and Government Sales
  1-800-382-3419
  corpsales@pearsontechgroup.com

For sales outside of the U.S., please contact

  International Sales
  international@pearson.com

CONTENTS AT A GLANCE

TABLE OF CONTENTS

FOREWORD

There is a funny paradox in design. We often think that what we are trying to overcome are bad ideas and bad design. But actually, I don't see that as the real problem. After all, those ideas and designs should be easy to address by a competent designer. No, in my opinion, the real "enemy" is just the opposite: not bad design and ideas, but great design and ideas. In fact, the better the idea, the bigger the problem that it presents. Let me explain.

Bad ideas and design are generally relatively easy to displace. However, great ideas of the past get serious traction...and deservedly so. They then get entrenched, and with that, their establishment carries with it a huge inertia—an inertia that continues well past the "due date" of the original idea.

One such example is the basic WIMP (windows, icon, menu, pointing) interface that was developed in the 1970s, and that made its commercial debut with the Xerox Star 8010 workstation in 1981. The WIMP, or graphical user interface (GUI), was a brilliant innovation that built on at least 20 years of research, flowing from MIT's Lincoln Lab and the Stanford Research Institute, through Xerox PARC. What it did was bring us into a world where computers not only started to work, but could be used by mere mortals like you, me—and more to the point—our parents, our grandparents, and our children. This was a great idea for its time. No wonder it took hold—thank goodness it did.

However, this strong hold—although welcome at the time—creates all the bigger problem for the software engineer, designer, and most importantly, the end user of today and tomorrow. The problem is that in the interim, technology, design, and needs have not stood still. Yet, to a very large extent, the inertia of the whole ecosystem around this past success has constrained our ability to deliver on the full potential of these more recent insights and innovations. Users were used to a way of doing things, schools were set up to teach the established way of building things, and professionals—who were always under pressure to deliver—tended to rely upon what they knew in order to deliver what was asked for. Things were complex and expensive, so taking a risk on new ideas and approaches was, understandably, not the norm. In short, the normal tendency is to approach the future looking in the rear-view mirror, rather than through the windshield.

And yet…. New ideas and designs did emerge, much in the same way that the concepts underlying the WIMP/GUI design emerged in an earlier era. And, along with the awareness that emerged, came a growing aspiration for a different way of working and for a different kind of experience. In essence, the field had started to mature. Just as civil engineers are not cheered because their bridges let you cross the river and don't fall down, it was no longer impressive or adequate that things actually worked and were usable. These are things that competent engineers and designers should be able to deliver if they deem themselves to be professionals, and are things that consumers and end users should be able to take for granted. That is where we are in our industry now. Things kind of work, they are kind of usable, and we, like our civil engineering counterparts, are kind of professional.

But that is not enough. Not by a long shot.

We can do better, and our customers deserve better. The frontier has shifted from making things work and be usable, to a place where those things are delivered economically, and with an outstanding user experience—one that reflects the task, the user, and the social/physical context. The bad news is that to deliver this, we have to overcome the engrained inertia of the WIMP/GUI elephant that lies in the room. The good news is, just as there were 20+ years underlying the emergence of those concepts, so is there for the technologies that are going to enable us to move beyond this heretofore entrenched *status quo*.

And that is what brings us to this book and what it represents.

It is naïve to assume that an established technology or idea is going to be displaced magically by some great new idea. The history of technology—captured in what I call "The Long Nose of Innovation"—simply does not reflect that. Things take time—typically 20 years—to get established. (Even the mouse, which was an obviously great idea, took 30 years to get broadly established!) Now, for anything to happen, at least two criteria need to be met, as follows:

1. There has to be a real problem and real value resulting from its solution.

2. There has to be a reasonable cost/benefit relationship.

The problem, as I see it, is the limitations on our ability to deliver the quality of user experience imposed by the existing tools, techniques, and practice. In a nutshell, the value, and a key component of the quality experience that we aspire for, is grounded in improving the dynamic flow and behavior of our designs—to recognize and build on the notion that the modalities used and the transitions within our interactions are prime ingredients in shaping the experience. The designs that result need to work in a way that—at the same time—are consistent with our expectations, given the technology used, who we are, what we are doing, why, and where, and yet still surprise and delight.

Achieving that is what will lead us from the frontier into the next, more refined, stage in the evolution of our industry.

But if that is the value, how do we make it happen? How do we establish the eco-system that enables us to achieve the needed cost/benefit balance? It seems to me that there are at least three ingredients necessary if we are to have the chance of displacing an established great idea of the past:

1. **A foundation of research and ideas** on which to build, which have been sufficiently refined to be ready for prime time—to be rendered into wide-spread practice.

2. **A set of tools** that enables practitioners to render into practice these new concepts, without having to start from scratch—that is, it is just as important to pay attention to the computer-developer interface as it is to the computer-user interface.

3. **Training resources** that do everything possible to help developers and designers through the transition from the old to the new, in terms of knowing how to understand the ideas and use the tools.

What excites me about where we are in the industry, in general, and with this book, specifically, is that we are at an inflection point that I have dreamed about for a long time.

First, I know that there is at least 20 years of research that informs the transition that we are in the process of making. I have been in the thick of it personally and have seen what has been done at a number or academic and industrial labs.

Second, with tools like SketchFlow, we finally have an enabler that not only lets us spend as much time designing transitions as it does screen shots, it lets us do so in a designerly way—by sketching—that enables us to explore a range of different designs before committing to any one of them. Thus, the path is set to enable us to not only get the design right, but to get the right design.

And last, but not least, we have resources like this book that greatly facilitate the ability of designers to acquire the requisite skills to take advantage of these 20+ years of research, and the resulting tools, and deliver the great potential that lies within their power.

Chris and Sara are uniquely positioned to do this book. Not only are they great teachers, writers, and UX practitioners, they live in this world where, on the one hand, they have access to some of the most creative UX designers in the world. On the other hand, they have direct access to the engineering team that built SketchFlow, Blend, and so on, and many of the researchers who helped develop many of the underlying concepts. Taken together, what this means is that the book that they have produced goes far beyond mere enhanced documentation. Their concern is not so much what button to push to do what in using the tool; rather, it is understanding the underlying concepts. In short, it is about design and the implications on design of the tools covered.

I welcome this book and what it represents. But most of all, I welcome the inspired designs that will stem from it. It is a really welcome addition to my desk—not just my bookshelf!

—Bill Buxton

Principal Researcher, Microsoft Research

ABOUT THE AUTHORS

Chris Bernard is a 17-year veteran of the design and technology industry. He is a passionate advocate for advancing the practice and discipline of innovation at the intersection of design, technology, and business.

Sara Summers is a 13-year veteran of the design industry. She has a personal mantra of design democracy—happy, healthy designers and developers working and playing together to create beautiful, inspirational products.

DEDICATION

This book is dedicated to my parents. They've instilled in me a sense of curiosity and optimism that I use every day, fighting the words of the cynical or those who say "It can't be done." This book is dedicated to my family, Christine, Ben, Ellie, and Erin, for giving me the patience and support to write this book. This book is dedicated to all my professional colleagues who provided the enthusiasm and mentoring to bring this book to life. Finally, this book wouldn't be possible without Sara Summers' talent, patience, and enthusiasm as my co-author.

—Chris Bernard

Books are seldom written in isolation; much thanks and gratitude goes to Thirteen23, especially Lee Brenner for the long hours and amazing ideas; Chris Bernard's vision, drive, and quick wit; Branden Hall's honest and wise perspective; my brother, Kris Geist, and his literary savvy and skilled problem solving; and my parents, Michael Summers, Jane Procise, Pam Summers, and Kerry Geist, for their relentless trust, belief, and ethics. This book is for you and anyone who has ever sought to change something for the better.

—Sara Summers

ACKNOWLEDGMENTS

A special thanks to Bill Buxton, Jon Harris, Roger Martin, Laurence Moroney, Doug Olson, Christian Schormann, and Arturo Toledo for their support and insights in creating this book and for how they inspired and challenged us. Thanks to Steve White and Kirupa Chinnathambi for their technical guidance and to Fred Gerantabee for his contributions to the resource section of this book. Thanks to Vijay Kumar and the Institute of Design for allowing us to share some of his methods in this book. Great books need great editors, and we had many of them, including Loretta Yates from Pearson and our technical editor, Branden Hall. Finally, a special thanks to Nathan Hancock and Harry Caldwell for their support.

—Chris Bernard

Thank you to all the people who challenge and inspire me to think, experiment, and grow: Nathan Hancock, Harry Caldwell, Chris Bernard, Brian Gorbett, Kris Geist, and all the good people of B3S.

—Sara Summers

WE WANT TO HEAR FROM YOU!

As the reader of this book, *you* are our most important critic and commentator. We value your opinion and want to know what we're doing right, what we could do better, what areas you'd like to see us publish in, and any other words of wisdom you're willing to pass our way.

As an associate publisher for Que Publishing, I welcome your comments. You can email or write me directly to let me know what you did or didn't like about this book—as well as what we can do to make our books better.

Please note that I cannot help you with technical problems related to the topic of this book. We do have a User Services group, however, where I will forward specific technical questions related to the book.

When you write, please be sure to include this book's title and author as well as your name, email address, and phone number. I will carefully review your comments and share them with the author and editors who worked on the book.

Email: feedback@quepublishing.com

Mail: Greg Wiegand
        Associate Publisher
        Que Publishing
        800 East 96th Street
        Indianapolis, IN 46240 USA

READER SERVICES

Visit our website and register this book at informit.com/register for convenient access to any updates, downloads, or errata that might be available for this book.

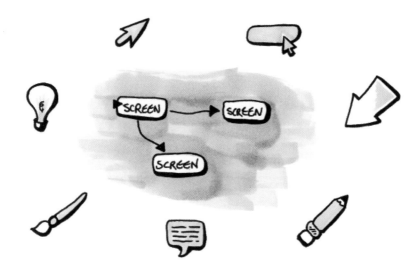

INTRODUCTION

This section introduces you quickly to the concepts and differences between sketching and prototyping and gives an overview of everything Dynamic Prototyping with Expression Blend covers. It also gives you an explanation of how different sections of the book are arranged.

What's a prototype? This seemingly simple question can have many answers. Throw the word dynamic in there, and things can get even more confusing. If you're contemplating purchasing this book or have already taken the plunge, you might be doing so because you're frustrated with the status quo when it comes to prototyping for interaction—or you may even be uncertain about why sketching and prototyping is something that should become part of your design process.

Bill Buxton has one of our favorite definitions of how we create and design experiences—or rather how we should create and design experiences. It's illustrated by something Bill defined as the dynamics of the design funnel, and he's been gracious enough to let us recreate it for you here.

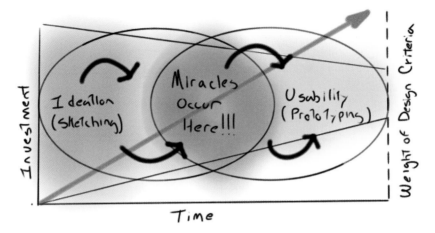

Figure 0.1   The dynamics of the design funnel shows us the continuum of how sketching and prototypes help us make great experiences. Idea and figure courtesy of Bill Buxton with a few modifications.

The design funnel illustrates two disciplines and two concepts. The disciplines are sketching and prototyping, and the concepts are ideation and usability. Sketching is valuable for idea generation because it's fast and enables ideas to be explored quickly and cheaply. More refined designs can be tested at later stages of a project by building prototypes to test the usability of the ideas that we've decided to focus more of our attention on—and this is how we define a prototype in this book—as a tool to help test the usability of an idea with design criteria. The further we get into the world of prototyping, the more invested we become in process, and the more focused our design becomes; this is represented by the funnel in our illustration. As we transition from ideation to usability, the weight of the design criteria we use for our project takes on more importance, and it requires a bigger investment in time and money. This is represented by the arrow in the graphic. Finally, this is not a linear progression; it's iterative, and the circles represent the iterative nature of this process. It also means our criteria and rigor isn't constant in a smart and innovative design process; we want less rigor, not more, in the ideation process; as we move deeper into a project, we want to slowly but certainly ensure that we've got consistent, vigorous, and valid criteria to evaluate our prototypes.

Now if sketching weren't such an important and critical part of prototyping, then perhaps we'd be working with PrototypeFlow instead of SketchFlow in Expression Blend. But the reality is the sketching and prototyping are different activities that we do at different stages, and great prototypes always start with great sketches. SketchFlow in Expression Blend is designed to let you engage and leverage both activities, and it helps us get to when the miracles occur in good experience design—which we feel is in that intersection of sketching and prototyping.

Many of the existing processes that we use for prototyping were never created for the world of agile design and development or the nuanced world of interaction design. Today, the entire soul of a product or service may hinge on the inherent quality of an interaction, how fast parts of an application load on a device, the gentle bounce of an icon after you've selected it, or the physics or fluidity of an item as you manipulate with your fingers, mouse, stylus, or other input device.

In software design, what we're really describing is the transitions that take place between the different states of an application. In the applications that bring us joy and are simply fun to use, it's the transitions, or the journey, we take between states in an application that brings those experiences to life.

Many creative disciplines have well-established processes and tools that enable us to do our jobs. But for those of us resigned to showing the dynamic nature of what we build in software—especially when it comes to transitions—we are often stuck using the hand-me-downs of our peers. We think SketchFlow in Expression Blend is a killer application for quickly and easily defining, developing, showing, and sharing the transitions that make for a great experience.

By incorporating sketching and prototyping into our design and development process—which we simply call dynamic prototyping—we are able to use sketches and prototypes to determine not just what *to* build but what *not* to build. We are able to iterate in a consequence-free environment and refine and identify the details of interaction design to make products and services that are competitive and differentiated. We get to define and show the states of an application, but we also get to provide equal and perhaps more attention to the transitions. We can do this currently with a variety of tools, but SketchFlow for Expression Blend represents one of the first tools that simplifies how we do this today, while still enabling the designer to play an active role in designing and showcasing dynamic interactions without resorting to code.

WHO SHOULD READ THIS BOOK?

This book will be useful to anyone who wants to get a thorough understanding of how to create dynamic prototypes with SketchFlow in Expression Blend and learn the basics of dynamic prototyping.

SketchFlow functionality was introduced in Expression Blend 3. If you're using a later version of Expression Blend, some of the detailed information provided in this book may no longer be current. However, the fundamentals of understanding SketchFlow and Expression Blend shouldn't change, and we'll provide free updated content at www.dynamic-prototyping.com to cover breaking changes

The target audience for this book is professional designers, tasked with creating interactive and dynamic prototypes without having to rely on a developer or knowing code to bring their solutions to life. Our approach presumes that you want to leverage existing design tools that you currently use and are familiar with, but we also encourage you to focus on simplicity—you'll start the design process with pen, paper, or, perhaps, digital tools that mimic the act of sketching. No matter what your day-to-day role is, or even if you have more than one of the following, you'll find this book a valuable resource.

Visual Designer, Information Designer, Information Architect, or Interaction Designer

This book should strengthen your familiarity and competency with dynamic prototyping and the functionality enabled by SketchFlow in Expression Blend, even with no prior knowledge of the tool. This book also serves as a great foundation for learning more about the full functionality of Expression Blend.

Design Planner or Researcher

You may find that SketchFlow in Expression Blend is a useful tool for getting ideas off of a whiteboard and into the hands of clients for iteration and feedback when dealing with remote or displaced teams.

Motion Graphic Designer or Front-End Technology Specialist

If you frequently use dedicated prototyping tools to collaborate, you may find that SketchFlow in Expression Blend is a powerful new tool in your arsenal—especially if your existing tools require a great deal of scripting and coding to develop dynamic prototypes.

Usability Specialist or Design Strategist

You may find that SketchFlow in Expression Blend is a great tool for testing low-fidelity concepts with potential users of applications and services or as a way to present ideas and concepts to key stakeholders.

Software Architect or Developer

You may find that you are often thrust into playing the role of a designer in your projects and day-to-day activities, you'll find that the techniques put forth here will enhance your ability to do better work. This book shouldn't, however, be regarded as a replacement for having the capability and skill of a professional designer on your project team.

SketchFlow for Expression Blend is easy to learn and can be used to create dynamic prototypes for a variety of mediums, from design to business problems. It's a subset of the very powerful, but more complex, functionality of Expression Blend—a tool designed to create Rich Internet Applications (RIAs) for Microsoft's .NET platform.

This book is focused on the tasks that are essential to effective prototyping using SketchFlow in Expression Blend. The reference section of this book provides a charted course for deeper understanding and continued learning with Expression Blend. Dynamic Prototyping with SketchFlow in Expression Blend should be regarded as a complement to books that focus on Expression Blend in its entirety. This book is designed to give you a deep and comprehensive understanding of not just how to use SketchFlow, but also to help you understand how to bring core concepts around sketching, ideation, and concept exploration to your design process—or how to simply add a design process to your current workflow if you don't have one. Consider Dynamic Prototyping with SketchFlow in Expression Blend to be a hybrid of books that focus on design process agnostic of technology and software instruction manuals that tell you the how and not the why of how things work.

WHAT'S IN THIS BOOK?

Expression Blend is a professional design tool that is really a WYSIWYG (What You See Is What You Get) tool for creating applications that run using Windows Presentation Foundation (applications that run on Windows PCs), commonly known as WPF applications and Silverlight applications (cross-platform applications that can run in a browser or out of a browser on different platforms, including Windows, Macintosh, and Linux platforms). Both WPF and Silverlight are part of the .NET platform. The power of the .NET platform is that it lets developers use a similar set of skills and tools to write applications for PCs, for the Web, and even for devices. Tools like Expression Blend extend this capability to designers who work on products and services designed to take advantage of the .NET platform.

Expression Blend enables you to work with video, text, 2D animation, 3D animation, bitmap images, vector art, audio, advanced typographic and printing functions, data, and code to create these types of applications.

This book will focus on are the features that are required to enable you to be successful in SketchFlow.

This is important because SketchFlow itself is a tool that enables designers to quickly and easily start using Expression Blend and to be productive without a complicated and demanding learning curve. In fact, as designers ourselves, we think SketchFlow is the best way for designers to *start* using Expression Blend. It's important to note, however, that even if you don't want to create applications that take advantage of the .NET platform, SketchFlow in Expression Blend can still be a powerful tool to utilize in your design workflow.

We cover all the features of SketchFlow with which you need to be familiar, including the following:

- Design, sketching, and prototyping **best practices** and **design patterns**.

- Understanding the Expression Blend **interface** and getting your **workspace** set up to work with SketchFlow.

- How to **import** freehand **sketches** into Expression Blend and bring them to life with SketchFlow.

- Creating **navigation flows** that show the **screens** and **interactions** in your application.

- How to refine your application with SketchFlow **styles** that enable you to build real **controls** and functionality into your prototype.

- How to create **reusable assets** that save you time and energy in your projects and professional practice.

- How to use **animation**, **navigation**, **states**, and **behaviors** to add complex interactivity in your applications.

- How to integrate real or simulated **data** sources to showcase complex functionality.

- How to **annotate** your work and package your dynamic prototypes and **distribute** them so stakeholders can provide **feedback**.

- How to create professional design **documentation** automatically with SketchFlow that you can pass on to stakeholders and colleagues in projects.

We've also included a thorough, but optional, reference section you can learn in more detail about some of the key technologies behind Expression Blend, including sections on the following:

- The .NET framework

- Extensible Markup Application Language (XAML)

- The C# programming language

- Windows Presentation Foundation (WPF)

- Silverlight

HOW TO USE THIS BOOK

Every individual has different learning styles. There are four main parts to this book and they can be reviewed in or out of sequence depending on your learning style.

PART I

Part I introduces the fundamentals of the design process that use sketching and prototyping techniques. We also discuss patterns and practices for dynamic prototyping that we've found particularly effective with SketchFlow in Expression Blend. If you need a basic overview of design process, thinking, and practice and how dynamic prototyping enables it before diving into the basics of the tool, start here.

PART II

Part II shows you how to use SketchFlow in Expression Blend to quickly build a prototype. You'll find a basic overview of how to be productive in SketchFlow that can be completed in less than a few hours. If you're the type who doesn't like to read the manual but are new to Expression Blend, start here. We'll introduce all the key concepts of Expression Blend's interface and nomenclature here in great detail so it will be easier for you to navigate about Expression Blend in other sections and chapters.

PART III

Part III takes a deep dive into the functionality and workflow of SketchFlow in Expression Blend. If you're someone who enjoys learning every nook and cranny of a tool before you're comfortable, we'll spill the beans on everything, including the following:

- The SketchFlow interface

- Assets, styles, and components

- SketchFlow animation and states

- SketchFlow behaviors

- Data

- Annotations, feedback, and documentation

PART IV

In Part IV, we focus on applied knowledge. If parts I through III are a bootcamp Part IV is where we drop you off in the forest and you put to work everything you've been taught. If you're the type who learns best in a tutorial-style of environment, this is the best place to start. We take you though a dynamic prototyping project, starting with a creative brief and all the artifacts we'd typically inherit in a design-focused project; we then create an actual dynamic prototype and even discuss how to begin the detailed design process using Expression Blend.

REFERENCE

In the Reference section, we go deeper into the technology that makes all this happen, including .NET, XAML, C# WPF, and Silverlight. Finally, we provide curated resource lists and recommendations on how to continue learning about Expression Blend, prototyping and design, and WPF and Silverlight.

FAQ

Dynamic prototypes? Sketching and wireframing with my current tools works just fine for me. Why do I need this?

In the world of rich interactive applications, if a picture is worth a thousand words, then an interaction is worth a million. For example, imagine having to create a document that would describe the interface of the iPhone, the Xbox, or TiVo without interactivity, gestures, or motion. Our current static processes, ignore the transitions that must exist in our software and interactive experiences. It's far easier and more effective if we can actually design and show these transitions as part of our design process. We can do that with a variety of tools today, but it can often be labor intensive and time consuming. Should it really take five or six different tools to create a simple prototype? Wouldn't it be nice if we could take our sketches and bring them to life?

The moment design of a product begins, the collection of design documentation becomes outdated and often unmanageable unless documentation is constantly updated with each progression and iteration of the project. Big, complex documents are often difficult for stakeholders to review and understand. Sometimes what you document and think you explain clearly really isn't clear, leading to a miscommunication with the client, which often isn't discovered until much later in the project when changes are costly.

You shouldn't abandon techniques and processes that work for you, but we think you'll find that SketchFlow in Expression Blend offers a faster and easier way to demonstrate interactivity and create documentation that can be used in creative briefs, project specifications, and design documents.

If you're constantly being asked to do more, but still maintain high quality at an even faster pace, tools like SketchFlow for Expression Blend can be very useful in your design process.

I'm a designer, not a developer. Won't SketchFlow in Expression Blend be too difficult for me to learn?

A good ski instructor can teach someone to ski in a day; this doesn't mean you'll become a master of the carve, skiing down the most difficult runs of the mountain by lunch, but you should at least be able to have fun. SketchFlow for Expression Blend makes Expression Blend fun and accessible to less technical, or even non-technical designers. As a tool it gives you power that typically is only available to those that spend a great deal of time learning how to code.

Most designers can learn to be productive in SketchFlow in a matter of hours. You can gain confidence in the powerful features in SketchFlow for Expression Blend within a few days without bothering with code.

Once you learn how much fun SketchFlow in Expression Blend can be, you may find that you want to delve deeper into the considerable capabilities of Expression Blend. This book is a great way to start. We provide plenty of resources and links should you choose to learn some of the features beyond the capabilities of SketchFlow, but these are optional things that are not required knowledge for using SketchFlow.

However, we strongly encourage any designer to endeavor to understand the elements of what they are working with. If we look at classic artistic and design movements like Bauhaus or even the discipline of architecture, there is often an expectation around understanding the materials that you work with (textiles, photography, concrete, or steel) that is often missing from the interaction design process. You'll find that you're perhaps a better designer if you begin to learn the underlying characteristics of the medium. You don't *need* to do that to use SketchFlow, but we suspect you'll be a better designer and developer as you make those efforts over the course of your career.

My team already has a number of prototyping tools. Why should I learn one more?

If you've spent years learning the ins and outs of prototyping tools and come from a world of Adobe Flash and/or Flex, you should find the learning curve on even advanced functions in Expression Blend to come to you very quickly. In fact, you'll probably discover that you possess about 90% of the skills and capabilities to start learning how to be productive in using Expression Blend if you've been working with Flash, Flex, and ActionScript 3.0.

If you require an application that easily lets you work with sketches in a dynamic fashion, you'll find that SketchFlow does things that other tools currently do not. This includes using traditional animation techniques to create and explore transitions, adding interactivity and linking without code, and creating documentation and sharing feedback—all within one tool.

If you regularly work with teams that create solutions that ultimately target WPF or Silverlight, you'll see that Expression Blend enables a powerful workflow that makes designers first-class citizens in the design process, which allows for round-trip design and iteration that simply isn't available on other platforms. (You can learn how this is possible in the Reference section of this book, which discusses XAML.)

I don't use a PC for my daily work. Can I still use SketchFlow for Expression Blend on a Mac?

Microsoft Expression Tools only run on Windows at the moment. Although this may seem odd, there are some simple reasons for why this is currently the case. Fortunately, there are some easy workarounds for those who find SketchFlow for Expression Blend to be a killer application in their designer toolbox.

Microsoft Expression Tools, most commonly called Expression Studio, were actually designed using the very technology they are designed to help you create (WPF and Silverlight applications). For example, Expression Blend is a WPF application, and so are many parts of Expression Design. By using WPF, Microsoft is able to create new features and versions of the Expression Studio suite far more quickly—in fact, Version 3 of Expression Studio is the third revision of the software in just slightly over two years.

This level of speed comes at a price; it's nearly impossible to move that quickly and support multiple platforms.

In the professional design tools space, this is less of an issue than it was even a few years ago, as most computers can easily run a variety of operating systems natively or through a function called virtualization.

For example, most current users of Apple computers can run Windows on their computers just as effectively as they can run OSX. You can either do this using the Bootcamp feature of Intel-based Apple Computers to run Windows natively on your computer, or you can explore using special virtualization software that enables you to run and use Windows and Windows applications within OSX.

The bottom line? If SketchFlow for Expression Blend makes sense in your design workflow, the barriers to incorporating it are modest, regardless of your primary design operating system.

One feature of SketchFlow in Expression Blend is the ability to preserve assets into production—by doing that, my focus is more on the end product than a prototype. Are you sure this is a tool for prototyping?

One of the most valuable things a designer can do with a prototype is throw it away. The more effort and care put into the prototype, the more likely that a team can become blind to continued exploration or the marriage to bad ideas.

SketchFlow in Expression Blend is designed first and foremost to enable you to leverage the power of sketching and showcase interactivity using animation—perhaps the most effective way to demonstrate complex interactions without writing code—currently a popular method of prototyping among many designers.

But sometimes, our prototypes are not just about concept exploration; sometimes we need to know if something is even possible. This is typically an iterative step in prototyping. In most traditional workflows, we leave the low-fidelity world of sketching and move into higher-fidelity methods because we have to. SketchFlow for Expression Blend lets you seamlessly embrace this evolution and work with real controls, data, behaviors, and (if needed) code to show the most complicated interactive concepts.

SketchFlow can actually make these complex controls look like the same thing you'd sketch on a piece of paper. This is important because it can keep stakeholders focused on what's important—the idea, versus the details. In this stage of the creative process, this is a crucial area of focus.

For projects whose ultimate destiny is WPF or Silverlight applications, SketchFlow projects and the documents they create become valuable resources that can dramatically accelerate production. The analogy that comes to mind is how you might create an illustration for a comic book: Use a pencil to rough in an image, use an inker to build on those initial sketches, and finally use a colorist to add additional detail. Coupled with the copy, a comic book slowly comes to life. SketchFlow for Expression Blend elevates the control that a designer can have in the final result when creating an interactive application.

We won't promise, nor would we recommend, that you take assets and code created for a dynamic prototype wholesale with you into production; it takes away from what the core process of sketching and prototyping should be, iterating quickly and without consequence. But we suspect that those who work with WPF and Silverlight will find that many of the assets and components used in dynamic prototyping can be used to massively accelerate the production process.

SUMMARY

SketchFlow in Expression Blend is a game-changing tool for creating dynamic prototypes for:

- Validating design research and insights.

- Sharing brainstorming concepts and rough sketches.

- Beginning concept exploration.

- Bringing hand-drawn sketches or digitally created sketches to life in dynamic prototypes.

- Generating consensus and feedback.

- Creating design specification documentation.

Regardless of the final form factor of your output (service, application, product, business idea), SketchFlow in Expression Blend can help you get there—quickly, iteratively, and without code.

SketchFlow in Expression Blend has added benefits for those who are using it to design software or applications that take advantage of WPF or Silverlight, including the following:

- Dozens of controls that can be skinned and linked to simulated data early in the design process with SketchStyles (low-fidelity themed controls that work like a real application control, but look like a sketch) that later can be converted to production assets quickly and easily.

- Great workflow that allows simple importation and manipulation of high-fidelity artwork created in today's most popular design tools.

- Deep integration into professional asset management and application lifecycle management workflows that make the design process a first-class citizen in the development process

So, enough talk. Let's go learn about sketching, prototyping, and SketchFlow!

PART I

THE THEORY BEHIND
SKETCHING AND
DYNAMIC PROTOTYPING

1

WHY SKETCHING AND PROTOTYPING ARE IMPORTANT

It's easy to think that sketching and prototypes are the latest in a long line of design and development trends. But in fact, there's a great deal of science behind why sketching and prototyping are good for us. To understand this, we need to go back to the mid 1950's, where two scientists began the long process of trying to decode the messages our retinas send to the brain.

At the time, most of science assumed that our brain was like a video camera, with our eyes as the camera lens, recording nearly everything verbatim. And just like a photograph, if we zoomed in on the "picture" our eyes capture, it would be a tidy series of tinted dots. Then this perfect constellation of points would flatten into a 2D image and directly transport into the brain for interpretation and storage.

Yet, this isn't at all what happens; it's far more complex and unusual. So when David Hubel and Torsten Wiesel started chipping away at the dark veil surrounding our brain's sensory processing, what they found earned them the Nobel Prize.[1]

Figure 1.1   This bare bones representation is almost instantly digestible. Our brain can compute and recognize it faster because of the simple line work.

So how does it work? In a nutshell, our eyes output uniquely coded signals that our brain receives and interprets into motion, depth, and color signals, to list just a few. These hieroglyphic symbols are ordered by importance and then decoded and processed by the brain. Essentially, cells in the visual cortex initially react and are attracted to straight lines and angles of light. This means that our neurons favor light contrasts over lightness alone, and straight edges over rounded ones, and that the genesis of perception starts as a jumble of angles, edges, and lines. Hubel and Wiesel figured out scientifically what artists, designers, and animators had known intrinsically for centuries.

We can actually see these theories at work in many art movements that defined the twentieth century. The anti-figurative aesthetic, which

1 "Brain Mechanisms of Vision," by David H. Hubel and Torsten N. Wiesel, Scientific American, v241 n3, p. 150–162, Sept. 1979.

dominated the art of Matisse, Picasso, Marcel Duchamp, and Georges Braque, created a way to engage the raw impulses that make art pleasing.

Cubism and abstract art culls interest by pinpointing fundamentals of what our brains find stimulating and attractive—abstraction, bare form, hard lines, and a spectrum of contrast. These methods were continued by the minimalist movement, reflected in the Bauhaus teachings, modern architecture, and even furniture design, literature, and music. The overwhelming response and acceptance of these art and cultural movements is no happy accident; it plugs directly into the visual processes of the brain.

The more "done" something appears, the more narrow and incremental the feedback.
—*Kathy Sierra,* Creating Passionate User Interfaces

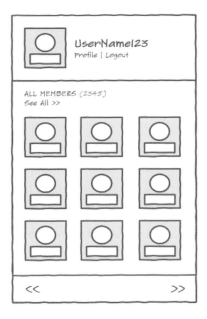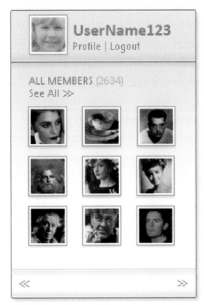

Figure 1.2   Lo-fidelity visuals not only help with solution-focused feedback, but they are instantly understood by the viewer.

The genius behind this enchantment and arousal with little more than some canvas and paint can be replicated in what we do as designers, and it forms the foundational thinking for what makes sketching and prototyping fantastic techniques for solving problems.

When we set out to create great solutions, or mold them into something to display and present a story to persuade our audience, our work is (with varying degrees of success) activating and stimulating the brain. Rough sketches, done in a few minutes can, arguably, be more effective in communicating our intentions or ideas than a picture. And through drawing and art, we can connect more instantaneously with every audience. The more we refine, exact, and perfect the designs we present, the more limited and inflexible the feedback from stakeholders becomes. The truth is, we NEED sketches.

REVEALING DIRECTION

As in most things great, one of the most amazing design magazines (and a favorite of this book's authors), *Critique*, is long defunct. Tucked inside its cover are to this day some of the most renowned thinkers in the business and craft of design. Milton Glaser, the father of the iconic, ubiquitous, "I heart (love) NY" logo, contributed often. While researching the contrasts of an artist's preliminary drawing to their final work, Milton wrote, "The sketch or rehearsal reveals the thought process of the creator in a way that finished works are unable to do." This act of drawing conveys much more than what is illuminated on paper; it tells us a story and guides what we do next. The destination is bound tightly to the journey and path we take to get there. The magic of what we *learn* from our own exploration in sketching or observing that of another is didactic.

> *What becomes obvious is that the process often reveals more than the work itself.*
> —*Milton Glaser*[3]

Most of us have come into our careers with computers at the forefront of every aspect of our daily tasks. We are dependent upon the instantaneousness, connectivity, and perfection that the computer provides. But what we make up in ease and speed we lose in direct brain cognition. The perception, problem solving, and analytical visual deductive processing are all bettered by practiced sketching. The mastery of software alone cannot create appealing design or compelling, intuitive solutions. Technology presents us with amazing potential but can also impose roadblocks to the creative process. As designers, and even developers, we are conceptual architects—exercising our idea muscles is a must.

3 *Critique Magazine,* Autumn 1997, p. 28–29.

This discussion—our brains versus a computerized world and potential creative hindrance of mechanical tools—will likely rage on forever. What's more valuable is the notion that we must devise a conducive environment, methods, and tools for idea capture and collection into a form by which to communicate them. For the simplest of reasons, sketching is one of the most effective means to ideate; humans have been drawing for as long as we have been Homo sapiens. And if you avoid constant self-torment with regard to the results of your sketches, you will be able to initiate creativity at its most elemental prime.

IT'S THE IDEAS PEOPLE

Plato, Socrates, Michelangelo, and Da Vinci had many hats: philosopher, poet, engineer, architect, painter, and inventor. Today, however, if Michelangelo was a co-worker, we would likely call him "the idea guy." He might go on a little too long, or come off a pinch righteous at times, but he would be the person everyone would look to, to turn a problem on its ear. These days, it seems that not many people don themselves with the "inventor" title, but thinkers, creators, and pioneers are everywhere. No matter the industry: Big ideas, disruptive change, and the advancement and betterment of all products and daily life comes from someone (or a group of someones).

If you are now thinking that you wish you had an "ideas guy or gal" at the office, STOP! The inventor, pioneer person can easily be you. Even a small amount of experimentation and education can make a dramatic difference in your ability to generate ideas. A search online for "idea" literature quickly takes you deep into a philosophical study, spanning everything from individual freedoms to altering reality. Although fascinating, this is not the most handy when tackling a client or industry problem. What's more applicable is the concept of devising a method or an environment where frequency of ideas increases. We're going to frame this goal generally because there are several vastly different ways to attain ideas, but let's plant a few seeds.

Here are three pathways to finding ideas; pick one or try them all to see what works best.

THE ORGANIC

Go outside, walk, explore, hop a fence, write, sketch, and photograph what comes to mind. Take yourself out of your daily routine and environment. Shackled to your desk? Swap out the things you have on it often. Pictures, postcards, art, toys, markers, pens, and books should be rotated in circulation. If you're a talker, listen more. If you're the quiet type, ask more questions and fuel more conversations. Date, document, and sketch; then reflect and chart your progress.[4]

THE STICKIE

Focus on the outcome and perception of your idea, with these tested tenets. Is your idea simple, unexpected, concrete, credible, emotional, and does it tell a compelling story? Keep in mind that you could just as easily observe the idea. Great concepts are not always "created." Jot down and/ or sketch all the iterations; having this mental history in a physical form is priceless. And while you are at it, observe and document good design experiences you discover throughout the day, as well as bad ones. Train your brain to pay attention to the details of each. Soon you will be able to have a much deeper understanding of what exactly makes something well designed.[5]

THE SCIENTIFIC

Become your own expert or "lead user." From Eric Von Hippel's research on solution or needs spotting, Hippel reveals that "lead users" (or power users) have a keen sense of future directional product success. And if you don't have time to become one yourself, go find, interview, and research the people who are. Avoid a phone interview if at all possible; observing your interviewees in their environment will prove to be far more productive and rewarding; spotting ideas, visually, in real time. Write, sketch, and tape record during the sessions.[6]

Note that the key to each method is to always be drawing, writing, and gathering as you go along. This unlocks the true power of idea generation—consciously capturing and collecting without concern of the immediate outcome. As with every step in the design process, the

4 *IdeaSpotting: How to Find Your Next Great Idea* by Sam Harrison
5 *Why Some Ideas Survive and Others Die, Made to Stick* by Chip Heath and Dan Heath
6 *Creativity in Product Innovation* by Jacob Goldenberg and David Mazursky, p. 201.

evolution of what you create becomes the storied vehicle to success. Conveying what you have learned not only maps a creative process that people can understand and learn from, but helps you further your own development.

IDEAS ARE CEMENTED IN PURPOSE

We have all heard the phrase, "the medium is the message," which stems from the book of almost the same name (rumored to have been misprinted), *The Medium Is the Massage*, by Marshall MuLuhan and Quentin Fiore. In it, the two men predict (the book was published in 1967) and illustrate how media leaves us as passive participants as it happily abducts our senses, leaving little room for interpretation from the viewer. This is extremely important for two reasons. First, we designers unwittingly ask too much of our stakeholders and fellow teammates, when we show them a few static wireframes and expect them to "get it." Designers should impart the daily practice of creating visuals that have a true symbiotic relationship with not only the end user and final product, but WITH the entire process of developing and communicating the project. Second, if we have all been spoon-fed this technicolored, submissive media experience at every turn, we just don't realize what is missing when we don't have it. So, even though WHAT we are designing is deeply complex, requiring weeks of brain strain on our part, we shouldn't present it that way to others.[7]

Walking clients carefully through a few visual phases can do wonders to remove some of the unseen miscommunication. Tangible, handmade work also appeals to our senses in a way that can subconsciously connect our instincts to our mind. The following sketching steps are certainly not the only way to go about enhancing conveyance, but the guide is a great place to start. At its core, sketching and visual processing are for you and your team. Envisioning success and achieving innovation are nearly impossible without an element of "serious play." And if your boss or manager finds this concept to be difficult, gently remind him or her that it is far less expensive to spend time sketching and prototyping than it is eating the cost of a failed product. Buy him or her a copy of *Serious Play* by Michael Schrage; it should be your office bible.

> *Games are the most elevated form of investigation.*
> —Albert Einstein

7 *The Medium Is the Massage* by Marshall MuLuhan and Quentin Fiore

Ask yourself these questions as you work through the sketching/prototype phases:

- Is there a way to turn parts (or ALL) of this exercise into a game?

- Are you fighting the good fight? Does this design have Relevance? Performance? Precedent?

Take note of other parts of the product design process that often create frustration or confusion. Would a quick sketch or lo-fi prototype help? Visually step stakeholders and team members through a project at each interval, as follows:

- **Sketched ideas**—Detail concepts in their most basic form, but be mindful to include the emotion and intent for user success. The medium (a simple sketch) lets the client know that this is an idea and helps keep the conversation focused there. These should be posted in the meeting room, so everyone can physically interact with the sketches and so you can organize and prioritize on the spot. Working spatially and visually in real time produces better results and reinforces stakeholder confidence and conversation. You are prototyping to better prototype; everyone must crawl before they walk.

- **Dynamic sketches**—When you have created some solutions you would like to proof further, scan and bring them into SketchFlow. Experiment and exhibit some foundational navigation, basic animation, and descriptors to refined sketches. Proof and test the viability of your ideas; if something doesn't work or can't be achieved the way you imagined, go back to sketching. Enlist the team to ideate around the issue, but treat it like a sprint. Keep the visual medium simple, but advance the conversation toward functionality and critical problem solving.

- **Sketchy style prototype**—A more thorough exploration, expounding on navigation, behaviors, animations, content, data, functionality, and user success via task flows. Build out the important task scenarios; using SketchFlow, retain the scanned sketches that add continuity and context, but replace elements like buttons, with working, sketchy styles. This is where a more informed user experience conversation can begin. Stakeholders can now see and articulate on how the product FEELS.

The goal for each step is the same: Let the sketching and prototyping shape and inform us about what we do next. The result of this is conversation where everyone is on the same page: seeing, feeling, and sharing the same experience. This is also the golden ticket to sketching and prototyping. If you can walk out of a meeting with the feeling that everyone had a productive conversation around the ideas, then you've hit a home run.

There are also larger things at play as well. The old business models that worked well for us in the last century have increasingly less relevance today. It began with the simple actions and changes by individuals and the tool in which they exacted their voice: the Internet. Now, our savvy clients are no longer impressed with a protracted, hierarchical, heavy-handed process—not only because the consumer has demanded it, but because the mechanics of power and control have drastically shifted. We have moved beyond an "us versus them" mentality, but designers need to bring that concept into the project process. So despite the barriers, forge ahead, and ask for forgiveness instead of permission.

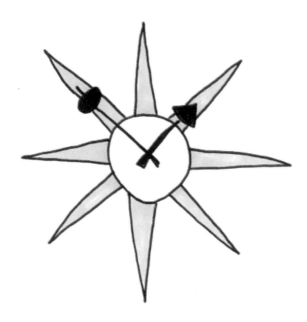

2

DESIGN PROCESS

Workflow, process, patterns, and methodology are simply a way of life; we typically take advantage of some formalized practice to aid the projects to which we toil and the resulting products we launch. This is especially true of projects or endeavors that involve technology. And, if technology would stay put for a minute, we could reuse the patterns from the last successful project—alas, technology is a constant of change. How do we keep up? Pick the "right" methods? Learn and adapt?

> As a rule, software systems do not work well until they have been used and have failed repeatedly, in real applications.
> —David L. Parnas, Ph.D.

For several years, the tech industry has become fascinated with failure; stories of failure, learning from failure, and celebrating failure. This is not at all coincidence. As technologists, we are bound to an eternity of failed attempts, in part because of the nature of business and management, the current software used that can't keep up with what we are tasked to do, but more importantly, the complexity of what we are required to create has exponentially increased. Humanized interfaces, gestural touch technology, and intuitive, predictive, user experiences; this is cause for revolution in every facet of how we think of and execute on ideas.

So now what? How can we expect to change what has historically been a frustrating, pride-swallowing battle? A journey back in time, to how other industries successfully built products in a time of disruptive change, is a great start. The industrial innovation surrounding the mass production of cars, the advent of advanced innovation in architecture practice, and the engineering books that document the techniques used are all ripe for exploration.

It may sound odd to seek-out groundbreaking design processes from a nearly 20-year-old engineering reference but we can learn quite a bit from *The Mechanical Design Process* by David Ullman.[1] Design process for engineers has been explored, tested, and documented in vast detail, because of the high overhead—production cost, expense of manufacturing, and considerable time to take product to market. The following are a few powerful examples of the engineering process that have been adapted to both the design and software engineering process. Most importantly, Ullman discusses why the prototyping process is so critical to our work. To whit:

- Whenever possible, organize the talent around the project.

- Exact measurements or outcomes are not important when prototyping a proof of concept; it's a learning tool.

- Build it twice: once to fail and second to succeed.

- Don't plan for a set number of prototypes. Take what is learned from the first prototype and apply to the second. Rinse, repeat.

- The more complex the function of the product, the longer design prototyping will take.

- Reduce the problem you are trying to solve with the product into one inclusive statement.

- Every phase of product design is iterative; requirements included!

- The human requirements ARE functional specs.

1 *The Mechanical Design Process* by David Ullman

At its most basic level, we can describe the design process as it relates to sketching and prototyping with the following model.

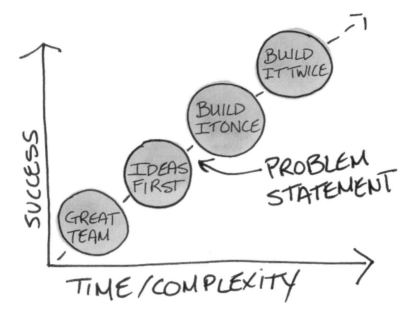

Figure 2.1   *The preceding lessons simplified in a bubble chart.*

But the act and discipline of design is more nuanced, and it's about far more than aesthetics and surface elements of a given solution or artifacts—in fact, what many folks outside the profession of design consider design to be is only scratching the surface.

Creating the form or appearance of an object or artifact is certainly a part of the design process, and it's often referred to as graphic design, visual design, or communications design. Because it's the most visible and tangible output of design, it perhaps pushes aside some of the other realms of design that are also critical.

Fundamentally, design process is about developing and communicating insights. There are two major influences that we think are important when it comes to the idea of sketching and prototyping.

One is focused on the work of Roger Martin and his thesis around how organizations need to seek validity versus reliability.[2] Martin's work

2 *The Design of Business: Why Design Thinking Is the Next Competitive Advantage* by Roger Martin, p 44.

resonates specifically around our need to balance incremental innovation through refinement of existing knowledge with the need to enable breakthrough innovations—essentially the difference between a version 2.0 product or service versus something nobody has seen before, or thought they needed.

Typically, many organizations focus on developing evidence for future product needs based on past outcomes. They use a limited number of objective variables to remove judgment and bias from decisions to support innovation, along the lines of "Our customers told us they want this" or "This is what everyone else is doing, and they are successful." Martin characterized this type of *substantiation* as reliability (looking into the past to make an informed judgment about the future). Designers are often called upon to focus on *substantiation* based on future events. This means that they use a broad number of diverse variables. Using processes that integrate judgment and that acknowledge the reality of bias is what design processes are used for. They are needed because most organizations make decisions based on facts, or what Martin called *reliability*. Design operates more in the mode of validity, often asking people to take a leap of faith, and the insights and recommendations can't always withstand the scrutiny of reliability.

At this point, you may be thinking that it's because those insights may not matter if they can't be backed up with reliability, but the reality is that we make decisions based on validity every day: It influences the cars we buy, the people we choose to spend our time with, and the type of phone we buy. Tapping into the gestalt that motivates those decisions is what design thinking and design processes are engineered to facilitate.

Martin characterized the difference in skill sets between designers and business decision makers and their propensities via something he called the predilection gap.[3] Organizations that are successful at innovation often have folks that are grounded in theories and practice that value both reliability and validity. Organizations that skew toward reliability often have difficulty innovating or recognizing good ideas. Organizations that skew toward validity often have a hard time getting their good ideas into the marketplace. It's actually possible to be good at both of these things and not have folks that can serve as translators between these two schools of thoughts as well. The result is often paralysis in an organization.

3 *The Design of Business: Why Design Thinking Is the Next Competitive Advantage* by Roger Martin, p 54.

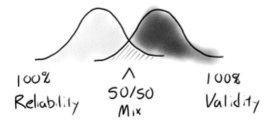

100%
Reliability

∧
50/50
Mix

100%
Validity

Figure 2.2   *A sketch that illustrates Martin's theories.*

(Printed with permission from Roger Martin, author of *The Design of Business: Why Design Thinking Is the Next Competitive Advantage*, Boston: Harvard Business Press, 2009.)

So, if we can acknowledge that design can be more than just about aesthetics and form and that validity is an important component of innovation, what's the process that designers use to enable success?

Although there are multiple books on this subject, and some of the names may change, the typical process that designers go through is fairly straightforward. If you ever hired a product design or innovation firm, you would most likely be exposed to a process such as this—or it would at least be the process applied to solving your problem. If you were to explore the techniques being applied in academia around design education and strategy, you would also find that these are the techniques that many designers are being exposed to in graduate and undergraduate education when it comes to learning about "design thinking." Here we'll use some examples from one of the author's previous work under Professor Vijay Kumar at the Institute of Design at the Illinois Institute of Technology.

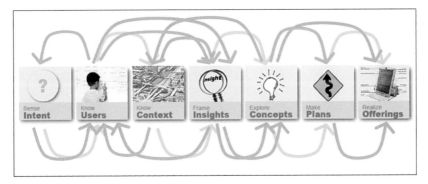

Figure 2.3   *An example of the steps and non-linear nature of a design process taught at the Institute of Design by Professor Vijay Kumar. (Image printed with permission from Vijay Kumar.)*

A TYPICAL DESIGN PROCESS

Design processes are about a journey of discovery. There are numerous techniques that can be applied to each stage of the design process, and each stage is designed to build on the other. Design-driven innovation is different from business- and technology-driven innovation in that is starts with a focus on understanding your customers or users first versus starting with a technology or a business.

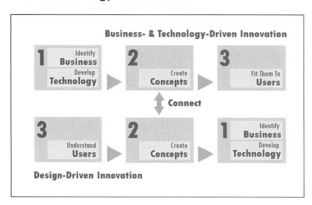

Figure 2.4 *The journey that occurs in a design process around design innovation and how it differs from business and technology innovation. (Image printed with permission from Vijay Kumar.)*

Most design processes contain the following steps. For large projects, it can take weeks or months to go through all of these phases, but talented design planning teams can also accomplish these steps in a matter of days for focused efforts. Here's an overview of what those processes look like when we follow the techniques and practices that the Intitute of Design employs.

DEFINITION AND INTENT

Design process starts with an idea or, more often, a hypothesis—something you are trying to prove or disprove. This definition state is where designers state their intent, or where the business process is framed and where a research plan is hatched.

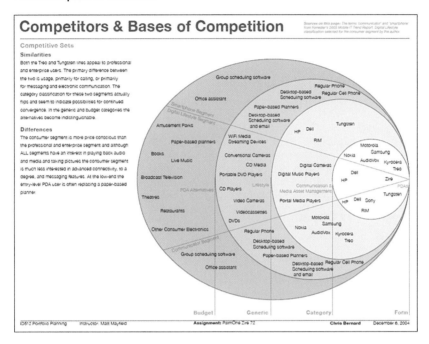

Figure 2.5 *Some definition efforts begin with an attempt to capture a snapshot of a landscape that influences a problem space. This is an example of a product mapping completed for a Portfolio Planning Class at the Institute of Design.*

RESEARCH

The second stage of a design process is focused on research; it can take many forms, but one key difference from the typical "stakeholder" interviews and secondary research that we might be familiar with is that this research typically takes the form of what is often called contextual or ethnographic research. Direct observation and anthropological techniques are often used.

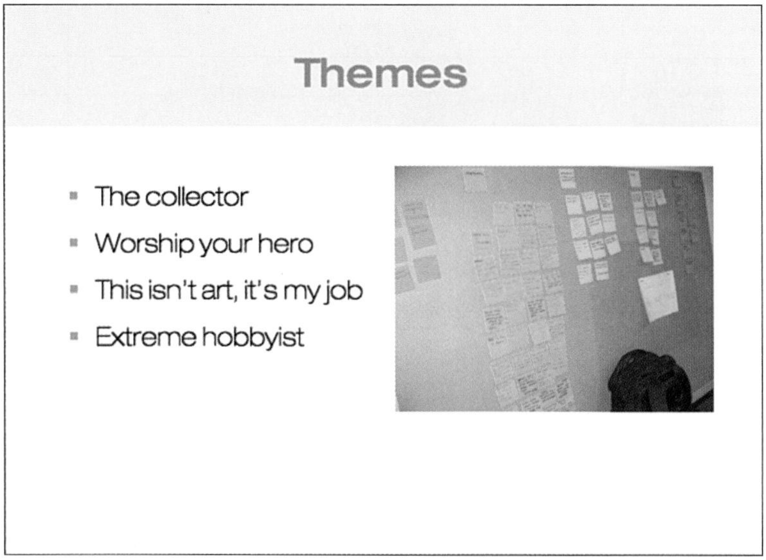

Figure 2.6 *Insights or observations from contextual research are often clustered or cataloged at collection or soon after. This is an example from an Understanding Users Class at the Institute of Design.*

ANALYSIS

The next stage is really one of analysis: processing and organizing all the data that you've collected. Often one of the biggest challenges for designers is not coming up with ideas, or collecting them, but figuring out which ones are the most important to pursue.

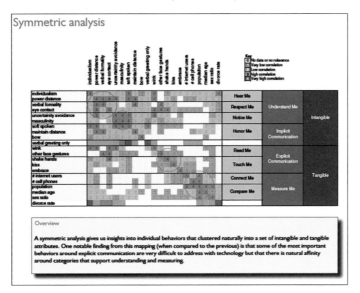

Figure 2.7   *Even designers use spreadsheets from time to time; here we see a morphological sort of data and attributes derived from primary research. This is an example from a Design Analysis Class at the Institute of Design with Professor Vijay Kumar.*

SYNTHESIS AND IDEATION

This is at the point where most people think the design process begins, and that is around the phase of synthesis or ideation. This is the point in the process where we start to develop and flesh out some of the themes and memes that come out of our analysis process. It is also the phase where tools like SketchFlow can start to become useful.

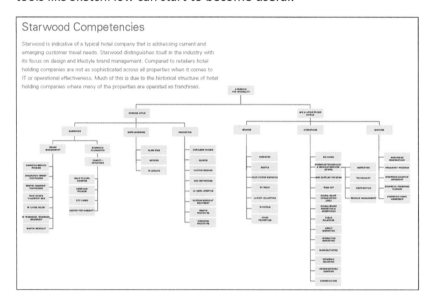

Figure 2.8   In this example from one of the author's student work, analysis of data enables us to identify competencies for a sample customer. This is an example from a Design Strategy Workshop at the Institute of Design with Professor Vijay Kumar.

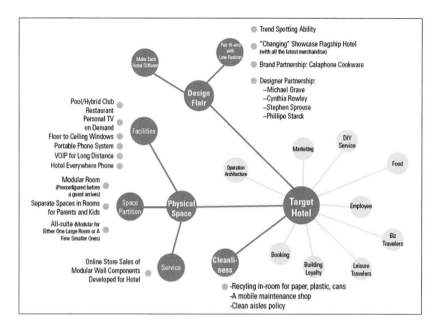

Figure 2.9 Affinity mapping helps designers and business makers uncover new opportunities. This is an example from a Design Strategy Workshop at the Institute of Design with Professor Vijay Kumar.

By looking at competitor offerings and matching them with a different company, teams can uncover new business opportunities. Here is an example of student work of one of the authors; it was identifying competencies and needs that would allow for a new business to be created, which would deliver new value to an existing customer segment.

PLANNING

Have you even been frustrated when you ask someone for an estimate and a plan and their first response is, "It depends." We often roll our eyes at consultants and companies that suggest a six-week project to figure out what the *real* price of a project may be. But the reality is that for complex problems that require breakthrough innovation, if *someone* hasn't gone through a process of research, analysis, synthesis, and ideation, the estimate you receive will be useless or wildly inaccurate. Another way to think about this is that solving hard problems is, well, hard. If it were easy, we wouldn't need to go through all these steps, and we would always make smart choices all the time.

CONCEPTUALIZATION AND PROTOTYPING

Many traditional processes have this phase, and it's often called a macro or high-level design process. It's often the stage where we plan out a slice of a project or develop multiple initial concepts to help us drive toward our final decision. For many people who don't use a fully realized design process, this is often where SketchFlow might first be used.

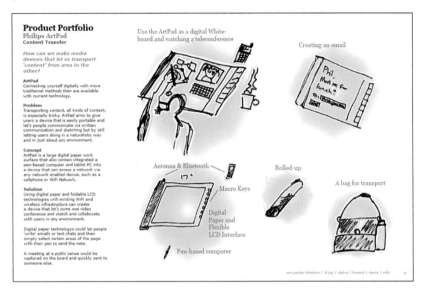

Figure 2.10   In this example from one of the author's student work, we see an encapsulated design process that features intent, a problem statement, conceptualization, and a potential solution. This is an example from a New Product Definition Class at the Institute of Design with Professor Chris Conley.

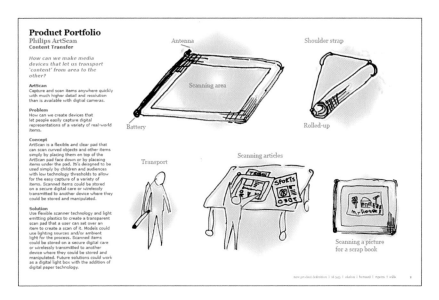

Product Portfolio
Philips ArtScan
Content Transfer

How can we make media devices that let us transport 'content' from area to the other?

ArtScan
Capture and scan items anywhere quickly with much higher detail and resolution than is available with digital cameras.

Problem
How can we create devices that let people easily capture digital representations of a variety of real-world items.

Concept
ArtScan is a flexible and clear pad that can scan curved objects and other items simply by placing them on top of the ArtScan pad face down or by placing items under the pad. It's designed to be used simply by children and audiences with low technology thresholds to allow for the easy capture of a variety of items. Scanned items could be stored on a secure digital care or wirelessly transmitted to another device where they could be stored and manipulated.

Solution
Use flexible scanner technology and light emitting plastics to create a transparent scan pad that a user can set over an item to create a scan of it. Models could use lighting sources and/or ambient light for the process. Scanned items could be stored on a secure digital care or wirelessly transmitted to another device where they could be stored and manipulated. Future solutions could work as a digital light box with the addition of digital paper technology.

Labels: Antenna, Shoulder strap, Scanning area, Battery, Rolled-up, Transport, Scanning articles, Scanning a picture for a scrap book

Figure 2.11 Another example of the same encapsulated process. This is an example from a New Product Definition Class at the Institute of Design with Professor Chris Conley.

PRODUCTION AND IMPLEMENTATION

This phase is often known as a micro or detailed design process. In many cases, a designer might not even have been engaged until this stage of the process with a mandate to "Make it pretty" or "Make sure our customers love this"—which may be an impossible task by this point. SketchFlow and technologies like WPF and Silverlight offer a powerful combination when using SketchFlow and a design process because they allow a designer's work and vision to translate seamlessly into the development process.

SENSING AND FEEDBACK

Great products are never really finished until they are abandoned. New releases, features, and innovations follow the lifetime of a product or service. Good design processes acknowledge this and ensure that a mechanism is in place via process or technology to capture, judge, and act on feedback and insights that are collected over the lifetime of product. Just as SketchFlow is a great tool to use at the beginning of a project, its utility can also be realized to support shipping projects and services that need to evolve.

WHAT ABOUT AGILE PROCESSES?

Increasingly, design processes are being combined with agile methods. There are two primary ways to accomplish this. The most common way is to incorporate design processes in each sprint or release of a product. The most valuable way—and some designers might argue the *only* way—is to incorporate design processes in an initial phase zero that takes a long-term and holistic view of project needs before moving into agile processes.

FURTHER READING

The Reference section of this book provides recommendations on other authors' books and work to reference if you'd like to learn more about design processes. Employing design processes into your existing workflow is not a trivial task; in fact, you might not even be convinced that you should at this point. Although it's beyond the scope of this book to be exhaustive in articulating the value of a formal design process, we'll discuss some basic patterns and practices in the next chapter that you can incorporate into your work.

3

PATTERNS AND PRACTICES FOR INNOVATION

In this chapter we will talk about some patterns and practice that will help you get the most out of sketching and prototyping with a focus on techniques for brainstorming and ideation.

The philosophy and psychology of great human experiences is often difficult to visualize, even though we have all experienced them in our lives. There are two theories that are useful in assisting with organizing the task of people-friendly products. The first is the Kano model, which we have conveniently attempted to re-imagine for a design process (see Figure 3.1).

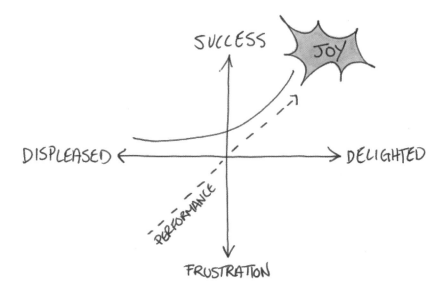

Figure 3.1 The Kano model for user experience.

Seeing tests and describes the psychology of human need in the context of experiencing art. The desires outlined paint an intricate portrait of how to architect human experience for satisfaction.

Enjoyment increases learning, and increased learning leads to understanding, which encourages more enjoyment.[1]

The practice of human experience:

Perception: "I can do this, and it is enjoyable!"

Emotion: "I don't feel dumb or frustrated!"

Engagement: "I can explore and personalize!"

Communication: "I know where I am, and there is feedback to guide me!"

1 *The Art of Seeing: An Interpretation of the Aesthetic Encounter* by Mihaly Csikszentmihalyi and Rick E. Robinson

But what does creating great experiences look like, and how do you start?

It is important to first consider how vital it is to capture creative ideas, the moment we have them. The everyday, inconsistent use and definition of the words "creative" or "creativity" can disguise the scientific relevance and the effect it has on the design process. In the context of thoughts and ideas, behavior is novel. We will never have the same thought or idea the same way twice. We don't put our shoes on in the exact manner we did the day before. Thought, behavior, and ideas are incrementally, generatively different from one moment to the next. In short, all humans have the capacity for creativity, in ever-evolving infiniteness.[2]

For this reason, brainstorming and ideation sessions are so immensely critical to producing powerful experiences. The art of capturing these thoughts, when they happen, enabling an environment conducive to having them, helps foster the magic formula for discovery, toward innovative product design. The true difference between those described as "creative" and the rest of the world is the cognitional ability to capture thought. A camera, sketchpad, pen, or pencil is all you need to seize ideas; remembering to bring them with you is helpful also.

TEAM SKETCHING FOR IDEAS

One of our long-standing pet peeves with design processes is the isolation and siloed division of labor that often occurs. It never seems connected to anything that resembles team work. Indeed, everyone has a job title and has some things they are particularly good at, but everyone also has the ability to generate ideas. Start with a team meeting—a brainstorming session that everyone involved with the project can attend. Make it fun, a "no bad ideas" environment (the potential for judgment or negative evaluation has been shown to inhibit creativity). Candy, snacks, beverages, pens, markers, stickers, lots of sketch paper, and toys drastically improve mood and inevitably set the appropriate tone. Describe the purpose of the session, as Alan Cooper famously stated, "If it was magic, how would it work?" Make sure that you convey that there are no constraints other than time—no limits, no judgments or critiques, just an ideation stream.

2 *Cognition, Creativity, and Behavior: Selected Essays* by Robert Epstein

If your team needs context beyond the high-level concept of the product, add a small amount of structure; that is, ideate on one part or function of the product. Or, our personal favorite, use props with a twist; present four items that relate to the project and one completely unrelated item. For example, if the client is an online furniture retailer, bring in fabric swatches, measuring tape, a vase, and a mirror; then add the dissociated item, a fake mustache. If you are looking for even more "out of the box" ideas, present your props to a 5- or 6-year-old child and record how he interacts with and talks about them.

> Sketching Tip: Typically, the first idea in your head seems obvious and possibly not worth exploring. Sketch it out anyway to mentally and physically "move past it."

Now with the premise and mood set—beverages, pens, and props in place—start sketching (Figure 1.2). Request that each person generate four or five different ideas; beautifully crafted drawing is not the goal. However, place a time limit (5–10 minutes maximum) for each round. Why does this matter? Remember that report or project you finished at 4:30 am… because it was due in the morning? Mimicking that same pressure and adrenaline charge builds excitement and produces better results. This may be one of those "trust me; it works" moments. Set a stop watch; the proof lies in the ideas.

Figure 3.2 *Initial ideas sketches should look as lo-fi and rough as what we have here.*

With your first round of sketches in hand, show them off to the team. For large teams, break into subgroups of 5–7 people and begin discussing the concepts. Each person should have the limelight for a few minutes to briefly talk through his or her ideas. Remember, this is a criticism-free zone—nothing kills excitement and creativity faster than, "That won't scale!"

After some lively discussion, take your favorite idea and visualize it further with another timed round of sketching. This time, give 10–15 minutes, allowing for a little deeper exploration. By now, you will want to create something that is self-describing, moving toward the true purpose of prototyping. These sketches should attempt to instantly communicate the idea, in the same way a comic strip simultaneously conveys movement, emotion, and storyline.

VISUAL STORYTELLING

Figure 3.3   We've been using sketching techniques to communicate our collective history for a long time.

Communication by way of story is the collective history of all people regardless of culture. Storytelling is not only the way we talk but, more importantly, how we are ultimately understood by others. It's the difference between putting someone to sleep with a string of unillustrated facts or the inability to ignite emotion, or creating excitement and action with a succinct tale of human experience. Accurate communication is almost never derived from content alone; the majority is a combination of verbal and non-verbal cues—vocal tone, gestures, eye contact, and facial expression.

What does this tell us? It is our job to recreate this experience in every facet of our work in design, presentation, and the foundation of how we express ideas. If understanding and acceptance is the greater goal, we must consider the subtleties of successful storytelling not only for stakeholder approval, but for the entirety of the products we create. Thankfully, we have great patrons of visual language and narrative to guide us: comic book artists.

COMIC NARRATIVE

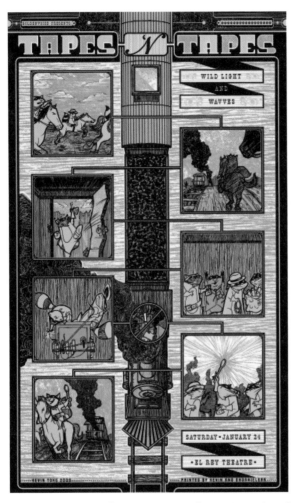

Figure 3.4 *Tapes 'n Tapes poster*. Illustration printed with permission from Kevin Tong.

The essence that gives comics their mass appeal is the articulate focus on the subtle nuances that define human emotion and experience. It almost appears effortless, although if you have ever tried to write and illustrate one yourself, you know that it's far from easy. Eliciting response from often just a few squares filled with graphics and a pinch of text takes practice and a thoughtful study of the daily socio-human dance. Yet, even though we may make products or software, this is exactly what we are also responsible for—to honor nuance, to engage and reward, to study and mind the psychology of the audience, and paramount to all else, to tell a fantastic story.

So, how do comic artist do it all, often in black and white and with such limited real estate? *Making Comics* by Scott McCloud describes some choices or guidelines to aid your visual story and to move you toward clear and instant communication.

Figure 3.5   *The same concepts that make comics work can be applied to our sketching and prototyping work.*

MOMENT

Show what is most important and remove the extraneous. This provides focus, and prevents someone from getting mired in the details.

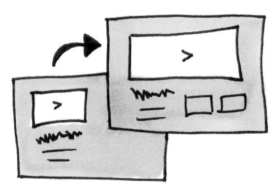

Figure 1.6   *A simple sketch that shows a change in state.*

FRAME

Define the space; this can help define size in reference to other elements or objects. This may not be as useful if you are designing a desktop or browser experience, but if you are making a tangible product, this could be very handy.

Figure 3.7 *Contrast helps us frame what's important in a sketch.*

IMAGE

Utilize any and all conventional graphics and symbols to communicate effectively. This is the foundation of design language—apply liberally.

Figure 3.8 *Words, simple shapes, and the flow of a line all converge to communicate an idea—in this case, speed.*

WORD

Reiterate what is displayed graphically with words. This is good for describing emotion or sound effect that accompanies an interaction. In truth, most prototypes will include words to affirm the sketch.

Figure 3.9   *Line art and the liberal use of a finger can indicate a state or transition early in the design process.*

FLOW

Lead the eye toward the focal point with arrangement. If you are highlighting an interaction or motion, one sketch could simply describe what that piece looks, sounds, or feels like. Dynamic prototyping lets you take this to the next level by actually implementing the gentle bounce of an icon or pulsing throb of a button in need of selection.

Refining your visual storytelling skills with some of these tricks will help greatly absolve the roadblocks in communicating ideas to everyone. But with the complexity of software and products today, your design battle is not over. Next, you take your new expertise into the realm of dynamic interface design and prototyping.

COMMUNICATING DYNAMICALLY

We mentioned earlier that our process and the things we produce along the way need to have symbiosis with the end result. The mechanical design book we read about and the industries that utilize its methods—automotive, film, and architecture—are well seasoned in the mastery of prototyping. Most of the things we create from here on out will likely have a good amount of discrete human interaction, and the only way to sell this to our stakeholders is by allowing them to experience it for themselves. Otherwise, we are reduced to static images that don't describe the emotion involved in completing tasks, and the hand-waving dance we perform to make up for it. Thankfully, we can conquer both issues by creating prototypes that perfectly exhibit the intricate interactions that *define* the product and experience.

BUILD TWICE FOR SUCCESS

> *Plan to throw one away; you will anyhow.*
> —Frederick Brooks, The Mythical Man-Month (1975)

One of our all-time favorite interviews is an email conversation between Peter Merholz and Pixar's Michael B. Johnson, who for the past 13 years has run the Moving Pictures Group at Pixar. Johnson's specialty has been developing a pre-visualization system along with lighting and animation tools to assist in the massive task that is the animated movie. Possibly more impressive, Johnson redesigned the whole story and editorial production pipeline to operate 100% digitally—which is no small feat. As he describes the process and experience of making each movie, he reveals, "Pixar loves their films so much, we make them twice." He goes on to describe the savings in time and money this technique provides and what is learned by building the movie as a rough sketch, but then he drops a bomb: "If you are trying to build a prototype that you want to use as a blueprint, it should exist in the same medium as the final product."[3]

Johnson is right, and the success of Pixar's last decade of hit films is the proof.

To create a working prototype, in its intended medium, gets us several important things we didn't have before: an accurate idea-testing environment and a tangible way to work together; designers and developers as one happy family. It also frees us to focus on the dynamic and interactive nuances that define human experience, which we can

3 Peter Merholz's conversation with Michael B. Johnson, www.adaptivepath.com/blog/2008/07/14/conversation-with-michael-b-johnson-of-pixar-part-1/

instantly turn around to get buy-in from our stakeholders. So, when we use the word "dynamic," it describes more than just having interaction or motion in what we create. Dynamic becomes how quickly and efficiently we can work in the constant flux of technology and project development. Productivity has been provided to us, inherently.

As a result, our process becomes more open, responsive, and honest. Yes, honest. As designers for technology, we've never been enthusiastic about work that is a "hack," or "duct taping" a product prototype together only to admit later to the client that all the beautiful motion we displayed was actually an animated .gif. These are the same ills the agile manifesto was trying to cure almost 10 years ago in software development. If we can keep our process from becoming dogmatic, we will then be truly nimble and proactive through each phase of design and development—and be honest along the way.

You may be wondering if we're contradicting ourselves here, but we're merely talking about patterns and practices along the lines of the prototyping continuum. There will always be room for a thick permanent marker and a clean sheet of paper, just as there is room to use animation to simulate complex ideas. But as your project evolves, so should the fidelity of your craft, and the tools you use to iterate should support that process.

DESIGN PROCESS PATTERNS

Let's start this section with a huge disclaimer: Your team, its culture, and the things you create together are unique. All the "best in show" references on process and design can only take you along part of the journey, because *people breathe life into ideas*. Some of these processes will fit, but others won't, and you may already have some of them in place. With that in mind, use this section to augment, educate, and otherwise guide you and your team.

It may sound surprising, but the design process is similar in some ways to accounting. How? Both, despite preconceived notions, are a blend of art and science but in opposite ways. In design, our goals for success often appear as intangibles, but we use a good deal of process and rigor to arrive at them. In accounting, the outcomes are often represented as facts, but in truth, the processes that we use to arrive there have a healthy dose of art applied. Design objectives like effortless integration of empathy and generosity, and ease of user adaptation and acceptance—all while fostering an enjoyable, intuitive experience—can be tough to land in a world that likes facts.

Thankfully, we can look back to the industries and leaders that came before us, and harvest some tried and tested principles. The process patterns outlined next are a mixture of architecture, film, and traditional product-engineering practices, which in several instances, the technology world has forgotten.

If your project manager or team lead takes one look at the amount of upfront thinking and design strategy work in the first few sections and glazes over, remind him or her that this lightweight time in the beginning saves untold hours and dollars in the final, more expensive production and testing stage.

RESEARCH, INTERVIEW, OBSERVE

Take the time to listen, tinker, investigate, be a student, and let the client and power users guide our process, scope, and strategy. This stage is all about learning; do you need to gut the product that is in place today, or toss it in the scrap heap and start anew? What are the known and unseen problems? Break down any mysterious problems into smaller digestible chucks; embody the spirit of a scientist. But it is not just about the numbers—it's deciphering the depth of cognition and emotion of the people we are designing for. By focusing on the culture, motivations, habits, and inherent behaviors, we can begin to shape the entire scope of the project. This ethnographic research or "mental modeling" is the psychology of your users in their unique environment: direct, first-hand, and holistic observation. If you find that your power users have developed their own lingo around the product, record the words and their meaning and adopt it. Observe, interview while documenting, and graph the results, but remember to analyze and study what you find *with* your team and stakeholders. Create visuals that illustrate your findings, so everyone can see and physically interact with the results. Out of this discovery, a clear, synthesized strategy can be formed that you will carry with you through the rest of the project. Make no mistake: If there is "no time" or money for this phase, fight for it. This *is* what sets "run away," successful products apart from the competition.

Recommended Further Reading on User Research: Remote Research: Real Users, Real Time, Real Research *by Nate Bolt and Tony Tulathimutte.*

IDEATE, SKETCH, EXPERIMENT

Now it's time to become the scientists of joy and magic. Problems should be puzzles to solve, and hurdles lead us toward further incubation, giving us necessary pause to fully understand what we are making, who we are making it for, and what would make the product truly great. Begin having the brainstorming, team-sketching sessions we described in the "Team Sketching for Ideas" section of this chapter. From there, prototype the key features and functions. Now that you have some ideas to concept and proof, build those out in SketchFlow with your sketches. Start testing and iterating on known problems, devise several possible solutions, and test them with your power users. Have your test subjects provide feedback via the feedback player. Then, open all the feedback at once in Blend and look for patterns. Even with just a handful of results (a good magic number is six), the common threads should be fairly obvious. Iterate and continue to share and showcase results and changes with the team and your stakeholders. Start experimenting and exploring the interactions, sounds, and functions that are not only important to the product and client, but that exhibit the joy and compelling nature of your ideas. Remember to survey your iterations. Does this feel consistent, reliable, explorable, enjoyable, intuitive, and meaningful? Then take what you have made and build scenario prototypes that chart a successful completion of a task or tasks.

DESIGN, TEST, SURVEY

Once you have built out and elaborated on the scenario prototypes, begin to add more connective tissue to each. Thread similar tasks and features together and test, observe, survey, and collect feedback again from your power users. Keep in mind that one of the most pleasing aspects to great user experience is the absence of abruptness. If an interaction solution isn't testing well with your users, make sure it seems responsive and smooth before you go back to the drawing board. Remember to also test with new users of your experience as well. Power users know how things work but new users must really rely on the metaphors and patterns we are creating. Sometimes they spot problems a power user would never see. Often subtle changes to the experience can be the cure for bleary feedback like, "I am not sure why, but it just doesn't feel right." After iterating, tweaking, and presenting your findings to stakeholders, it is time to put it all together in SketchFlow. Design as much of the entire experience as possible in *components* (grouped features and tasks); add real data, working functions and controls. Once you have built enough of the application to take stakeholders through nearly all of the mission-critical experiences and features, write out 5–7 key task lists and test them on your team. This is a benchmark moment; after you present this high-functioning prototype to the client and have them test and run through the task lists, the historically expensive parts of the process lie directly ahead. Approving a hi-fidelity visual look and feel can be time consuming; however, if you work within Blend and create reusable styles for the approved templates and look and feel, this activity can become a bit less daunting. We show you how to create, augment, and design styles in Part IV of this book.

Now that you have created a visual treatment on likely the beginning screen or page of the product, select two or three other critical, connected pages to explore. Remember to maintain the same interaction and transition experiences. Test just these screens with your team. Does it feel like you thought it would? Does it retain the essence and emotion that the prototype had? Then package only those pages, send them off to your stakeholders, describe your thoughts around the aesthetic choices you made, and ask them to submit feedback through the SketchFlow player. Load all the feedback into Blend and compare each stakeholder's comments to the other. Watch for patterns; if you see similarities, address and change those first.

Upon visual design approval, it's tempting to run off and "pound out" the rest of the project. Don't! The participatory relationship you created with the team and clients is at stake. Devise a check-in schedule; encourage everyone to be engaged and involved. This is absolutely one of the best ways to keep a client for life. They will likely never stop bragging about you either.

BIG IDEA:
Build your style or UI guide for the entire project right now. All the hard work you put into componentization, interactions, and visual styling can be turned into a "cliff's notes" catalog to aid the whole team throughout the rest of the project. This won't be a quick task, but it will save everyone's time and dissolve a large amount of frustration in the upcoming production phase. Identify and document all reusable elements: buttons, controls, feature sets, text styles, behaviors, and styles. List everything you

want to capture in the style guide and task each team member with collecting and documenting designated parts. Designers should collect the experience assets they are most familiar with; developers should compile the behaviors and discrete repeated code and interactions. Everyone should then be in charge of updating their sections, in the event of changes during or after the production stage. We explore how to create this style guide in Part IV of this book.

EXECUTE, RELEASE, ITERATE

This is it...where rubber meets road. Now you can *prove* that you've put your money where your mouth is. Every second of work you did before pays off right here. Time in this stage is valuable, but thankfully you are merely adding the finishing varnish and gluing all the moving parts together—moments away from showing it off to the world. Your team should continue to gut-check the pieces that each person is working on. Joint ownership and responsibility in the production and execution phase are critical and keeps the team energized and focused, and helps keep any one team member from getting myopic. The magic word here is *efficiency*; if you have to iterate on an unforeseen issue here, treat it like a sprint. After the sketching and idea-proofing sessions, you and your team should be able to breeze through any last-minute problems. All the stages of the process before give you the competitive advantage now; the time spent learning, understanding, experimenting, and iterating afford you the luxury of productivity. Estimating your development time and quality assurance testing become easier and takes less guess work. The components you have already created are pre-tested and approved, so sew each set together and keep your eye on the experience and performance. Make sure the transitions are smooth and test for lag, slowdown, or anything that isn't consistent to the whole. After some QA testing (if you don't have a QA team, you and your team should take on the task), launch it (even if it has to be a private beta), invite your power users to try it out, and if you feel good about your product, invite the stakeholders to watch users test via live video.

EVALUATE, AMEND, RELEASE

Now that you have gathered feedback from power users and your client, it's time to sit down and examine what you've accomplished. Is there something glaring you've missed? Or is it tweaks and user interface refinements? Grab your team and review. Make an aligned, solid plan for the changes you decide are best for the users and the business strategy; then present that to the stakeholders. Give them firm launch dates and an outlined plan of what care-taking will be necessary to track user adoption and how success will be measured. (If this is a large project, like a management or operations system, the maintenance and service-level agreement needs to be discussed and signed off on before the project begins.)

TUNE, LIFE CYCLE, DEBRIEF

After the product has been rolled out and live for a period (two months or so), refinements may be necessary. Metrics and trends should be studied; problem areas or pages should be reassessed. It's time to interview your power users, collect their insights, and observe their new task flows. Are they using the product as you intended? If not, how and why? They may really enjoy using it, so they may not realize they are working in a way that is different than what you had designed. Watch and record how they execute everyday tasks and document any inconsistencies. From this data, devise a plan that creates a vision of how to manage growth and adapt to user needs and demands. Take the data and the new game plan and propose a product life cycle, or future strategy to the stakeholders. Map out how to scale growth and performance, and schedule the incremental tuning and maintenance. Match the product goals to the client's business objectives. Ultimately, you want to become an invaluable part of their success model. It is never too early to begin the "next-generation" conversation. Sharing your ideas on increasing customer satisfaction, furthering the relationship with users, and illustrating what is beyond the horizon will help ensure that your clients continue to come back time and again.

FURTHER READING

Ideas often get built on other great ideas, and we easily could have written much more on what we just briefly covered in Part I of this book. We highly encourage you to look deeper at the authors and sources we quote here and suggest that the books we call out become a part of your design and development library. See the reference section for more recommendations to explore these topics in greater detail.

SOME FINAL THOUGHTS

Best practices evolve and change over time; the technology we use, client needs, and user needs change too. If you can't walk into work tomorrow and gut everything (most people can't), pick your battles and piecemeal change one day at a time. Keep your team excited, open, and talking. Take notes on ideas, issues, little wins, and challenges that you, your team, and your clients reveal. The best products in the world didn't come easy; compromise, sacrifice, frustration, mistakes, and humble pie are part of every project. This is not to say that it can't be a little better next time. Stay true to what matters: have good intentions (they're not everything, but they sure help), focus on the goal, have a mantra, be a good listener, measure data and people equally, make sure everyone is up-to-date and involved, throw things away, and break your toys. What designers and developers do is complex ball juggling, so it makes sense that we are reticent to accept the hypervelocity of technology change, or feel overwhelmed and complacent at times. Don't stay stuck; keep your chin up and find your inner Buddha—not everyone gets to sketch, brainstorm ideas, and play with colors all day.

In this chapter we've learned how some simple design patterns and practices can get us started with sketching and prototyping.

PART II

LET'S BUILD A PROTOTYPE

4

GETTING STARTED

This chapter introduces the key fuctions of SketchFlow that support prototyping and establishes a common definition of prototyping that we can use when discussing prototyping techniques. We'll show you how to set up your SketchFlow workspace and create your first SketchFlow map. At the end of this chapter you'll know how to start a new project, set up your workspace, and build a SketchFlow Map for your project. In this section we're going to presume that many of the concepts around Expression Blend and its interface are going to be new to you. We'll introduce key concepts and names in bold in Part II. For legibility, we'll refrain from doing this in later sections.

LET'S BUILD A PROTOTYPE

By using a simple set of examples in Chapters 4 through 11, we show you how to do the following:

- Set up the workspace for SketchFlow in Expression Blend.
- Create a map that shows the flow, screens, and components that comprise your dynamic prototype.
- Import sketches and create content.

- Share and get feedback on your work.

- Use animation to simulate interactions.

- Add navigation.

- Create states that add interactivity.

- Annotate your work.

- Generate documentation.

- Begin working with data.

When you're done with these examples you'll have been introduced to all the major features of SketchFlow in Expression Blend and will be able to create, work on, and share SketchFlow projects using SketchFlow in Expression Blend.

> In Part I of this book, we covered the fundamental of effective prototyping and best practices. In Part III, we take a deeper dive into the features of SketchFlow and explain the program in detail. In Part IV, we apply this knowledge to a more complex tutorial project to work with advanced features.

No matter how we define the word prototype, there are some common threads that run across the discipline of prototyping. There are also many tools that we can use to create a prototype—including a simple pencil and paper. So, why should we use a tool like SketchFlow in Expression Blend? Let's see if we can answer that:

- Prototypes are artifacts that can represent, prove, and demonstrate the functionality and viability of an idea, be it a structure, product, service, software, website, or device.

- Prototypes are useful in collecting feedback and demonstrating actions or steps based on the receiving of feedback.

- Prototypes should be something that can be created quickly and inexpensively—particularly relative to the final outcome.

- Prototypes should have the ability to showcase, demonstrate, or enable an individual to interact with a proposed solution.

- Prototypes should be something that we can easily walk away from and start over with.

Prototypes are extremely valuable in design for determining what to build versus how to build it. Sometimes the act of prototyping itself can lead to breakthroughs or epiphanies that are harder to come by with more linear processes.

Increasingly, prototypes can have their place in more detailed design and definition activities. When they do, the following can be useful attributes as well:

- The ability to create, evolve, leverage, and reuse libraries and design patterns.
- The ability to carry some assets, code, and structures into production versus discarding.

With SketchFlow in Expression Blend, we are concerned with dynamic prototypes. SketchFlow can facilitate a variety of prototyping and concept exploration, but our primary focus in our introductory chapters will be on using SketchFlow to design an interactive application.

When we say dynamic, we're talking about the secret sauce of interactivity that's often too difficult and time consuming to demonstrate with static or physical prototyping methods. Today, this type of interactivity is often too costly and time consuming to demonstrate by creating actual code to showcase interactivity. Or, when we do create this interactivity, we must often use tools that don't enable us to leverage code, frameworks, or other technical patterns that may also be a critical part of our solution.

SketchFlow's ability to use animation with quickly generated sketches can overcome these barriers in traditional waterfall processes and can enable designers to work with interactive concepts earlier in the design process in a rapid and iterative fashion. This makes it easy to explore multiple options or even start over without making big investments in development to prove ideas. As the design process moves into production, SketchFlow enables us to leverage assets we are comfortable with or leverage design and technical patterns to add increased fidelity to our concepts.

As an agile development tool, SketchFlow enables designers and developers to work more iteratively through the design, proof of concept, and development process and begin the process of creating reusable assets and elements that can aid in the detailed design and development process.

Many of the techniques and strategies we outline in this book are universal and applicable to other tools, disciplines, and practices related to prototyping. Use them where they work best for you; along the way, we'll also discuss best practices that work well for us and give you tips and tricks on how to quickly get the most out of SketchFlow in Expression Blend.

SketchFlow solves some key challenges that existing tools and processes have when it comes to prototyping workflows and interactions. In fact, you'll likely find that regardless of your profession, SketchFlow in Expression Blend can be a fantastic tool to use to generate, explore, and get feedback on ideas around products, services, software, and business concepts.

SETUP

We're going to presume that you have Expression Blend installed on your computer—if this is not the case, you can go to www.microsoft.com/expression and download a trial. Note that you'll need to be working with Expression Blend 3.0 or later with a license key that enables SketchFlow in Expression Blend functionality. It's probably a good idea to ensure that you have Silverlight installed on your computer as well. The easiest way to check if you have Silverlight is to go to www.microsoft.com/silverlight and see if the page loads correctly. If the page doesn't prompt you to load Silverlight you should be in good shape. If you need to load Silverlight the page will provide instructions and guide you through the right steps.

In addition, Chapters 4 through 11 require some files that we've created for you; they can be downloaded at www.dynamic-prototyping.com. On the home page, you should see a welcome message and links where you can download files for each chapter or a single archive that contains all the chapters. For Chapter 4 you'll see directories called *Chapter Number_ Project* and *Source Art*. The *Source Art* directory will be the same directory you use for all chapters in Part II. If you are ambitious you can create assets from scratch as you read Part II but we're going to be learning a great deal of new concepts. We suggest grabbing the sample files before you begin.

For each chapter in Part II we have a new set of project files that include all the information we covered in the previous chapter. This enables you to jump right into chapters without having to work in a linear fashion. It can also be a learning aid. If you get confused in a chapter, simply look at the files for the next chapter to see what we are trying to accomplish. Or if you'd simply like a preview of what you are building, you can open the project files for the next chapter and view the output of that project.

SketchFlow in Expression Blend can only have one project open at a time, but you can have more than one instance of Expression Blend open at the same time if you'd like to to click back and forth between project files for different chapters.

SETTING UP YOUR WORKSPACE

When you launch Expression Blend for the first time, you are presented with a menu. If you've worked with Expression Blend in the past, you may see that it lists your most recent projects. You can select a new project or work with the *Chapter4* project we've created for you.

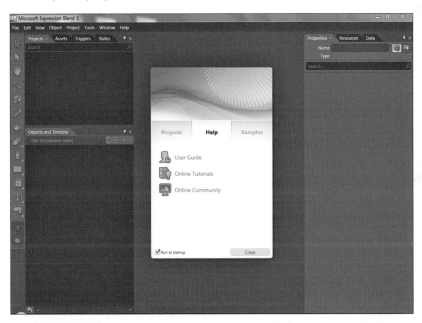

Figure 4.1   *The default screen you should see when you open Expression Blend for the first time.*

If you select the tab labeled **Projects**, you are presented with a dialog box that contains a number of options. For now, we want to create what is called a *Silverlight 3 SketchFlow Application*. Select **New Project**.

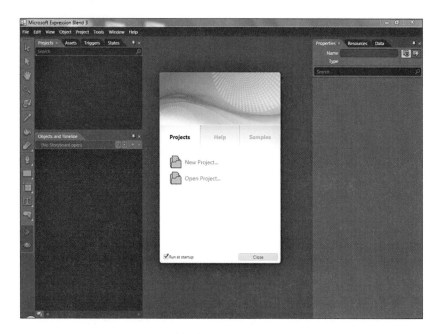

Figure 4.2 *You can open an existing project file or create a new one.*

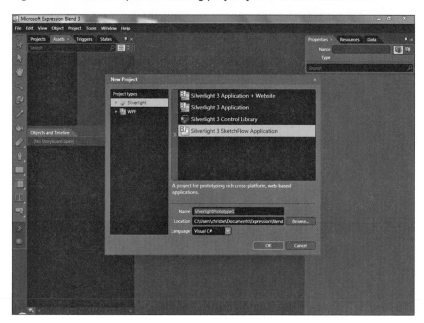

Figure 4.3 *Project selections that are available with Expression Blend.*

Name your project *SilverlightPrototype4* and click OK or open the *Chapter 4* project that we've provided for you. If you're creating a new project, Expression Blend creates a directory in your documents folder to save all your projects and their assorted files. This folder is called Expression in your documents folder. We suggest storing your projects here by default and copying new projects into this directory when you download or get projects from others.

When you create new projects, you may also notice an option to select a programming language; in most cases, you leave this as Visual C#, as we do now. We explain the differences between some of these options in the Resources section of this book.

Creating a Silverlight SketchFlow project enables us to package and distribute this application with the Silverlight SketchFlow Player so we can share our prototypes in the browser on PCs and other computing platforms. Alternatively, we could create a WPF SketchFlow application if we were designing a solution focused on a Windows application that we'd only need to use, see, or share on a Windows platform.

Technically, Silverlight and WPF applications have some very big differences. From a SketchFlow perspective, you'll find the capabilities to be identical with a few minor differences will cover in later chapters. Refer to the Reference section to learn more about the differences between Silverlight and WPF.

At this point, you probably have a workspace that looks similar to this.

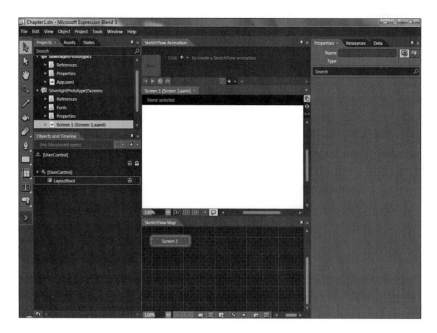

Figure 4.4   A workspace for SketchFlow at a computer resolution of 1024 by 768 pixels.

This default view is for the Design workspace in Expression Blend. For now, you don't need worry about what all of these panels are. In fact, you're going to simplify your workspace and save a special Workspaces file that you can use when working with SketchFlow projects.

If you're curious about all of these different parts of Expression, we do a comprehensive overview in Part III that describes the Expression Blend interface in detail.

What we want to do is get our interface to look something like Figure 4.5.

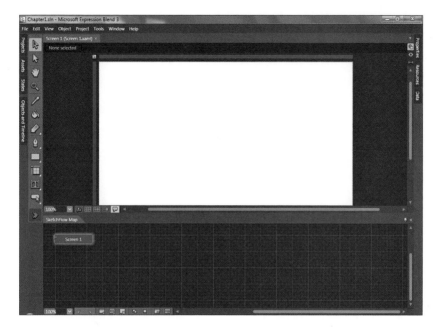

Figure 4.5 *A workspace we've optimized for SketchFlow projects.*

So, how do we do that? First, let's close a few panels that we don't need.

If you look from left to right across your screen, notice that there are a number of tabs that run across the top of the screen. Find the panel labeled **SketchFlow Animation**.

Figure 4.6   *The SketchFlow Animation Panel.*

In the upper-right corner of that panel, you should see an **x**. Click that **x** to close the panel. You can always go to the **Window** menu to reopen any panel or even reset the program to a default view.

Now if you look to the left of the screen, you see a three-tab structure below the application menu.

Figure 4.7   The tabs for Projects, Assets, and States.

To the right of that panel, find the **x** icon, but also notice a white icon that looks like a pushpin. If you click this button once, it appears to actually collapse the projects, assets, and states panels, but what it really does is enable a feature named Auto Hide. As we work through the chapter, you'll see how useful Auto Hide can be. Let's enable it for a few more panels. After enabling Auto Hide for the last panel, you probably noticed that it caused the objects and timeline panel to move to the top of the screen. Enable Auto Hide for that section and then do the same for the right side of the screen, enabling it for the **Properties**, **Resources**, and **Data** panels.

When you're done, you should have a screen that looks like Figure 4.5.

This is a simplified view in Expression Blend that is ideally suited for quickly building prototypes with SketchFlow in Expression Blend. In fact, let's go up to the **Window** menu and save this Workspace. Go the **Window** menu and select the third item in the menu entitled **Save as New WorkSpace**.... Select a name for the workspace—we suggest just calling it *SketchFlow*. Now, with future projects, you'll be able to easily configure this workspace by selecting the *SketchFlow* workspace you've just created.

UNDERSTANDING YOUR WORKSPACE

If you've used animation or imaging software before, what you now see in Expression Blend should look pretty familiar to you.

THE ARTBOARD

The top portion of the screen is the Artboard. The white screen you see on the Artboard is similar to a canvas that you'd see in other graphics applications. It's best to think of this canvas as a blank sheet of paper or screen. This screen is a work area where you can add elements that you've imported into your SketchFlow project or to create new items directly on the design surface.

Figure 4.8 *This screen is where you'll actually import and work with sketches or create elements from scratch using controls and drawing tools available in Sketch-Flow.*

Many of the conventions we're familiar with in design tools are present in Expression Blend. For example, select the Artboard and use the Control and + or – keys. You should see the Artboard zoom in and zoom out. If you have a scroll wheel on a mouse attached to your computer, you should notice that it works the same way. If you hold down the space bar, you should see that you can drag the Artboard around on the screen.

You'll also notice some controls and settings that surround the Artboard. We cover those in the later chapters of this book, as they are not important for what we're going to do now. You will find that most controls are self-explanatory in Expression Blend if you mouse over them and wait for a context menu to appear.

THE SKETCHFLOW MAP

The next portion of the screen below the Artboard that takes up the most space is the **SketchFlow Map**.

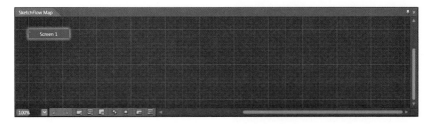

Figure 4.9   The SketchFlow Map panel.

It is here that we'll actually begin most of our work with a SketchFlow project. On the bottom of this panel, there are controls to control the zoom level of the panel, undo or redo actions, and add and subtract elements, as well as controls for fitting all elements or selected elements on to your screen.

Notice that there should be a box on the screen in blue that is labeled Screen 1, this box is called a node. This is a graphic representation of the white canvas you see on the Artboard.

Mouse over that screen, and you should see that a panel appears below the node. You're presented with some options in the form of icons; mouse over each icon and read the description.

Figure 4.10   This box in our SketchFlow Map represents a screen in our application and is called a node.

You can create new nodes that attach by default to the node you just created. You can create new connectors to existing nodes and create a special type of node that represents a component screen, which is discussed later.

Finally, you'll see the last icon labeled **Change visual tag**, which enables you to change the color of your node.

*Figure 4.11   Changing the color of our node with the **Change visual tag** feature.*

CREATING YOUR FIRST SKETCHFLOW MAP

Now, in our particular case, let's presume we're helping out a friend at a shoe manufacturer to design some software to enable customers to select and customize a shoe design in a new flagship store they are opening. Your friend would like to design software that will not only work on computers in the store, but eventually even work on a customer's computer, phone, or gaming console.

The first thing your colleague does is draw you a picture that shows you the basic details of the application. She knows that customers in the store will need to set up a profile, design their shoe, and then be able to save and order their creation. She would like your help in creating a simple presentation that demonstrates how this software would work.

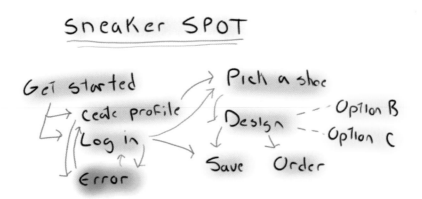

Figure 4.12   Our simple sketch shows a potential flow for our application.

From this sketch, you decide to quickly represent what this application flow would look like in SketchFlow in Expression Blend. See if you can recreate what's in the picture in Figure 4.12. All the nodes you create will be connected screens in the application.

Because we have hidden our work surfaces when we started our project, the Auto Hide feature automatically shows and then hides specific panels as you create new project assets. This may be a bit disconcerting at first; as you continue to work in SketchFlow, however, you'll find that this method gives you just enough information and feedback about the assets you're creating, while letting you continue to focus on the **SketchFlow Map** and Artboard. If you're working with Expression Blend on a higher-resolution monitor, you might find that it's easier to leave some of these panels open after you get more familiar with the functionality of Expression Blend and to disable Auto Hide. You'll also notice that as you add each node that the Artboard for that node will be opened each time you create a new screen.

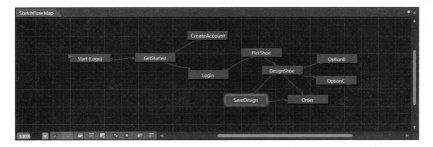

Figure 4.13   A recreation of the sketch.

Now, spend some time with the flow you have just created and see if you can make some changes to your flow by color coding a few nodes and their connectors. This is something that is simple to do, and color coding can help you quickly draw attention to and visually organize important areas of the application—such as error states or groupings of components in your applications. In the **Project menu**, you can even change these colors by selecting **SketchFlow Project Settings**.

Mouse over one of the blue nodes and right-click with your mouse. A dialog box appears that gives you a number of options; these options duplicate some of the options you also see when you access the contextual panel that appears below a selected screen. You'll be able to rename, delete, or even change which screen appears first in a SketchFlow application by using the **Set as Start** selection for a node. The last icon, labeled **Change visual tag**, lets you change the color of the screens.

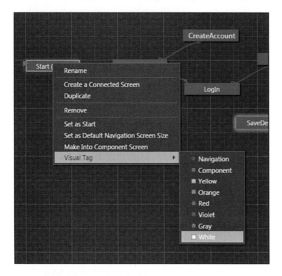

Figure 4.14   Editing visual tags for a node.

Now, mouse over the actual connectors. You'll notice that you have simple options here as well. In addition to being able to color code these connectors, you can also indicate what type of **Transition Style** will be used to transition from screen to screen. Leave this in the default **Fade** setting for now, but take a moment to look at some of the other options. They can be useful for adding simple but powerful transitions that can mimic the interactivity of an application.

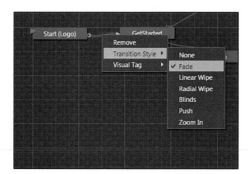

*Figure 4.15   We can use **Transition Style** to control the transitions that occur between screens as we navigate from one screen to another at runtime.*

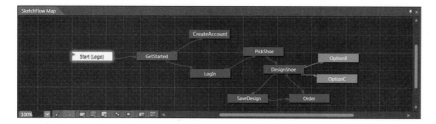

Figure 4.16   Our SketchFlow Map with nodes and connectors that we have color coded.

At this point, we've created a simple structure and guts for what could be a dynamic prototype. Because we haven't added any content to the screens, created in the map, they should all appear blank on the Artboard. Next, we'll start adding content to our application to bring these screens to life.

Before we move to the next chapter, we want to do one more thing. Select the *Start (Logo)* screen in the **SketchFlow Map** panel by double clicking it. Then, access the File Menu and select the option **Close Other Documents**. This closes all the files that we have open in our project except for our *Start (Logo)* screen.

Figure 4.17   When our workspace gets too cluttered, we can can close documents that we've left open but don't need to work with right now.

SUMMARY

In this chapter we learned how to create a project/solution, set up our workspace, simplify our workspace for SketchFlow projects, and create our first SketchFlow Map.

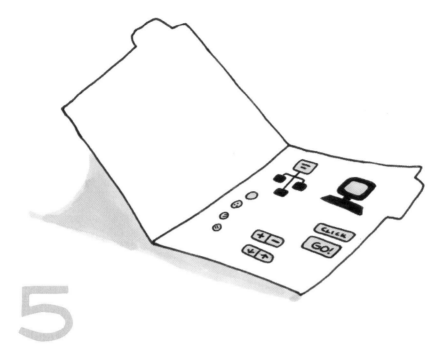

5

IMPORTING AND CREATING CONTENT

This chapter shows us how to work with content. We're going to show you how to import content that you've created in other programs into SketchFlow in Expression Blend and how to create content within the tool. At the end of this chapter you'll know to get assets into SketchFlow and how to create items directly on the Artboard in Expression Blend.

You can continue using the project you used in the last chapter or open up the project files for Chapter 5. We've also created assets in our *Source Art* directory that you should have downloaded earlier. Inside of *SourceArt* should be a directory called *Sketches*. This includes some quickly sketched screens that we can use to complete this chapter.

sneakerSPOT

Figure 5.1   Screen assets that you can use in this chapter.

Let's import these files into our project. We'll need to open our **Projects** panel to accomplish that.

Figure 5.2   The Projects panel.

As the Projects panel opens from Auto Hide mode, you'll notice a lot of files that we don't really need to worry about right now mixed in with some files that have names from our SketchFlow Map. All we're going to do right now is create a new directory called *Sketches* to import our sketch files into so we can use them in our project. Navigate over to the Projects panel and open the area of the project called **SilverlightPrototype5Screens**; right-click, and you should see a context menu.

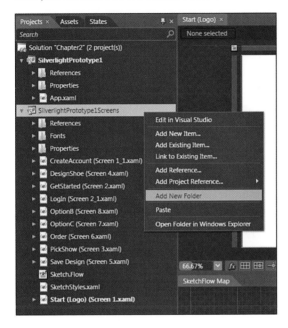

Figure 5.3 *Adding a new directory in the **Projects** panel via a context menu.*

There are a number of options. The ones we care most about for SketchFlow are the following:

- **Add New Item**, which lets us create a new item in our project.

- **Add Existing Item**, which lets us import existing assets into our project.

- **Link to Existing Item**, which lets us link existing assets into our project, which may be useful if you're working with specific assets that may change—such as photography or video assets that may change over time.

- **Add New Folder**, which lets us create new directories to house elements.

Let's select the option to create a new folder and import the sketch assets that we'll use for this project.

Figure 5.4   Our new directory as it appears in the **Projects** panel.

Once we've created our new folder and named it we should right-click and select the **Add Existing Item** option. This will open Windows Explorer and we can navigate to our *SourceArt* directory and import those items into our *Sketches* folder. When you're done, the folder should look like this, although you may be missing a few elements or they may be named differently if you've created your own.

Figure 5.5   The newly created directory with our added pictures.

ADDING CONTENT TO A NAVIGATION FLOW

After we've added our content to our *Sketches* folder, we can simply navigate to the correlating screens in our flow and drag these elements onto our canvas. For example, let's go to our first screen in our flow and drag out our logo sketch onto the Artboard. You might notice as you move your mouse over each item in your *Sketches* folder that a small thumbnail preview of that file will appear.

Now let's select the node labeled *sneakerSPOT* in our **SketchFlow Map** and double click it. Take the corresponding image labeled *sneakerSPOT* in our *Sketches* folder and drag it onto our Artboard. We can do that with all our images and their corresponding screens in our **SketchFlow Map** with the exception of the Log In screen, which we address in a moment.

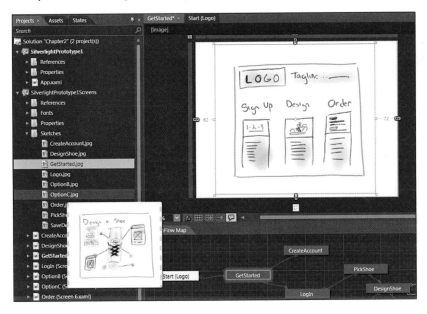

Figure 5.6   Images that we've imported and added to our Artboard.

Now is also a good time to get in the practice of saving our work on our project. When working with multiple screens and adding elements at once, we are in effect editing multiple documents at once that need to be saved. You can use **Control + Shift + S** to save all open documents in a SketchFlow project. When you close a project, it's possible that you might have open documents that you haven't saved. SketchFlow prompts you to save these items before it closes the project.

Figure 5.7 *A dialog box prompts us to save changes we've made to individual screens in a project.*

TOOLS AND ASSETS FOR CREATING CONTENT FOR A NAVIGATION FLOW

Creating content directly in Blend for a SketchFlow Map requires understanding the tools and assets options available. Let's see how some of these tools and assets work that we eventually use to create content for our Log-In Screen.

THE TOOL PANEL

There are only a few real key features of the **Tools** panel that you'll use extensively with SketchFlow in Expression Blend.

Figure 5.8   The **Tools** *panel that we use to access items that let us design directly on the Artboard.*

If you use other design tools, most of these controls should look familiar to you. We'll briefly cover the ones we need here.

Figure 5.9   *The Selection tool.*

The **Selection** tool is used for making basic selections of objects. Depending on what objects you select, you should be able to move and manipulate objects on the Artboard, including the ability to scale and rotate. You can quickly select this tool from the keyboard by selecting **V**.

Figure 5.10   *The Pan tool.*

The **Pan** tool enables you to pan the **Artboard** or **SketchFlow Map**. You can quickly activate this tool by pressing the space key on your keyboard.

Figure 5.11   *The Zoom tool.*

The **Zoom** tool enables you to zoom in or magnify parts of your workspace. You can quickly select this tool from the keyboard by selecting **Z**.

Figure 5.12 *The Pen and Pencil tools.*

The **Pen** tool enables you to create paths where you define each node, or if you're familiar with Adobe tools you'll find this tool works identically to the Bezier path tools in Adobe Photoshop and Adobe Illustrator. The **Pencil** tool enables you to draw freehand paths. With either tool, you can actually create simple sketches and wireframes directly in SketchFlow, although we prefer to create our sketches freehand or with a tool optimized for sketching, such as Autodesk's Sketchbook Pro. You can quickly select the **Pen** tool from the keyboard by selecting **P**. You can select the **Pencil** tool by selecting **Y**.

The remaining tools are not typically used in SketchFlow projects. The **User Guide** (which can be launched from Expression Blend by hitting the F1 key when you're in Expression Blend) also covers the functions of tool bar items in great detail.

ASSETS

Assets are where you'll spend most of your time when working with SketchFlow in Expression Blend; this is where the most frequently used project components for SketchFlow reside. Let's take a look at what's in the Assets panel.

There are two ways to access assets. One way is directly from the **Tool** panel.

Figure 5.13 *Accessing Assets from the **Tool** panel.*

This window appears (see Figure 5.14).

Figure 5.14   *Assets when exposed from the **Tools** panel.*

There are a lot of items in the **Asset** view from the **Tool** window. For the most part, you'll only use assets that are available to you in the **Project** and **SketchFlow** categories. Here are a few tips:

- SketchFlow has a collection of assets that have a sketch **Style**. This style looks like hand-drawn art, but all assets have access to the same functionality as any normal control in an Expression Blend Project. It's an incredibly useful way to add controls and functionality to dynamic prototypes that have started with sketching but need to evolve.

- You can discern this style from other styles in the Asset panel because it's appended onto the end of the asset. For example, in the **Tools menu**, you could add a **ListBox**; this adds a **Listbox** that has a default WPF or Silverlight style. However, there is also a **ListBox-Sketch** that adds a **Listbox** with the same functionality, but it will look hand drawn.

- You can **Search** for assets. For example, in the preceding view, you could type **text** in the search box and filter, and only the assets with a **text** in their title will appear. If you find yourself struggling to locate an asset, it's always a good idea to make sure the **Search** box is clear of any text.

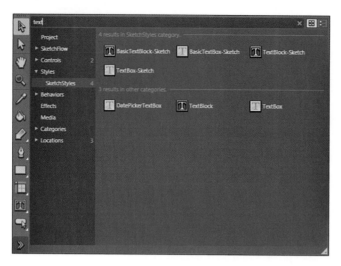

Figure 5.15 *Shows how the SketchStyles asset menu appears with a search parameter of text.*

Another way to see assets is through the use of the **Assets** panel. In general, we find that the **Assets** panel is the most convenient way to access things when working with assets as you get familiar with SketchFlow.

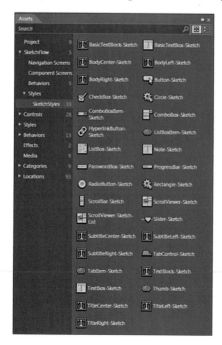

Figure 5.16 *Looking at assets with the Assets panel.*

ADDING CONTROLS WITH THE SKETCHFLOW STYLES

Now let's actually use **Tools** and **Assets** to create content in our project. Find the *Log In* screen and open it. Instead of adding a sketch to this screen, we are going to use some of the components available in SketchFlow to create the Log In screen. There are a few advantages to doing this.

One, we're actually using User Controls available to us via Expression Blend. This means that instead of making things that look like text boxes, dialogs, and buttons, we are using actual User Controls that work and have behaviors built into them that you would expect. For example, a button has selected, unselected, and hover states, and text entry boxes accept text input when our prototype is running.

Two, even though the controls are fully functional, we can apply a Style to them that looks like a sketch, enabling us to keep the essence of our prototype low-fidelity—a critical step when we want to focus on the interaction of an application versus how it looks, or to keep stakeholders from presuming things are finished when they are not.

See if you can create the following using **SketchStyles** in the **Assets** panel.

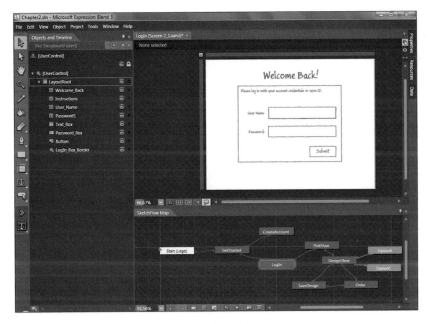

Figure 5.17   Creating a Log In screen using Assets.

We'll give you some hints....

The **Rectangle-Sketch** for our border box.

Figure 5.18   *The Rectangle-Sketch asset.*

The **TitleCenter-Sketch** for our "Welcome Back!" copy.

Figure 5.19   *The TitleCenter-Sketch asset.*

Here are **BodyCenter-Sketch** and **Bodyright-Sketch** for the other copy.

Figure 5.20   *The BodyCenter-Sketch and Bodyright-Sketch assets.*

The **TextBox-Sketch** for our "User Name" box.

Figure 5.21   *The TextBox-Sketch asset.*

Here is the **PasswordBox-Sketch** for our "Password" box.

Figure 5.22   *The PasswordBox-Sketch asset.*

The **Button-Sketch** for the Submit button.

Figure 5.23   *The Button-Sketch asset.*

As you create this screen, you'll probably have to use the arrow tool or arrow keys on your keyboard to move around some objects and resize them. When you're done with this, it's time to move on to the next chapter and learn how we can share what we've created with others.

SUMMARY

In this chapter we learned how we can import content that we've created elsewhere into SketchFlow; how we can create directories to house this content in our project; and how we can create content directly on the Artboard with Tools and SketchFlow styles.

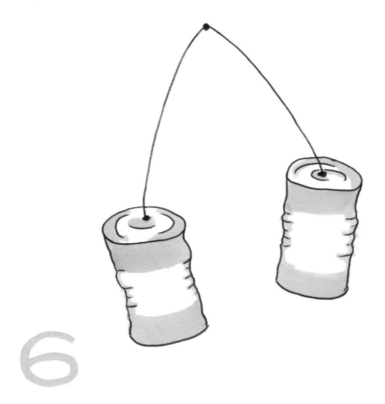

6

SHARING YOUR PROJECT AND GETTING FEEDBACK

This chapter shows you how you can take the work that you've completed thus far and share it with others. We show you how to build your project, share it, and allow individuals that view your project to provide feedback within a special feature of SketchFlow in Expression Blend called the SketchFlow Player.

BUILDING, RUNNING, AND DISTRIBUTING YOUR PROJECT

Sharing and getting feedback on your work in the early stages of conceptualization is a critical part of both design- and agile-focused projects, and SketchFlow is a useful tool for sharing concepts both inside your team and to external stakeholders. SketchFlow makes it extremely easy to share your dynamic prototypes and get feedback on them. The first step is to actually run your application. You do this by going to the **Project** menu and selecting **Run Project** or, as an easier way, by simply hitting **F5** on your keyboard.

When you build a project, you are actually compiling all the code to run your project—and updating certain files and assemblies based on changes you are making in your project. Occasionally, you might get an error when trying to build your project in SketchFlow after significant project editing, something that is displayed via the **Results** window. Typically, rebuilding your project again should allow it to compile successfully if you encounter this.

Figure 6.1   *This shows the Project menu and the Run Project selection. We can also access this feature from our keyboard by selecting F5.*

If you're using a SketchFlow project in WPF, this creates an instance of the application that opens and presents the SketchFlow Player application, the interface that enables people to see your project. If you're building the SketchFlow project in Silverlight, Expression Blend creates an instance of the SketchFlow Player that is hosted in a browser. Like any Silverlight application, you'll be able to share this application with anyone who can view it in a web browser and operating system that supports Silverlight.

You can take these files and distribute them in a number of ways—one way to do this is by going to the **File** menu and selecting **Package SketchFlowProject**, which creates a directory with all the files that are required for playback. For WPF, this creates an executable file that can be played on a PC. For Silverlight, this creates a directory of assets that comprises a Silverlight application that can be viewed in a browser.

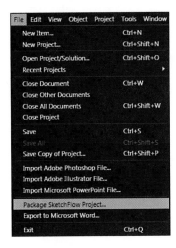

Figure 6.2 *We can collect our project for distribution by going to the File menu and selecting Package SketchFlow Project.*

You also can do the following:

- Email the files.

- Host the file on a computer or server where stakeholders can access them.

- Distribute the WPF application via the Web as a click-once application for download.

- Host SketchFlow projects created in Silverlight in a browser, which stakeholders can view on the browser and platform of their choice.

- Distribute or host the WPF SketchFlow Player on a server or website.

The SketchFlow Player looks identical regardless of whether it's in WPF or Silverlight. The exception is that a SketchFlow application built in Silverlight will be surrounded by the browser chrome—which you can, of course, remove in browsers that have a full-screen capability.

Figure 6.3 shows how the application looks with the SketchFlow Player in a browser.

Figure 6.3   *An example of a SketchFlow application presented with the Sketch-Flow Player in a browser.*

NAVIGATION IN THE SKETCHFLOW PLAYER

There are four ways to navigate in the SketchFlow Player, as follows:

- By using the **Navigation** panel.

- By using the **Map** panel.

- By overlaying the **Map** on the Artboard.

- By activating interactivity within the application itself (something we haven't done yet with our project, but will tackle next).

By default, the SketchFlow Player displays the Start Screen, which we renamed *sneakerSPOT*. In effect, this screen is the *Home*, or what we call the *Default* screen, of the SketchFlow project. In the Navigation panel, we should see a link to the *Get Started* screen.

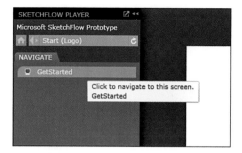

Figure 6.4 *This shows us a tab that would take us to the Get Started screen.*

You may notice a zoom bar at the bottom of the screen. This zoom bar enables us to zoom in and out of the screen to look at details or resize the application for the screen on which we're viewing it. Let's select the *GetStarted* label.

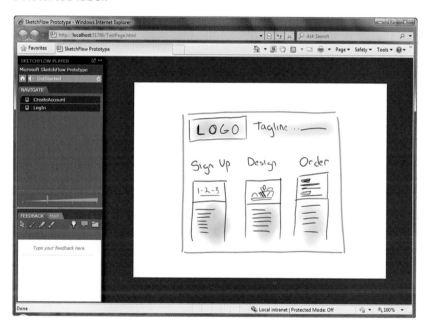

Figure 6.5 *The SketchFlow Player is now showing our Get Started screen and links to the Create Profile screen and the Log In screen.*

Notice that the Artboard refreshes and that we are now on the Get Started screen. We can link to other screens in our application flow that connects to this screen—in this case, *CreateAccount* or *LogIn*. Let's select *LogIn*.

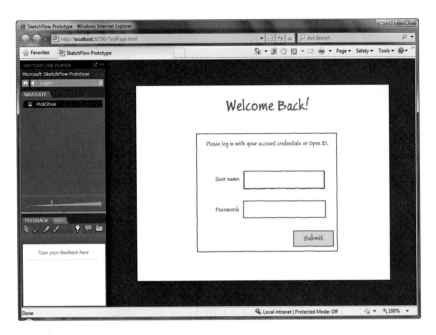

Figure 6.6 *The Log In screen with the controls we created earlier.*

Now we see the screen that we just created with various User Controls. See if you can enter your name in the User Name box; try entering a password in the Password text box, and then hit the Submit button. All of these controls can accept input, even though they look like a sketch. This is where the power of SketchFlow starts to reveal itself. Because we are working with real controls, it's easy to add interactivity to our interface by taking advantage of assets that are provided in SketchFlow. It's also easy to have some of these real controls follow us into production because they are the same controls that a developer would typically use to create this application in a WPF or Silverlight application.

If we want to return to the Home screen of our prototype, we merely need to hit the home icon.

Sometimes this linear navigation can mask what's available in a prototype. Take a look at our Feedback panel.

Figure 6.7 *The Feedback panel where a user can enter feedback about a project.*

By default, you should see a **Feedback** panel selection; select the **Map** panel. You should now see that the actual **SketchFlow Map** is available to the reviewer as well (see Figure 6.8).

Figure 6.8 *The SketchFlow Map displayed in our Map Panel.*

You can actually put your cursor on this panel and drag around the SketchFlowMap. In addition, you can use the zoom control to increase the size of the SketchFlowMap or even to pop an overlay of the map onto the Artboard (see Figure 6.9). Notice that the Map panels auto-update as you navigate through your prototype in overlay mode (see Figure 6.10).

Figure 6.9 *The zoom control.*

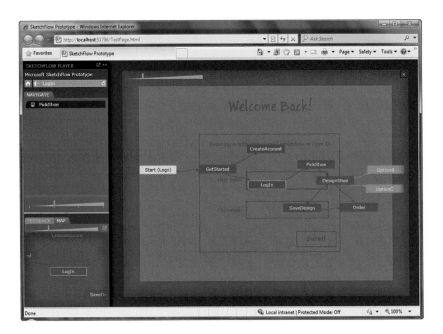

Figure 6.10   *The Map panel in overlay mode.*

We can also either close or break out the SketchFlow Player panel using these controls. For now, hiding the SketchFlow Player panel wouldn't allow someone to navigate through the prototype because we haven't added interactivity into the application itself—we'll tackle this in a moment.

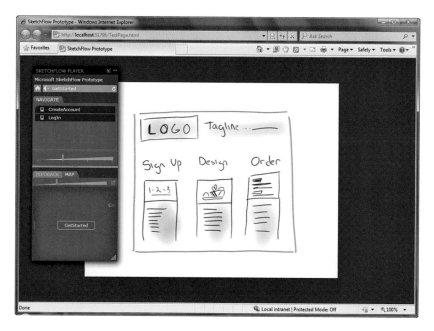

Figure 6.11 *This icon enables us to pop out or collapse the navigation controls for our SketchFlow Player.*

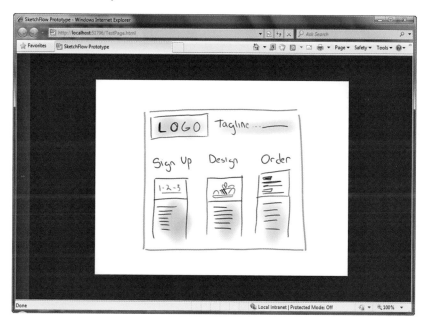

Figure 6.12 *This shows the SketchFlow Player controls in a collapsed mode.*

FEDDBACK IN THE SKETCHFLOW PLAYER

Now let's look at how we can use the SketchFlow Player to easily leave or create feedback. Make sure you can see the SketchFlow Player panel. Find the Feedback panel and select it.

This panel lets a stakeholder provide a variety of feedback in a number of ways, starting with the ability to insert type directly into the **Feedback Text Entry Box**. Every screen in an application gets its own instance of this feedback area. To enter feedback, simply start typing. Once you're done, you must click the small **+** sign to save the feedback. Let's investigate the feedback functions in more detail.

Figure 6.13   Entering feedback.

Here are the controls available to us when we provide feedback.

Figure 6.14   All of the feedback controls.

Figure 6.15 *The Arrow tool.*

The **Arrow** enables us to select a text box for direct text entry into the **Feedback Text Entry Box**.

Figure 6.16 *The Pen tool.*

The **Pen** enables us to add feedback directly on the **Artboard**, as does the **Highlighter**.

Figure 6.17 *The Highligher tool.*

The **Eraser** enables us to edit or remove feedback from the **Artboard**. The next set of controls actually controls what feedback is visible.

Figure 6.18 *The Eraser tool.*

Figure 6.19 *The Lightbulb icon shows or hides inked feedback or items that we draw directly on the Artboard.*

The **Lightbulb** icon enables us to show or hide inked feedback (from the pen or highlighter). When the **Lightbulb** is *on*, this feedback appears.

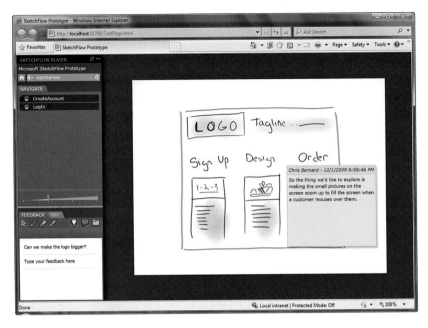

Figure 6.20 *The Annotation icon shows or hides annotations that the solution creator would include with the project to explain or call out features or items on a specific screen.*

The **Annotation** icon actually displays annotations inserted into the prototype by us in SketchFlow, something we discuss in Chapter 11, "Bringing It All Together." When the **Annocation icon** is on, the annotations appear.

Figure 6.21 *Exporting feedback by selecting the Show Feedback options icon.*

Feedback wouldn't be very useful if we couldn't do something with it. Here you can reset all the feedback—which removes it from the application, or you can export a copy of it that can be emailed. When you export information, it asks you for your name or initials and prompts you for a place to save the feedback. You can then email or post this feedback file, and it can be incorporated into your SketchFlow project (see Figure 6.22).

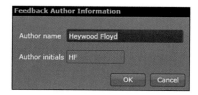

Figure 6.22   An example of feedback being exported.

Add feedback to your your project and then export this data to your hard drive. Create at least two unique sets of feedback that you can work with.

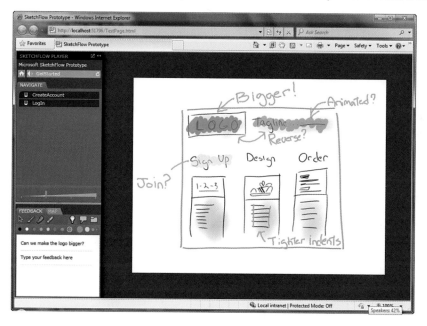

Figure 6.23   An example of feedback using inking functions on the Artboard.

VIEWING FEEDBACK IN EXPRESSION BLEND

If we return to our project in Expression Blend, we can see what that feedback looks like when we load it into our SketchFlow project.

The best way to do this is to go to the **Window** menu and select **Feedback**. This opens up the **Feedback** panel in the SketchFlow project.

Figure 6.24   Importing feedback into SketchFlow in Expression Blend.

Once that panel is loaded, your screen should look like Figure 6.25. (If you have previous feedback loaded into your project, it is also displayed in this panel.)

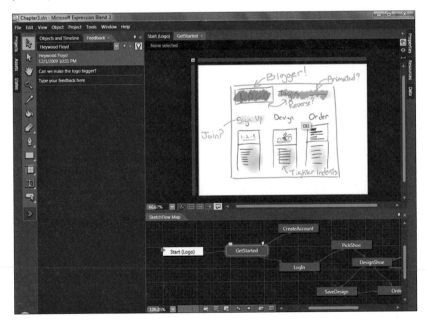

Figure 6.25   Viewing the feedback created in the SketchFlow Player in SketchFlow in Expression Blend with a Feedback file loaded into the Feedback panel.

We'll use the following controls to load feedback. Load some sample feedback that you've created.

Figure 6.26 *Adding additional feedback into the Feedback panel.*

You can load multiple sets of feedback but only view feedback from one person at a time. You'll see their text-based comments and any input they provide on-screen. You'll also notice in the SketchFlow Map that little icons appear on screens where there's been feedback from a stakeholder.

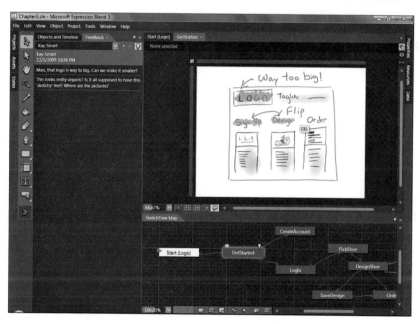

Figure 6.27 *The Lightbulb icon indicates that there is feedback for this particular screen in our project.*

When you're done with feedback, you can turn off the Lightbulb to hide feedback that appears on the Artboard and then close the Feedback panel, or you can remove feedback from the project by deleting feedback files that appear in the project menu.

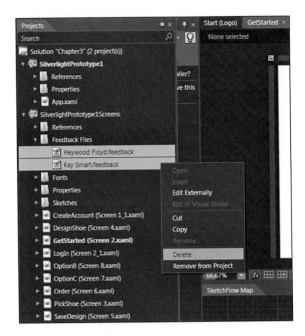

Figure 6.28   Deleting feedback from our project.

Many times in projects, it's difficult to go through all the necessary steps to prepare assets in a format where you can easily get feedback. In SketchFlow, it's easy to get feedback early and often and view that feedback in context, helping to create more informed designs based on stakeholder input or even just to facilitate better communication within a team. Now let's see how we can start bringing our project to life.

SUMMARY

In this chapter we learned, how to share our SketchFlow project with others; how to use the SketchFlow Player to navigate through our project; how to use the SketchFlow Player to input feedback on a project; how to export feedback from the SketchFlow player; and how to import feedback into SketchFlow in Expression Blend.

7

BASIC ANIMATION WITH SKETCHFLOW ANIMATION

This chapter introduces you to the animation features in SketchFlow in Expression Blend and shows you how to simulate a complex interaction using the SketchFlow Animation feature.

ANIMATION CONCEPTS IN SKETCHFLOW

As you collect feedback for a project, it's more than likely that you'll want to begin to explore how an application might work.

One of the simplest ways to do this is with animation. In SketchFlow, you can use animation to demonstrate what different interactions in your application will look like. Although Expression Blend has very advanced animation capabilities, SketchFlow has a special animation system called **SketchFlow Animation** that enables you to quickly create animations that can simulate advanced interactivity. Animation in SketchFlow is based on a system build into Expression Blend called the Visual State Manager, which we cover a bit later when we discuss states.

To understand how this tool works, let's go to the *SaveDesign* screen in our project. In this case, we'd like to show that a customer of sneakerSPOT could select shoes that he's designed and saved and then add them to shopping cart. The goal is to show that a customer could simply grab a saved design and then drop it in a shopping cart on the screen and have the screen auto-update with other saved designs.

It's entirely possible to build functionality that would show how this works programmatically or even within SketchFlow using a more advanced feature called **Behaviors**; however, with a little work with our sketches, we can use SketchFlow to showcase how this would work in a matter of minutes. This is important because in many cases the best approach is to quickly create multiple solutions to see which one ultimately works the best; animation is usually our best tool for doing these rapid investigations.

USING A PSD FILE WITH SKETCHFLOW ANIMATION

Open the new project files for Chapter 7 and if you get stuck during this chapter it may be helpful to look at the Chapter 8 files. The first thing we need to do is look at our current screen and determine what elements need to be animated (see Figure 7.1).

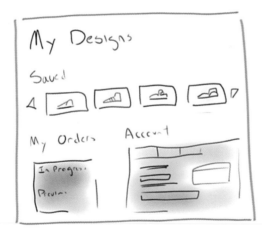

Figure 7.1 *The screen we'd like to animate.*

In our case, we actually took our sketch into Adobe Photoshop and quickly created a layered document with all of our assets that we'd need. We also removed the My Orders part so we could create a shopping cart with some of the User Controls and Assets available to us in SketchFlow.

We can import this Photoshop file into SketchFlow with layers intact so we can quickly start building our animation.

First, let's delete the SaveDesign.jpg from our Artboard. Next, let's go to our **Projects** panel and find our *Sketches* directory that we created earlier. Select the *Sketches* directory. This tells Expression Blend where to place our imported images in our Project folder structure. Expression Blend simply creates a new directory at the root level of our Project structure if we decide not to do that. Note that you cannot move this directory later without breaking your project, so planning as you structure your project can be helpful.

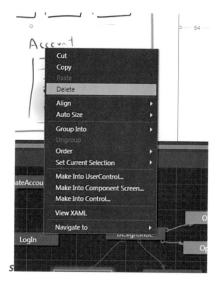

Figure 7.2 *Deleting our current image from the Artboard.*

Now let's import our Photoshop file, which will be in our *Source Art* folder in a subdirectory called *Animation Elements*.

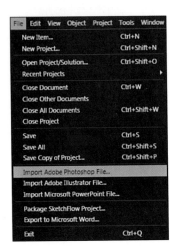

Figure 7.3 Using the File menu to select the Import Adobe Photoshop File feature.

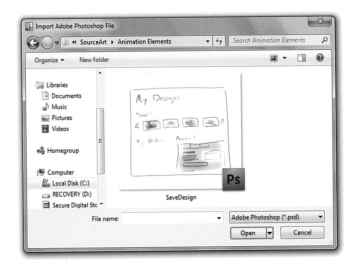

Figure 7.4 The Photoshop file that we'd like to import.

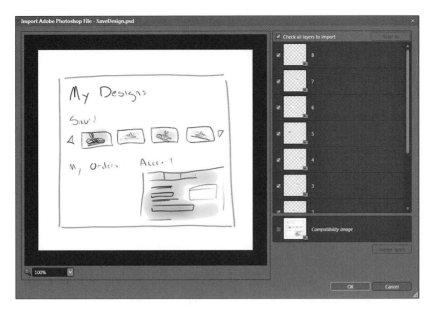

Figure 7.5   The Import Adobe Photoshop File dialog box.

In the **Import Adobe Photoshop File** dialog, we'll see that we can actually see all the layers in our Photoshop file and select which ones we'd like to import. For layers that are hard to discern in the dialog box, we can mouse over them and see previews of what's in each layer. In our case, we'll want to import all of these elements into our project, so we can select the **Check all layers to import** checkbox.

After you import all the files, it should place the items onto your **Artboard** for the *SaveDesign* screen. You may need to position the element a bit to center them on-screen.

To do that you may need to open up your **Projects** and **Objects and Timeline** menus as well and it may be helpful to turn off Auto-Hide on this panel as we work with it.

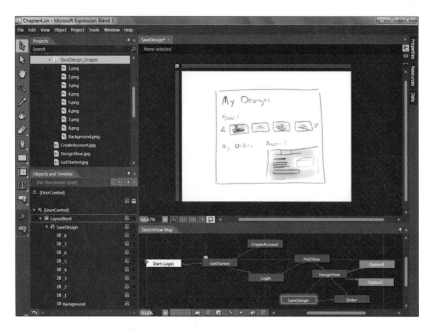

Figure 7.6   Our workspace with the Projects, Objects, and Timeline panel open.

Take note of a few things here. One, the Photoshop file has been added to our Projects directory in the Project panel as a collection of images. In our case, we added this collection to the Sketches folder we created earlier.

Two, we should see a collection of these images arranged in our **Objects and Timeline** panel. Let's take a look at this panel for a moment.

Figure 7.7   Our Projects and Objects and Timeline panel.

Notice that this panel might look very similar to layer panels you see in other programs. We also have controls to lock or turn off the visibility of different attributes. These are tools you use as you work in the SketchFlow interface, just as you would in other graphics programs. We don't, however, use these controls to control what happens to objects in a project at runtime.

UNDERSTANDING OBJECTS AND TIMELINES AND STACK ORDER

The **Objects and Timeline** panel is quite different than layer-based programs because neither SketchFlow nor Expression Blend use layers at all. In Expression Blend, we use what are essentially a series of containers that house the different objects and assets that we use in our application. These objects and assets can be elements we import into our project or simple objects we create within SketchFlow, including shapes or items from our **Asset** panel.

When we look at the **Objects and Timeline** panel, we are looking at a collection of objects that is arranged using a variety of these control elements. Control elements are used to do the following:

- Control the layout of our application.
- House objects, animations, navigations, and other interactions.
- Serve as nested containers for other control elements.

The most important thing to understand when you're looking at the **Objects and Timelines** panel in a SketchFlow project is the **Stack Order** of items. Because control elements are nested in a SketchFlow project (much like the layout of an HTML page), items that are at the root level appear at the top of the **Object and Timelines** panel by default—a mode called **Arrange by markup order.** Nested control elements are by their nature embedded in these **Root** control elements and therefore will cover any items that are nested below them. So, in this case, if we look at the *Save Design* element in the **Objects and Timelines** panel, the order of all the elements we've created is reversed from the structure of the file that we just imported if we were to view it in Adobe Photoshop. We recommend getting used to this structure because it's important to understand the hierarchy of Expression Blend projects as you get more advanced; however, if you find it odd for the time being, you can find a small icon at the bottom of the Objects and Timelines palette and select it. This enables **Arrange by Z order**, which will arrange items in order of which ones appear in front of other objects on a screen. For the projects that we've created for you in Part II, we've enabled the **Arrange by Z order** feature by default until you get familiar with how **Arrange by markup order works**.

Figure 7.8   *Items displayed in Arrange by markup order in the Objects and Timeline panel.*

USING SKETCHFLOW WITH ANIMATION

As you create more advanced interactions and animations in your project, the **Objects and Timeline** panel tells you a lot about your application. It tells you which items have animation or interactivity assigned to them, and it tells you which items are active in different **states** of your project. It also tells you the hierarchy of elements in your project, which is important when you start working with more advanced animation techniques.

Let's add a few items to this screen and then use the SketchFlow Animation panel to create some animation.

First, let's use SketchFlow styles to create a simple shopping cart on the screen below my orders. In our case, we've used the **Rectangle-Sketch and Button-Sketch** styles.

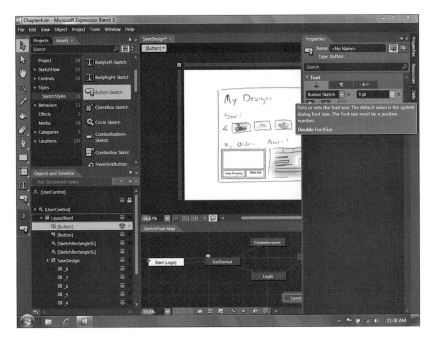

Figure 7.9   Adding SketchStyles to our Artboard.

When you're done, select all these items and see if you can group these items into a Canvas group. You may also need to show the **Properties** panel and adjust the **Text** category to change the size of the text in the buttons.

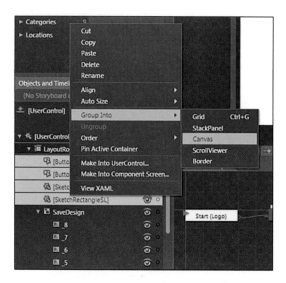

Figure 7.10   *Items created with SketchFlow styles and grouped into a Canvas, which is simply a grouped collection of our objects.*

Next, let's arrange some of our items in our **Object and Timeline** panel and on our Artboard. If we look at this panel, we should see the Canvas we've just created and a grouping object called **SaveDesign**. If we twist down the arrow next to that group, we should see all the nested objects that make up that group.

Look carefully at all the numbered items in the *SaveDesign* group. These numbered items are actually the different shoe images in our group. See if you can stack items _5–_8 on top of item _4 on the Artboard—in effect stacking shoes images on the right most shoe image. Remember if you haven't adjusted the Z order icon for the Objects and Timeline, you are arranging this so the higher numbers should appear at the bottom of the Objects and Timeline palette. You may need to resize a few items to make sure item _8 can cover all the other items. Now move the new Canvas group you've created and nest it in the *SaveDesign* group.

Figure 7.11   What our canvas looks like after we've repositioned some items and nested our Canvas group in our SaveDesign group in the Objects and Timeline panel.

WORKING WITH SKETCHFLOW ANIMATION FRAMES

Now, let's go to our **Window** menu and open up the **SketchFlow Animation** panel. Notice that we turned on Auto Hide for our SketchFlow Map so we have more room to work. The first thing we want to do is move our Canvas group to sit just above our background layer. This sets our markup order correctly so our shoes don't disappear behind the shopping cart area that we created.

Your screen should look like Figure 7.12.

Figure 7.12   *Turning on our SketchFlow Animation panel so we can begin to animate some elements into our project.*

If we look closely at the **SketchFlow Animation** panel, we see we have an item called **Base**. Base represents something unique in a SketchFlow project and Expression Blend itself. It's a default view with all your assets and all their settings that serve as a starting point before you begin to animate or change the values of items. The Base category can be confusing because it applies to a screen level in your SketchFlow project but can also apply to individual objects on your screen. The easiest way, perhaps, to avoid confusion is to simply note that every object in Expression Blend has a Base category and that screens are really just a complex object or user control. If this still doesn't make sense, try following along as we continue to explore animation and the Base concept should become more clear.

You should notice, right next to this Base category, a + control that we can use to create a SketchFlow animation. Click the **+**, and you should see a small icon appear that looks like a snapshot of your screen, which is a **frame**. **Frames** can be created by copying a **Base** screen or even other **frames**, which are now **states** in our animation. Now **frames**, which are really **states**, are different than our **Base** mode. The key difference is that in a **frame** we can record changes to our screen. As we add interactivity to our project to jump between **states**, Expression Blend does all the animation for us. It's a bit confusing that we use the term **frame** in SketchFlow animation while elsewhere in the application we use the term **state**. Both **frames** and **states** do the same thing but the interface into how we animate items is a bit different.

You'll also see a red outline that appears around our **Artboard**, which indicates that SketchFlow is in a **Record** mode, which can only happen when we're editing a Frame in SketchFlow Animation or creating or editing a state in our State panel, which we discuss later. This means anything we do on this **frame** will be captured and recorded in SketchFlow for whatever state you happen to be working in.

Let's move some items around on this screen.

Take the shoe labeled **item _1**, and drag it to our shopping cart. Scale it down and make it occupy roughly half of our cart. Next, grab **items _2, _3**, and **_8** and have them fill in the space left by removing item **_1**.

Your screen should look like Figure 7.13.

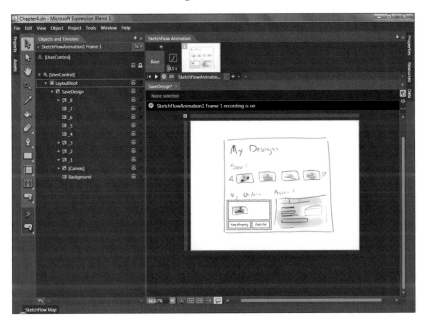

Figure 7.13   *What our screen should look like after we've moved some of these items around.*

Now select the **Play** button in the **SketchFlow Animation** panel. Notice that we've just created an animation that looks like we're dragging a saved item to our cart and that our **Saved** collection has auto updated and moved other saved item into its place.

If we go to our **Objects and Timeline** panel, we can see that items that are *active* in a given state have a red recording icon next to them. If we expand the *twisty* that is attached to each element, we can see that a **RenderTransformation** has been added to each item—which is a fancy way of saying we've moved items across the screen.

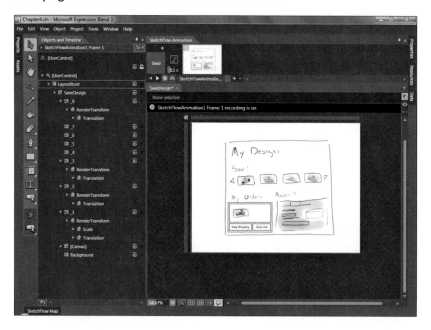

Figure 7.14 *Expanding our Objects and Timeline panel so we can see which items are animated in frame 1, which are the items that have a red dot next to them.*

SketchFlow determines automatically how to move the items across the screen when we create **frames**. If you've ever studied classic animation, you may see some similarities in how **SketchFlow Animation** and classic animation works. In effect, each **frame** or **state** is a **keyframe** for all the items on a given screen.

In classic animation, the lead animator on a project was often in charge of establishing the keyframes in a project, and then production artists would do the tween work or create all the images that are required to appear between each of the keyframes. In SketchFlow projects, Expression Blend does all the tween work when you build an animation with **SketchFlow Animation**.

Let's do some more animation. Click the **+** control next to **Frame 1** in the **SketchFlow Animation** panel (versus the **+** control next to the **Base** category). Ensure that **Frame 2** recording is enabled.

Figure 7.15 *Adding another frame to our SketchFlow Animation.*

Now, let's select the **Keep Shopping** button we created earlier. While that button is selected, let's go to the **Window** menu and open the **Properties** panel. You may need to find the **Scroll Bar** on this panel and scroll all the way to the top to see the **Brushes** category. When you find it, change the color of the button in the color editor. We do this by selecting the **Background** item in the **Brushes** category and selecting a color—in this case, we selected yellow. If you have room, it might be helpful to turn off Auto-hide for the **Properties** panel.

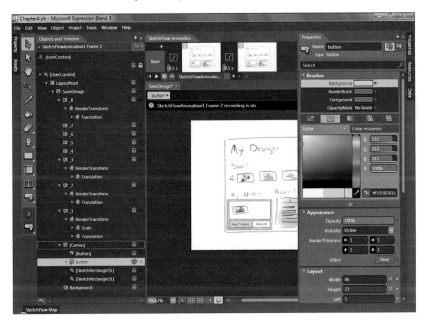

Figure 7.16 *Using the Properties panel and the Brushes category to change the color of our button.*

Now let's close the **Properties** panel and create a new frame by selecting the + control next to the second frame in your SketchFlow animation. Ensure that recording is on for **Frame 3**.

This time, grab **item _3** and drag it to the shopping cart. Then move **item _7** and **item _8** to replace the item you've moved. If you play your animation now, you should see that we simulate adding one item to the cart, selecting the **Keep Shopping** button and then adding another item.

There are two challenges, however. One, the timing is a little off. Two, the **Keep Shopping** button stays selected during our second transaction on **Frame 3**. We can fix this easily by changing the value of the **Keep Shopping** button back to white on **Frame 3** using the **Properties** panel. We can fix the timing by ensuring that the transition and time on **Frame 2**, where we simulate a button selection state, is much shorter. We do that by setting the transition during that time we spend on each frame.

If we select the Timer icon in the SketchFlow Animation panel and set the following times, our animation should look better.

Figure 7.17 *Adjusting the timing of our frames and transitions between frames for our SketchFlow Animation.*

In addition to the Play button and Timer icon, additional controls at the bottom of the SketchFlow Animation panel enable you to do the following:

- Go to the first frame or screen of the SketchFlow Animation.

- Play the animation.

- Turn on Fluid Layout, which lets SketchFlow automatically determine how elements should move from state to state when discrete layouts are used. In general, in SketchFlow you'll want Fluid Layout on in most cases; we cover this item in more detail in later chapters of the book.

- Controls for selecting which SketchFlow animation you want to work with and the ability to add or delete SketchFlow animations.

When we build our project and run it in our **SketchFlow Player**, we'll see that we can play the **SketchFlow Animation** with **the SketchFlow Player** controls when we are on the **Save Design** Screen.

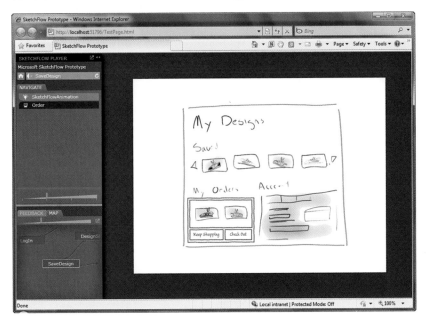

Figure 7.18   *These controls enable us to play our animation with the SketchFlow Player controls.*

SketchFlow animation is one of the easiest ways to build and demonstrate complex interactions without dedicating resources to building interactivity with scripting and code that is complex and time-consuming. It enables you to quickly get feedback on complicated interactions and communicate intent in an iterative workflow where many options can continue to be explored.

Let's build on what we've just learned about bringing our application to life by enabling navigation within our project itself, so we don't need to rely on SketchFlow Player controls for navigation.

SUMMARY

In this chapter we learned how to bring in a layered Photoshop file to Expression Blend; how to augment our design with SketchFlow styles; how to animate that file using SketchFlow Animation and the state model in Expression blend that allows us to set states and the transitions between those states; how to preview our work in Expression Blend; and how to preview our work in the SketchFlow Player.

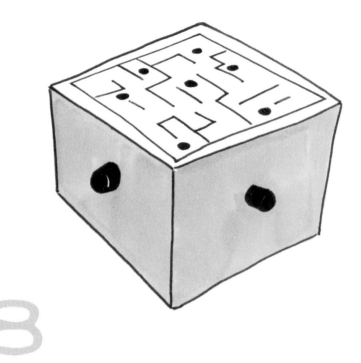

8

BASIC NAVIGATION

This chapter shows you how to make prototypes more useful by covering the navigation capabilities of SketchFlow.

Although we can use the SketchFlow Player to navigate through a prototype, we can make a prototype more dynamic when we enable navigation within the project itself. Let's look at how SketchFlow enables us to do this quickly. Open your Chapter 8 project files to get started.

ADDING NAVIGATION OBJECTS

If we look at our current **Get Started** screen, notice that we have three areas that would be nice to have linked to their corresponding screens of the application. These are the **Sign Up**, **Design**, and **Order** areas. It may be useful to display the **Objects and Timeline** panel as we show how to do this.

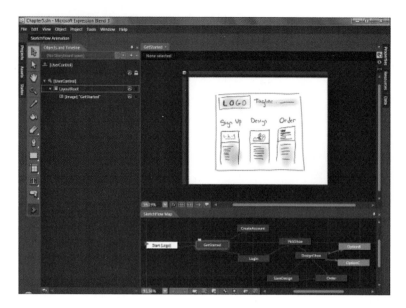

Figure 8.1 *We can see the three areas on our screen that we would like to add navigation to.*

What we want to do is add a rectangle to this screen—which we can select from the **Tool** menu. Once you've done this you can bring this screen to life with clickable navigation.

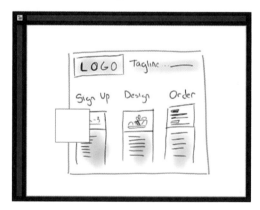

Figure 8.2 *Adding a shape to our Artboard that enables us to make all these items clickable.*

First, we change the **Alpha** of that rectangle to **0**, which makes it invisible; we then disable the stroke around the rectangle. Next, we position that rectangle over an area on our sketch where we want interactivity. We do this by using the **Properties** panel, much like we did when we were changing properties on our button using SketchFlow animation. You may find the Properties panel to be a bit overwhelming at first; it contains all the properties relevant to a selected object—which is quite varied in Expression Blend. You'll always find the color and alpha selections under the **Brushes** category at the top of this panel. If you don't see it, use the scroll bar to move to the top of the Properties panel (see Figure 8.3).

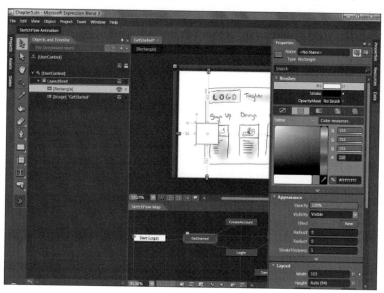

Figure 8.3 *The Properties panel as it would appear with the rectangle selected. Note the selected numbers in blue next to A, this is where we change our Alpha to 0.*

In Part III, we discuss the **Properties** panel in more detail. For now, however, all we need to do is look in the **Editor** category and set the **Alpha** to 0, which makes our object transparent. We then select the stroke in the **Brushes** tab and disable it by selecting the icon with a slash through it, which means that the object will have no visible outline around it. Because the object is transparent, it's still clickable, even though we cannot see it. This means we can attach behaviors to this item, such as navigation.

Figure 8.4 *Detail on brushes in the Properties panel.*

After you've done this, you should have a screen that looks like Figure 8.5. If you can't see the rectangle—after all, we *did* make it transparent—use the **Object and Timeline** panel to select it. Then use the Arrow tool from the Tool menu to move that item and position it around the sign-up box.

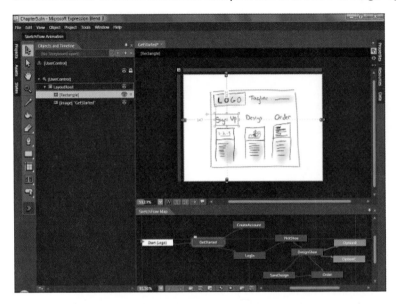

Figure 8.5 *Our transparent rectangle on our Artboard.*

Copy that element, either using keyboard shortcuts—**Control C** to *copy* and **Control V** to *paste*—or using the **Edit** menu commands. Place two new instances of the rectangle on the design and order sections of your sketch.

When you're done, it should look something like Figure 8.6.

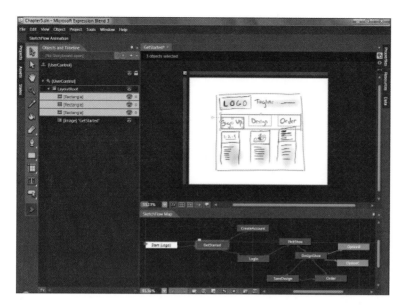

Figure 8.6   *Our rectangle copied and placed in multiple places on our Artboard.*

ADDING NAVIGATION BEHAVIORS TO OBJECTS

If you right-click on one of the rectangles and highlight the **Navigation** item, you should a list of items that we can actually link our rectangle object to.

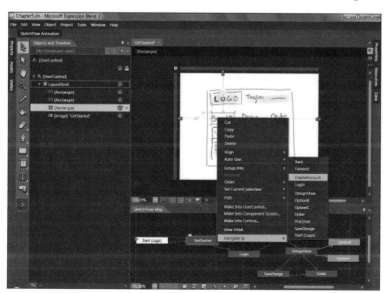

Figure 8.7   *Our contextual menu shows all the screens in our project that we can enable a link to.*

What you are looking at is a listing of all the screens that are available in your prototype that you can link to, including forward and backward links. See if you can wire up the other rectangles to link to their corresponding screens; then build your application and see if the linking is working correctly.

We can look in the **Objects and Timeline** panel and notice that **behaviors** have been attached to each of these shapes. Behaviors in SketchFlow are pre-packaged collections of code that can be used with different objects and assets in your project. The **NavigateToScreenAction** is a default behavior that ships with SketchFlow.

We can also notice that these links are now reflected as connections in our SketchFlow Map.

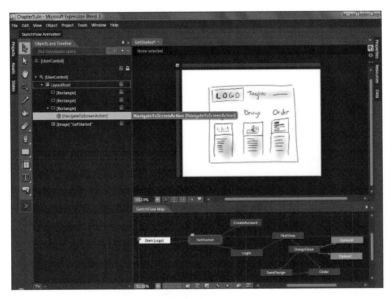

Figure 8.8   Our SketchFlow Map shows these new linkages between our screens because we've added navigation links.

The Objects and Timeline panel shows the behaviors attached to our objects that enable objects to link to other screens in our application.

Sometimes as your dynamic prototypes get too advanced, it may be helpful to dim these connections in the SketchFlow Map. We can do that by selecting the highlighted icon to dim those connections (see Figure 8.9).

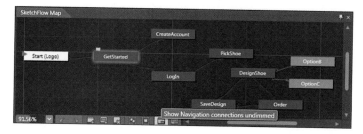

Figure 8.9 *We can dim the appearance of navigation links in our SketchFlow Maps for complex projects.*

If we look more closely at our application, we can quickly add navigation to other elements as well. For example, if we want to enable parts of the **Pick a Shoe** screen to link directly to **Design a Shoe**, we can easily enable different shapes or add buttons to enable that functionality.

When we have a fully enabled project, we can actually hide the interface of the SketchFlow Player if we want to do simple user testing of an application.

Figure 8.10 *An example of the SketchFlow Player with the SketchFlow Player navigation panel disabled.*

We've learned how to add basic animation and navigation to our sketches. Now let's see if we can add more advanced interactivity.

SUMMARY

In this chapter we learned how to add navigation to our sketches by created transparent objects and linking navigation behaviors to these objects so people can navigate through our project without using SketchFlow Animation controls.

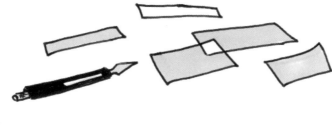

BASIC ANIMATION USING STATES

This chapter shows you how to add interactivity and animation to your project using the **State panel**. We show you how animation created with the State panel and the ability to trigger those animations with behaviors can create interactivity that can be activated directly within your prototype. Letting you move away from relying on the SketchFlow Player to drive interaction with your project.

UNDERSTANDING STATES

States let you add both simple and advanced interactivity to your SketchFlow project, and they are an integral part of Expression Blend when we work with Silverlight and WPF. Here we show you how states can be used in our SketchFlow project. In SketchFlow, states are most often used at the screen level of a project, but in reality, any object in a SketchFlow or Blend project can have different states and behaviors that trigger them. In fact, although it's a bit confusing the screens that you work with in SketchFlow are really just a special type of user control, which is an object that can contain content, other objects and controls. States are a way for you to alter a set of property values for these objects. You can edit or customize the appearance of existing states and create and define your own states.

If you have worked with the Web and CSS or done other interactive design, you may be familiar with concepts that are similar to what states can do.

For example, let's take a button in a given application. We can examine the Submit button on the **LogIn** screen that we created earlier.

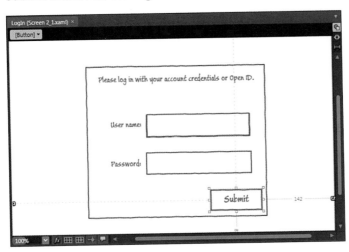

Figure 9.1   The submit button on our LogIn screen.

Buttons typically have different states in an application during run time. They may have a default or normal state, they may have a hover state, and they often give some indication when they are clicked (see Figure 9.2).

Figure 9.2   A default button with Normal, MouseOver, and Pressed states in SketchFlow in Expression Blend.

Most controls come with a set of default states that you can use as is, but it's also fairly easy to modify these states or create your own controls and define your own states for other assets in your project. (We explore this concept in more detail in Part III of this book.)

We can also use states in SketchFlow at the screen level to quickly define more complex user actions in a prototype. Let's see how that works.

A great way to think about states in SketchFlow is that they enable you to do two things, as follows:

- They enable you to alter the properties of objects in your SketchFlow project over time, such as visibility, color, scale, transforms, and so on.

- They enable you to create transitions between the states that can be simple or very complex.

As we discovered earlier when talking about SketchFlow Animation, every screen in a SketchFlow project has a **Base** condition that is, in fact, **stateless**. When you add new states, you enter a different condition for that screen—one where you can move objects around the screen and perform operations that may transform their size, rotation, or visibility; you can then enable SketchFlow to *transition* to these states when triggered via interactions in your project or the SketchFlow Player. A good analogy to think about is that a given screen in SketchFlow is like the stage that we'd use during a play. Over the course of a play, we may rearrange or add objects to the stage as the play progresses through different acts.

When you modify a state or create a state for a SketchFlow screen using either **SketchFlow Animation** panel or the **State** panel, you are creating a new state for that entire screen—every single object on that screen is part of that new state. Where this gets a bit confusing is that you can also set states for objects and controls that are on a screen at an individual object level as well. When you edit or work with states at an object level, you enter a different editing mode that is at the template editing level. We revisit what that means later, but for now keep the analogy of a play in your mind. Our Base condition for a screen is treating the screen itself as the stage for a play and all of its objects. New states that we create are simply positions in time on that stage where some of the objects may move or transform. In the last chapter where we discussed SketchFlow Animation, we focused on all linear progression through states via frames that were created in the **SketchFlow Animation** panel. In this chapter, we show you how by using the **State** panel to create new states that you can navigate to in a non-linear fashion to simulate different conditions in your application.

When you are editing a state, some features of SketchFlow may not be available to you unless you revert to the Base condition for your screen. In general, if you'll be working with a feature you can't animate—such as changing type or changing fixed values of an item, like margins or alignment—on your Artboard, you'll need to be on the Base condition for your screen that you want to edit. When you're in a state, SketchFlow will always want to animate or transition to whatever variables you are modifying in a given state.

A suggested best practice when working with states is to ensure that you always create a state that is a copy of your Base screen once you've configured and defined all the elements you need to create your states. This can be useful for advanced animations and linking and can help *set up* interactivity that you'll put into your dynamic prototypes. Basically, it provides a *default* state that you can easily transition back to from other states.

It's important to think about states carefully because after you've created a state group editing can become tricky. Basically to make global edits to a state group to an object that you've already altered in a VisualStateGroup, you need to make that change to your Base condition for your screen and then cut and paste that change into each state that you've created—or manually tweak the variables for each state using your Properties panel. If you're simply making an edit to stationary objects, you want to ensure to make those edits to the Base condition for a screen to ensure that they are reflected in all the states for that screen.

You'll find that both states and SketchFlow animation can be used to accomplish the same things. In general, we recommend using **SketchFlow Animation** for demo mode, where you need to quickly simulate complex interactions that benefit from a linear exposition. You might find that SketchFlow Animation may be an easier method for quickly concepting multiple ways to show something without having to worry about the nuances of how interactions with states that can be accessed in a non-linear fashion will work. We recommend using the **State** panel for subtle or complex changes that occur through the usage of the prototype or where non-linear interactivity is required such as showing what a screen may look like in an authenticated versus unauthenticated view or to show how a user may do complex navigation in an application. As you become more advanced with SketchFlow, however, you will find that both methods are useful in unique situations and that the state metaphor is often a more useful cognitive model than just using a timeline when *designing* interactions versus just demonstrating them.

The beauty of both of these models in SketchFlow is that Expression Blend does the hard work of creating all this animation for you automatically, doing the tweens that we discussed earlier. As we dive deeper into this functionality in later sections, we provide tips on how you can customize and tweak the animation and transitions that Expression Blend creates for you.

After we've created states, they are just like **Navigate To** functions. We can link objects and buttons to other screens of the application or to states that are available for the screen that we are on. We do this the same way we add navigation to objects on the screen via a context menu that shows all the SketchFlow Animation and States that are available to us. By attaching a SketchFlow Animation or state to an object, we are making that object a trigger to begin playing a SketchFlow Animation or trigger a state.

WORKING WITH THE STATES PANEL

Find your project files for Chapter 10 and let's take a deeper look at the Getting Started screen; make sure this screen is selected in your SketchFlow Map and visible on your Artboard. Make sure your **States** panel is open. We do this by going to our **Windows** menu. We can do the same to open our **Objects and Timeline** panel. It might be helpful after these items are open to ensure that auto-hide is turned off.

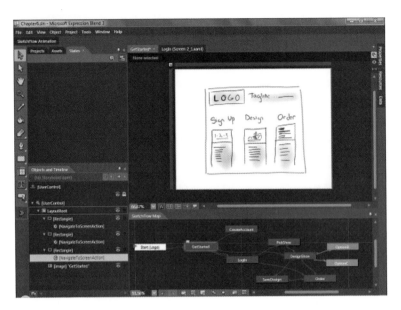

Figure 9.3 *The Window menu can be used to display both the State panel and the Objects and Timeline panel, which is open and available on the left side of the application.*

We now want to bring in some additional sketch work we've done. You may need to return to the **Window** menu to open up our **Project** panel. See if you can find the *Sketches* directory we created earlier; select it and right-click to bring up a contextual menu. Select the **Add New Folder** option.

Find the *SourceArt* folder we used in earlier chapters and look for a directory in that folder called States; add that folder to your Sketches folder.

You should have three files in your newly created *States* directory. What we want to do is set the **Base** category for this screen with these new elements on the **Getting Started** screen. Then we'll actually change the appearance of these screens on each new state that we'll create and use navigation behaviors to make it interactive.

Figure 9.4   *Here we see how we'd like to place these elements on our screen.*

See if you can get your screen to look like Figure 9.4. It may also be helpful to use Figure 9.3 as a reference. We've taken the *LeftColumn.png* and placed it over the 123 section of the left column and scaled it to cover that portion of the screen. Scale the image to make it much smaller. We've done the same to the right column with the *RightColumn.png* image. Then, we've taken the *ZoomArrow.png* and placed two instances of it on our screen. It may be helpful to lock the elements in the Objects and Timeline panel that you are not using while you do this. Because this is a low-fidelity prototype, it's not critical to make this stuff look perfect. Get as close as you can to what is shown in Figure 9.4. You'll find that you need to scale, and perhaps rotate, these items to make them fit properly on the screen.

Now, let's create three new states. We do that by first creating a state group. Select the icon reference in our **State** panel.

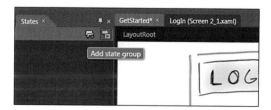

Figure 9.5   *Creating a new state group.*

This creates a **VisualStateGroup** for which we can then create different states.

Figure 9.6 *A new state group.*

This group needs the actual states we want to create. We add those states by selecting the **Add state** icon in the **State** panel.

Figure 9.7 *Adding states to our state group.*

See if you can add three states and then rename them as shown in Figure 9.8.

Figure 9.8 *Name all the states in our state group.*

Let's go into our **Left_Column state** and make the LeftColumn image we added earlier occupy most of the screen.

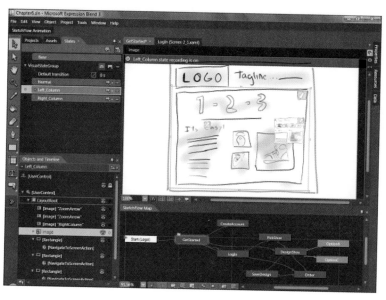

Figure 9.9   *Making our image fill the screen.*

Next, let's work with our two *ZoomArrow* elements that we added in addition to our LeftColumn and RightColumn elements. We want to do two things to these ZoomArrow elements: Make them invisible so they aren't seen in this state and set a parameter that collapses their visibility. These terms may sound odd, but we are ensuring they fade out during the transition *to* this state and that they can't be clicked *in* this state and cause unwanted behaviors.

We do that by going into the Properties panel and setting the **Opacity** to **0**. You find this setting in the **Properties** panel under the **Appearance** category. This makes them invisible in the *Left_Column state*, but doesn't remove them from the screen. Below that option you see an option to alter **Visibility** via a pull-down menu. Change that setting from **Visible** to **Collapsed**. This setting means the object can't be selected in this state, but it doesn't remove it from the screen. The reason we must do both of these things is because we don't want the object to disappear instantly once a transition to a state is complete, which is what would happen if we did not also animate its opacity.

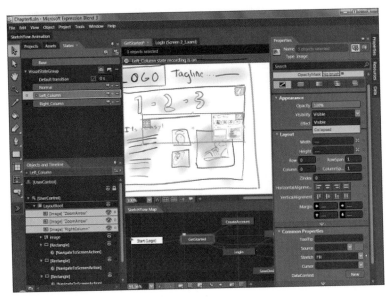

Figure 9.10   Altering Opacity and Visibility properties for objects on the Artboard.

Now see if you can do the same thing for the *Right_Column state*. When you are done, you may notice that some items are blocking each other.

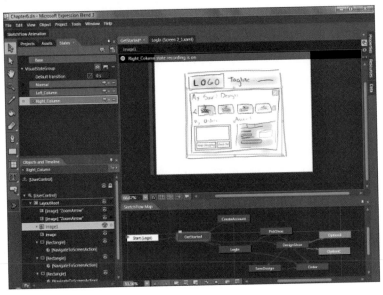

Figure 9.11   We have some objects blocking others because of their stack order in our Objects and Timeline panel.

CHAPTER 9 | BASIC ANIMATION USING STATES

This appears this way because of the **Stack Order** of items in the **Objects and Timeline** panel. We can alter the stack order or use the same opacity and visibility trick we did earlier.

If we go back to the States panel, we now have three states; we can see that although the elements are the same in each state, they are in different positions—some are scaled differently and some are not visible. If we go into our States panel, add a time duration to the default transition, and enable **Turn on transition preview**, we can see how we can navigate between each state. Each image will zoom to fill the screen for each state and then shrink to its original size when we select the normal state.

Figure 9.12   *Previewing our states and transitions.*

It is simple to do more with states. Suppose, for example, that we wanted to show that a special offer could appear where the tagline resides in the image during different states. We can use some simple text objects to simulate this. Let's go back to the **Base** category for our screen and create an element that appears during the *Left_Column state*. In this case, we used Sketch-Styles to create a rectangular box and add a body text element. We colored the rectangular box and adjusted the size of the body text element using the Properties menu.

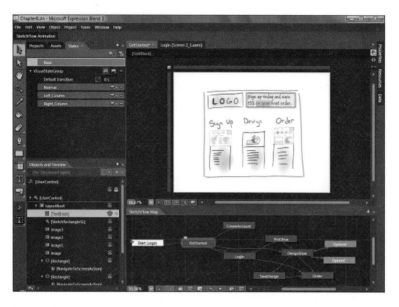

Figure 9.13 *Creating new objects to use in our VisualStateGroup.*

What we'd then like to do is actually select both of these elements from our **Base** category for our screen and copy them using **Control-X** on the keyboard or via the **Edit** menu. Now, go into the *Left_Column state* and paste in these elements.

You should notice two things after you do this. One, the elements paste in place into the *Left_Column state*. Two, if you click through other states, you'll notice that the elements are there but not visible. This is because SketchFlow automatically makes elements pasted into a live state invisible in other states. When creating new objects that need to appear in specific states, a suggested best practice is to always create and position those objects in our **Base** category view for a screen and then cut and paste them into the correct state. This keeps you from introducing unexpected animations into your work as you learn to get the hang of states in SketchFlow.

ACTIVATING STATES AND TRANSITION TIMING

We can also go into states and, using techniques we used earlier on the Getting Started screen, we can enable the Open and Close Arrows on our zoomed interface to activate the different states we've created for this screen. We need to do this for both of our smaller zoom arrows and once for the arrow on the fully zoomed interface. For our smaller arrows, we simply need to find them and right-click with our mouse so we can link directly to these states.

Figure 9.14   Linking objects to the different states that we've created.

For the large arrow, we need to create a transparent placeholder like we did for the Sign Up, Design, and Order links in our last chapter. In fact, we can simply copy one of these earlier items in our Base state and enable it for our zoomed interface.

Figure 9.15 *Creating a transparent placeholder for our close arrow.*

We've got one last item we must complete. We must go back into our **States** panel and enable a duration for the transitions between our states. We do that by entering a value in the **Default Transition** section of the **State** panel—which defaults to 0 seconds—or an immediate transition to the next state. In our case we'd like that transition to be gradual, so enter a value of 1 second.

Figure 9.16 *Entering a value for the transition between states.*

If we build and run our application, we should find that we've quickly created a highly interactive screen using states. Coupled with navigation

behaviors and **SketchFlow Animation**, it's very easy to bring our sketched ideas to life.

Here are a few things that we've found to be useful when using animation, navigation, and states:

- Objects can use multiple behaviors, such as triggering a SketchFlow Animation, triggering a state, and navigating to different screens. It is possible to have one object have a navigation **behavior** and activate a state. This might not always be your intention as you'll navigate away from a screen that has a state playing. Ensure that you don't have these overlaps if you notice things aren't working as expected. This can often happen when you copy elements and forget to remove behaviors and/or states before attaching new ones. To remove a behavior in SketchFlow, you simply need to right-click and find the active behavior (indicated by a checkmark or highlight) and select it to remove the checkmark or highlight.

Figure 9.17   Removing a behavior that has been activated previously for an object.

- Areas that are linked can overlap other linked areas, and this can cause unexpected behavior, making use of the **Visibility** feature and **Collapse** items that might trigger unwanted behavior in specific states can reduce risk.

- Pay attention to the **Stack Order** of items in the **Objects and Timeline** panel. Sometimes animations that seem impossible or difficult merely need to have items rearranged in the **Stack Order**. Use care in adding items to screens with active states; if working outside of the **Base** category for a screen, you may inadvertently begin animating objects that you don't intend to.

So far, we've already covered a great deal about how to bring our prototypes to life—but SketchFlow can enable us to do much more. Because we're in the digital realm and because SketchFlow is only part of a tool that is really designed to build fully functioning applications, it's very easy for us to incorporate data into our prototypes and concepts. Let's see how working with data can bring our interactive prototypes to the next level.

SUMMARY

In this chapter we've learned how to understand what states are and how they can be used; how to build Visual State Groups and add states to those groups; how to create and manipulate changes from state to state; how to create triggers or links that activate a state; and how to establish transitions between states.

10

WORKING WITH DATA

In this chapter we explore how you can use SketchFlow to designing with data. We show you how you can create sample data sources and use those data sources in your project to demonstrate complex interactions and linkages.

We can make our prototypes more dynamic when we work with real or simulated data. Working with data can bring forms and other parts of our prototypes to life and let users select and explore options interactively.

We're going to create a small sample data set and attach it the design column of our Getting Started screen.

Open your Chapter 10 project and go to the **Windows** menu and open your **Data** panel.

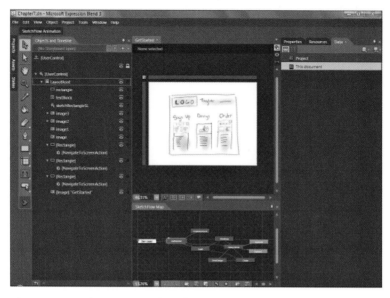

Figure 10.1   The Data panel in SketchFlow.

THE DATA PANEL

Let's look at the Data panel. A dataset is typically a collection of properties or values that we can define and use in different controls in SketchFlow in Expression Blend.

Next, let's discuss what some of the specific controls in the Data panel do.

When **List Mode** icon Figure 10.2 is selected, data can be dragged and added to controls as a list of items that might appear in a drop-down menu or list box.

Figure 10.2   The List Mode icon in the Data panel.

Figure 10.3   The Details Mode icon in the Data panel.

When **Details Mode** icon is selected, data objects are created that represent a single record or item of a data collection. In effect, this binds data to a property, such as a text box, versus entering that data manually.

Figure 10.4   The Add sample data source icon in the Data panel.

We select to the **Add sample data source** icon create a sample data source. We can generate this data randomly or use XML to import a sample set of data.

Figure 10.5   The Add live data source icon in the the Data panel.

Many people use Expression Blend to actually work with live data, and the **Add live data source** icon lets you connect your prototype to a live data source. In some scenarios, you might work with a developer that would enable you to use a feature such as this to bind to data that might be exposed via an API. An example of this might be a Twitter Feed, RSS feed, and so on.

Figure 10.6   Defining a new sample data source.

What we typically do in SketchFlow work with a sample data source in the prototyping stage. We define a new sample data source by selecting the **Add sample data source** icon and then selecting the option to **Define New Sample Data**. This indicates that we want to create a data source versus linking to a live one.

After you have done this you'll then be asked to name your new data source.

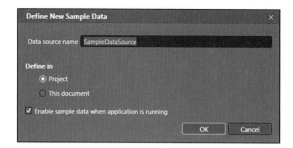

Figure 10.7   Naming a new sample data source.

Our new sample data collection is created with two properties by default, but we can easily add more.

Figure 10.8   A newly created sample data collection.

Let's add one more property to this data collection.

Figure 10.9   Adding a property to our data collection.

By selecting the plus icon next to our collection, we can add new properties. After we've done this, we can edit these values by selecting the **Edit sample values** icon.

Figure 10.10 A sample data collection with a new property and with the Edit sample values icon selected.

Here's an example of a view that lets us edit these data values (see Figure 10.11).

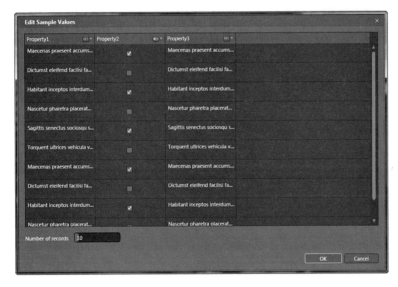

Figure 10.11 The Edit Sample Values dialog lets us edit the values our sample data collection.

WORKING WITH DATA PROPERTIES

We can modify the values for each property that we create in a project by selecting the data type and format for each property. SketchFlow makes it easy to auto-generate this data, and with smaller datasets, you can enter specific values easily. To get an idea of how this works, select the parameters option for our first category.

Figure 10.12   Changing property types for our sample data.

We can modify the values for each property by selecting a data type and format for each property.

Figure 10.13   Modifying the values for a property.

Next are examples of different formats available for auto-generated data.

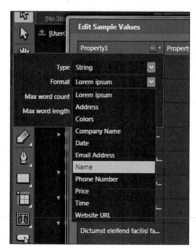

Figure 10.14   Formats available for auto-generated data.

Because we want to work with a small dataset, let's see if we can create the following data collection. What we'd like to do is make our collection look like the one shown in Figure 10.15.

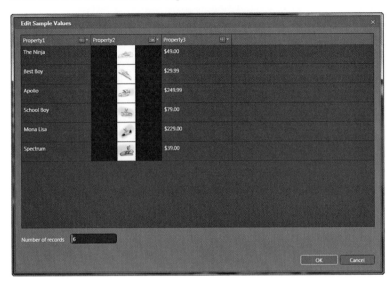

Figure 10.15   A small collection of sample data that we'll create for our proto-type.

We simply manually enter our item names for Property 1 and ensure that our total number of records is set to 6.

For Property 2, we must configure the parameter and point it to a directory with the photos we'd like to use. You'll see that SketchFlow inserts some generic icons for our use, but we'll use the Browse button to add items from our *Source Art* folder. Import the images that are in the *Data* subdirectory.

Figure 10.16 *Setting our image properties for the second property in our sample data set.*

To configure Property3, we set our type to String and our format to Price. We might find we want to tweak this data ourselves as well, so the prices don't look too odd.

BINDING DATA TO A CONTROL

What we now need to do is create the control to bind this data to. This allows the project to use our data at runtime. Normally, to create such a complex interaction, we'd need the assistance of a developer, but in this case, SketchFlow makes it easy for us to create these interactions ourselves.

We're going to go into our Assets panel for SketchFlow and add a control to the Getting Started screen called **ComboBox-Sketch**. This adds a user control to the Getting Started screen that will contain our data.

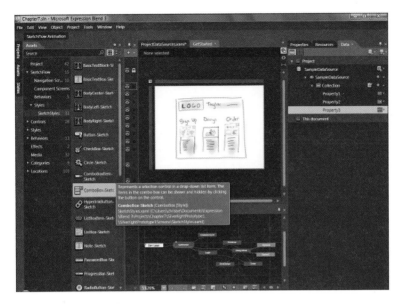

Figure 10.17　*Adding a ComboBox-Sketch control to our project from the Tools menu.*

Place that control over the picture in the center column of the Getting Started screen and keep it selected.

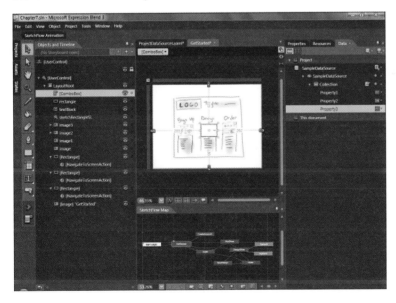

Figure 10.18　*Adding our ComboBox-Sketch control to the Getting Started screen in our project.*

Now we want to select that control. We simply select the collection in the Data panel and drag it onto our control.

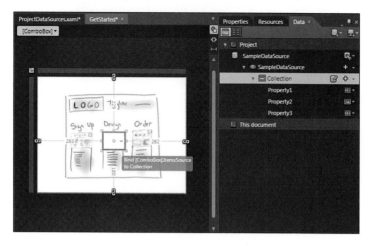

Figure 10.19 *Dragging our sample data collection to our control on the design surface.*

We can then build and run our application to see how this control works. We should see that the ComboBox now houses our data. The rest of the interactivity we designed earlier for this screen should still work as well.

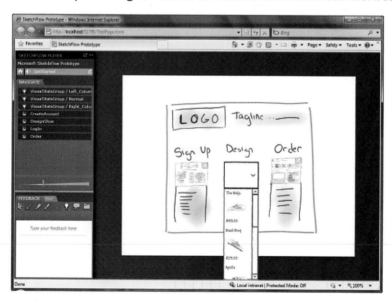

Figure 10.20 *Viewing our control in the SketchFlow Player.*

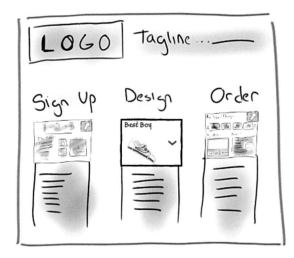

Figure 10.21 *Viewing a selected item in our ComboBox_Sketch control in the SketchFlow Player.*

Now one thing we might have noticed in running the application is that the ComboBox sits in front of some of our other elements that animate on the screen. To see this behavior you may need to run all of the animations on the *Getting Started* screen. We can fix this by going back to SketchFlow and changing the order of the **ComboBox** in the **Objects and Timeline** panel. Make sure that you're not in a Record mode for states when you do this or you'll find that SketchFlow won't let you make this change. This is easy to note because the Artboard will have a red border and record light on if you are in a state Editing mode.

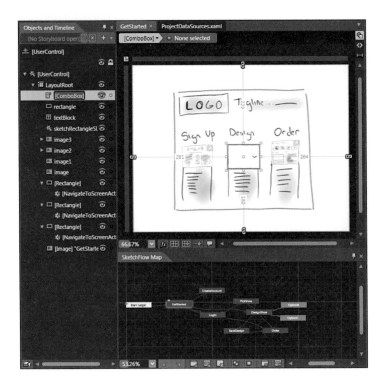

Figure 10.22   Checking the nesting order of our objects in the Objects and Timeline panel.

We've now moved the ComboBox in the screen hierarchy and should find that our prototype is working as expected.

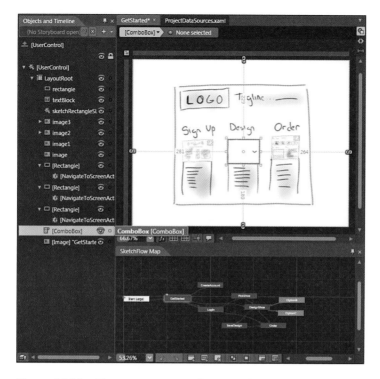

Figure 10.23   The arrangement of our ComboBox-Sketch control after we've moved it in the Objects and Timeline panel.

At this point, we've got an application that demonstrates some rather complex functionality and we've managed to build and assemble this functionality fairly quickly.

We are probably ready to package up our application and share it again. In fact, we might even want to generate documentation to support it and take some simple steps that will help us in the next iteration of the application as we continue to add more functionality. Let's see how taking some of these finals steps can help our project come together.

SUMMARY

In this chapter we learned how to work with data in our project by adding simulated data; create data collections; customize the data in those collections; create controls that can use data; and add data to those controls.

11

BRINGING IT ALL TOGETHER

We've now built a functional prototype from sketches that can communicate our ideas. This chapter covers a few other things we can do to make our project more manageable and understandable. We will learn how to create resuable assets so we can make changes easier as we enter more detailed phases. We learn how to annotate our work, and finally, we will learn how to generate documentation from SketchFlow that our design and development teams can leverage and that can serve as a foundation for artifacts we must create for project stakeholders.

ADDING REUSABLE ASSETS WITH COMPONENT SCREENS

Component screens are basically a collection of elements that we can use on multiple screens; they can make it easier to add screens to our project that have elements that might stay the same from screen to screen. Let's discuss how we can quickly create them.

First, let's take a look at our **Pick a Style** screen. Suppose we wanted to add some functionality to this screen with some extra navigation buttons.

Figure 11.1   The Pick a Style screen in our project.

Our goal is to make the screen look like this. We'll add some buttons to the screen using the **Button-Sketch** asset from the **Asset** panel and the **SketchFlow** category. We can then add **Navigate To**... actions to each button.

Figure 11.2   How we'd like our screen to look.

What would be helpful is if there was an easy way to take these buttons and link them to other screens without having to recreate them or copy them. We can do that by selecting these items and making them into a **Component screen**. We create a **Component Screen** by using our context menu. If we select these three objects and right click, we should see an option called **Make into Component Screen**.

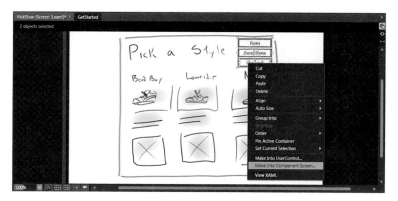

Figure 11.3   Turning a collection of objects into a Component Screen.

We'll then be given a dialog box where we can name our Component screen—which we've simply named Navigation. For simple SketchFlow projects, you'll want to leave the selection box unchecked and ignore the warning dialog.

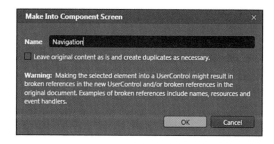

Figure 11.4   Naming our Component Screen.

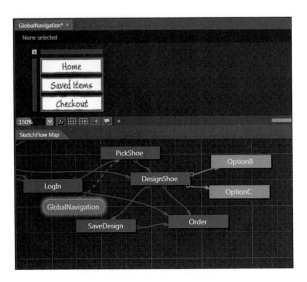

Figure 11.5 *The view of our new Component Screen on the Arboard and in the SketchFlow Map.*

What should happen next is you'll see a new screen added to our SketchFlow Map that shows the content that is housed in the *Navigation Component screen*. You may need to build your project quickly to have changes update. After you've done that, look at the Pick a Shoe screen. You should now see that it looks the same as before—but behind the scenes, what is now happening is that you have a reusable asset that is linked to the Pick a Shoe screen. See if you can add component connections to other screens, such as Design Shoe and Save Design.

You do this by selecting and dragging on the third icon in the contextual menu for a Component screen. If you drag on this icon to an existing screen, it inserts that component on the screen. You will find that once the Component screen is attached to a SketchFlow screen, you need to position it correctly on your screen.

In your **SketchFlow Map**, you can distinguish Component screens by their shape, their color (which you can specify), and the dotted line that connects them to other screens. After you have Component screens, it's easy to make changes on the Component screen that will auto-update throughout your project.

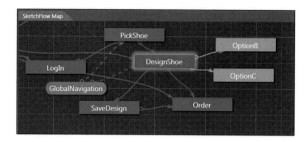

Figure 11.6   *Linking a Component Screen to another screen in our prototype.*

ADDING ANNOTATIONS TO OUR PROJECT

Earlier, we showed you how stakeholders could provide feedback via the SketchFlow Player. You can also insert annotations directly into your SketchFlow project on each screen. Both you and stakeholders have the ability to show or hide these annotations.

To begin adding annotations, we need to ensure that they are visible. We do this by ensuring that annotations are visible on the Artboard by enabling them; select the icon on the lower-left quadrant of the Artboard.

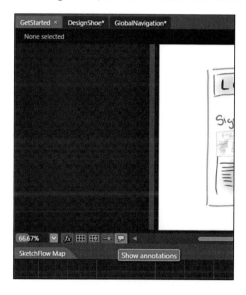

Figure 11.7   *Turning on annotations for our Artboard.*

We can then select any portion of any screen and use a keyboard shortcut or the Tools menu to insert a comment (see Figure 11.8).

Figure 11.8   Creating an annotation from the Tools menu.

Here we're adding a comment to the **Getting Started** screen, detailing what interactivity we've added. In addition, you'll see that we've loaded some earlier feedback we got from stakeholders as well. One of the things you'll notice is that feedback and annotations also appear in the SketchFlow Map itself, with a **LightBulb** for stakeholder feedback and with a **Comment Balloon** for annotations that we've added ourselves. In the **SketchFlow Player**, stakeholders can also view your annotations.

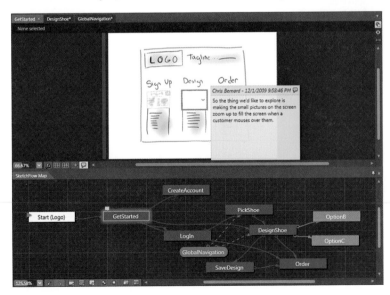

Figure 11.9   Viewing annotations in the SketchFlow Player.

CREATING DOCUMENTATION

Documentation is still a critical part of the design and development process. Often times, we must create vision documents, design specifications, and other artifacts to support the design process. SketchFlow in Expression Blend gives us great features to automate the document creation process by exporting the flow of an application and all of its figures and annotations into a Microsoft Word document. These documents serve as an excellent foundation for additional information that might need to be added to your documents and eliminate much of the busy work that goes into making these documents. With careful planning and annotation, these documents can live with the project as it progresses and be easily updated.

With our project completed—or in a state where we'd like to document what we have—we simply need to go the File menu.

Figure 11.10 *Accessing the Export to Microsoft Word feature from the File menu.*

After we select Export to Microsoft Word, we are presented with a dialog. If we have a standard template that we use for documentation, we can choose to leverage that as a starting point for our document.

Figure 11.11   The Export to Word dialog.

After you've selected the appropriate settings, your document is created.

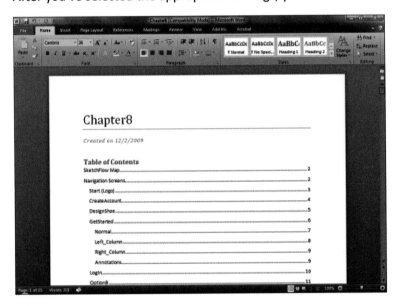

Figure 11.12   The Word document that SketchFlow has created for our project.

The document creates a table of contents, shows the flow for the application, and provides a collection of figures and any runtime annotations that have been embedded in the project.

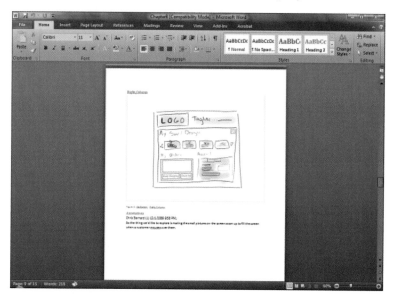

Figure 11.13   Some details from the Word document that SketchFlow has created for our project.

SUMMARY

At this point, you've worked with all the basic features of SketchFlow and should be able to be productive in creating dynamic prototypes quickly and iteratively. You've learned how to create a basic project flow, get assets into SketchFlow, quickly create a project flow, distribute your work, and get feedback. You also learned how to make prototypes dynamic by using SketchFlow Animation, navigation, states, and data.

You should be pleased with what you've learned to do with SketchFlow so far. However, if you are curious about how to unleash the full power of animation and data in your prototypes, and push into the creation of higher-fidelity work with SketchFlow in Expression Blend, we've got much more you can learn to make your dynamic prototypes sing.

Hopefully, this section has planted some seeds around how prototypes are just one of the many scenarios that SketchFlow can support in the design process. Dynamic prototypes help you explore how SketchFlow can become a key part of your ideation and design processes and dig deeper into best practice for integrating it with your existing workflow.

PART III

UNDERSTANDING SKETCHFLOW

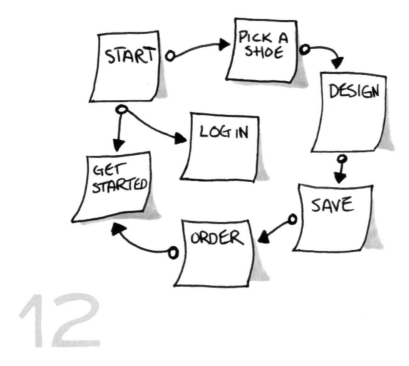

12

THE SKETCHFLOW INTERFACE

In this chapter we explore in detail the Expression Blend interface including splash screens, menus, and panels that surface the powerful functionality of the tool:

- Workspace

- Tools panel

- Projects panel

- Assets panel

- States panel

- Objects and Timeline panel

- SketchFlow Animation panel

- Artboard panel

- SketchFlow Map panel

- Results panel

- Properties panel

- Resources panel

- Data panel

- Feedback panel

- Application menus

As a powerful tool, Expression Blend can be intimidating when you first use it. This chapter helps you understand the different interface components. By the end of the chapter, you'll understand that you can make the interface work more simply for you by closing panels that you don't need at different phases of your project.

THE WORKSPACE

When you launch Expression Blend, you always see a splash screen.

You then see a three-tab welcome screen with a Projects tab selected and a display of previous projects you've worked with. In addition you see tabs that take you to the Expression Blend User guide, support communities, and a final tab that shows you sample projects you can explore.

Let's create a new project and name it SketchFlow Interface Project. Select the options to create a Silverlight 3 SketchFlow Application and leave all other settings at their default setting.

Now, let's take a look at your interface in depth as it relates to SketchFlow.

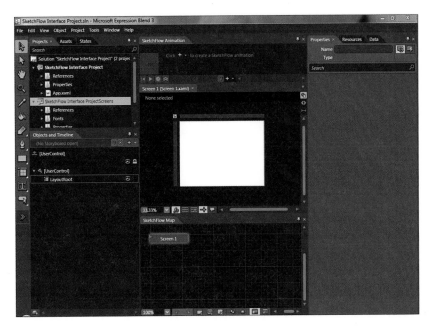

Figure 12.1   *The default interface for a Silverlight-based SketchFlow project*

In essence, when you look at this interface, there are three modes of controlling what happens in SketchFlow. The first mode includes all the options available to you in the series of menus that appear across the top of the screen. The second is all the options and items you can select in the panels that surround your Artboard. Finally, in the Tools panel to the left of the screen, you can use tools from that palette to directly manipulate options on the Artboard.

Blend 3 is a reconfigurable and contextual interface. This means that it's easy for you to attach and detach panels and put them anywhere you would like on the screen and also save these configurations. It also means that Blend will hide options that aren't available to you depending on what you're doing. For example, you won't see edit text options in the properties menu if you've selected an item where that feature wouldn't be available.

Let's take a quick look at how these different parts of the interface work. In some places, we'll defer detailed explanations until later chapters that explore parts of the interface in depth, as we discuss assets, states, animation, and so on.

The key to understanding SketchFlow is that there are always multiple ways to accomplish the same task. For example, you might select an item directly on the Artboard and manipulate settings in one of the panels by selecting an icon, or you may trigger the same action by using a keyboard shortcut or selecting the item from one of the application menu categories. Because SketchFlow and Expression Blend itself are robust and somewhat complicated, we've found that it's easiest to learn how to use the icons and contextual controls that are available to you in the panels and tabs that surround your interface as you learn the basics of SketchFlow. As you get more advanced, you'll find that using the menus and keyboard shortcuts might become easier.

THE TOOLS PANEL

We covered most of the Tools panel in earlier chapters. If you've ever worked with professional design tools, much of what you see in the Expression Blend Tools panel should look familiar.

Selection Tool
Direct Selection Tool
Hand Tool
Magnifying Tool
Eye Dropper Tool
Paint Bucket Tool
Gradient and Brush Tool
Pen and Pencil Tool
Radius, Ellipse, and Line Tool
Grid and Layout Tools
Text Tools
Control Objects ShortCut
Assets

Figure 12.2   The Tools panel.

The Tools panel defaults appear to the left side of the screen in Expression Blend. It can be detached and moved anywhere in the Expression Blend interface by grabbing the top of the tools panel and dragging it.

The Selection tool is for the basic selection of objects. Depending on what objects you select, you should be able to move and manipulate objects on the Artboard, including the ability to scale and rotate. You can quickly select this tool from the keyboard by selecting **V**.

The Direct Selection tool manipulates parts of an object or a collection of points. You can quickly select this tool from the keyboard by selecting **A**.

The Pan tool allows you to move around in the Artboard or SketchFlow Map. You can quickly activate this tool by pressing the space key on your keyboard.

The Zoom tool allows you to magnify parts of your workspace or zoom out to see more of your workspace. You can quickly select this tool from the keyboard by selecting **Z**.

The Eyedropper tool copies the appearance of another object to the currently selected object(s). This includes features related to Brush attributes (foreground colors, background colors, fills, strokes, masks), Appearance (opacity, stroke thickness, and so on), and Text (font family, font size, alignment, and so on). To use this tool, you select which object you'd like to alter and then use the Eyedropper tool to select the new object from which you'd like to copy attributes. You can quickly select this tool from the keyboard by selecting **I**.

The Paintbucket tool copies the appearance of the currently selected object(s) to another object. To use the Paintbucket tool, first select the object you'd like to copy attributes from and then select the Paintbucket tool. You can then paint other objects with these attributes. You can quickly select this tool from the keyboard by selecting **F**.

The Gradient tool and Brush Transform tool allow you to edit objects that have gradients applied to them. By default you see the Gradient tool in the Tool panel. If you hold and select the Gradient tool, then you see that you get an option to select the Brush Transform, too. These tools are used in conjunction with gradient settings that you would set in your properties panel in the Brushes category. The Gradient tool allows you to alter the gradient's direction and the colors or stops that make up your gradient directly on the Artboard by manipulating color stops and gradient position via line-based interface in the Gradient tool or a bounding-box interface with the Brush Transform tool. The way the tool influences your gradient depends on if you are editing a linear or radial gradient.

The Pen and Pencil tools allow you create paths and objects directly on the Artboard. By default you see the Pen tool in the Tool panel. If you hold and select the Pen tool, you see that you get an option to select the Pencil tool, too. The Pen tool allows you to create paths, which are collections of segments and points and determine if segments are curved or straight. If you've ever used a Bezier path tool in other programs, you find that the Pen tool works exactly the same way. When you add a point and pull with your mouse, Expression Blend lays down a control point that allows for curved segments and gives you handles to control the shape of your curve. As you create paths with the tool, you can alter the type of points you are creating by holding down the ALT or Option key on your keyboard to switch between straight or curved segments. You can use the Direct Selection tool to edit specific points of a path that has been previously created. The pencil tool enables you to draw freehand paths. If you use the pen tool with Fill Attributes disabled, you can actually create simple sketches and wireframes directly in SketchFlow. You can quickly select this tool from the keyboard by selecting **p**. You can select the pencil by selecting **y**.

The Rectangle, Ellipse, and Line tools are used for creating primitive shapes in Expression Blend—but for much of your work in SketchFlow, you'll create these shapes in a different way. You can quickly select this tool from the keyboard by selecting **L**. Like the Gradient and Pen tools you'll find the Ellipse and Line tools nested in the tool menu.

You won't use the remaining tools very often in SketchFlow projects unless you understand the underlying programming and layout frameworks that support WPF and Silverlight. The User Guide for Expression Blend covers the functions of these items in great detail and is a great place to start learning how these elements work. We do feel it's important to plant some seeds here, however, because it can be helpful to understand how to break down an interface into its fundamental components.

One way to think about why it's valuable to make an investment in understanding these concepts is to look at how professional design education is typically conducted. Many of us learn a great deal about the theories behind design, such as how composition, contrast, and graphical systems like grids help us create more compelling graphic designs. We also study typography, form, proportion, and scale. All the tools and concepts that support layout and the structure of interaction design are derivative extensions of this design education. In fact, the best way to think about layout tools is as a set of foundational elements that establishes the guidelines and rules for our interface.

Figure 12.3   A collection of Layout objects available in a Silverlight-based Sketch-Flow Project.

The Grid tool contains a variety of containers—similar to the Layout Root that we covered in earlier chapters. In fact, the Layout Root is a container itself, and in SketchFlow and Blend projects defaults to a Grid container. If you want to change the Layout Root to a different type of element, you can do this easily by right-clicking the Layout Root in the Objects and Timeline palette and selecting another option.

These containers, called Elements or Objects in Expression Blend, add functionality and capability to the applications and prototypes that you create. Depending on if you're working in a Silverlight or WPF project, you'll see a different collection of objects. WPF generally has more layout elements, text options, and buttons, whereas Silverlight generally has a subset of all of these options.

As you get more sophisticated in taking SketchFlow projects into Expression Blend or creating high-fidelity prototypes, you often find yourself breaking your sketches or concepts created in other tools (like Adobe Photoshop or Illustrator) into their core parts and using these containers to house the functionality that you'd like your application to have.

As an example, let's say that you would like to create an interface element that can house a number of objects and enable a user to scroll through objects when there are too many to fit in the window in which these objects reside. Let's say you also want to put a border around that object to call attention to it. You may, in fact, use a series of elements that are nested in each other to accomplish this.

For example, the root element may be one that lets you control your border, the next object may control how items populate the element and how they are spaced, and the final element may contain the actual scroll control for the interface element.

Typically, the order in which the items are added to these types of elements is important. Objects that are added to elements in Blend are called child objects of the elements in which they reside.

Refer to the User Guide to get a detailed overview of how to work with layout elements in WPF and Silverlight. Here we'll outline what some of these types of elements are typically used for.

A Grid object arranges child elements in a flexible layout of rows and columns, and can be used to create *liquid* designs and provide rules-based layout controls.

A Canvas object arranges child elements according to absolute x and y coordinates.

In a StackPanel object, any object that is created or added to it would be added to it in a hierarchal order—or as the last child in a stack. So, if adding a collection of items to a StackPanel, it would stack those items in the order that they were added.

In a WPF SketchFlow project, you can also use a WrapPanel object that is similar to a StackPanel except that it arranges child objects from left to right; then, when it runs out of room at the end of a panel, it *wraps* them in a new row. The orientation of a WrapPanel can be reversed so it stacks item from top to bottom or left to right.

In a WPF SketchFlow project, you can also use a DockPanel object to arrange child elements so they stay, or dock, to a specified edge of the panel.

A ScrollViewer object enables the scrolling of child objects that it contains. A ScrollViewer may only contain one child object and is an element that is designed to be used with other elements that can contain multiple objects inside it.

A Border object draws either or both a border and background around an element. An important thing to note is that you can only add one child element to a border container. A good rule of thumb is to nest a grid or canvas panel in a border panel if you'd like to nest more than one object.

In a WPF SketchFlow project, you can use a Uniform Grid object. Although it sounds similar to the Grid element, in effect what it does is arrange child objects within equal and uniform grid regions. In this way, it's more useful as a tiling device to lay out multiple elements with equal distance between them (for example, as an image list).

In a WPF SketchFlow project, you can also use a ViewBox object, which is useful for when you need to consistently scale a collection of child elements. Like some of the other elements detailed here, it only accepts one child element, so you typically nest another element within it that may contain more than one child object.

Figure 12.4   A collection of Text objects available in a Silverlight-based SketchFlow Project.

The Text tool enables you to easily create a TextBlock that allows you to display content that can't be edited, a TextBox so users of an application can enter data, and a PasswordBox that hides the data that is being entered. Just like with layout containers, WPF contains additional text options.

Figure 12.5   A collection of Control objects available in a Silverlight-based Sketch-Flow Project.

The button tool contains a variety of controls that would be useful in an interactive application. We've touched on how some of these controls work in Chapter 11, "Bringing It All Together," and in Section IV, we'll explore a few more. Many of these control objects are not used until later in the prototyping stage. We cover how the Sketch Style control objects work in Chapter 13, "Assets, Styles, and Components."

THE PROJECTS PANEL

The Projects panel contains all the files that you use in your projects. It looks complicated because a SketchFlow project is actually a collection of programs and all the files and libraries and reference assets that are designed to make a project run. If you are new to interaction design, one way to think of a SketchFlow project is to think about how you'd make a print document or a video. Typically, those types of projects are collections of assets, such as vector art, fonts, pictures, and so on. In a print project, the actual file you create may simply *reference* all of those other items. In a video, you may often use multiple video clips, audio files, music, and graphics to create a video. The final artifact you give someone may be one file, but if you wanted to make any changes to the project, or optimize it for other formats, you often want to go back to all the *assets* that make up the projects. In SketchFlow, you are basically dealing with the same thing, except some of the formats and what the files do may be less familiar.

Let's take a look at the current Project view in your project.

Figure 12.6 *The Project Panel contains all the elements that make up our project.*

Notice that there are two hierarchies that you can see in the Projects panel. The first one is labeled SketchFlow Interface Project. This collection of files is, in fact, all the controls and code needed for the SketchFlow Player itself.

If you twist down and look at all the files, you notice a References folder with a collection of files called DLLs that have a file structure that ends with .dll. These are the dynamic link libraries that are used to make sure your Silverlight or WPF applications function properly.

You'll also see a properties folder included with your solution that identifies any shared code that your specific application requires and how to bind to any non-shared code that is a part of your project. Also included is a code-behind file; in both Silverlight and WPF, much of your functionality is contained in XAML, a form of markup that derives from XML and controls many of the UI elements of your application. But your application is also supported with other computer code; this code—instead of being embedded in the XAML—is typically put in a code-behind file that ends with the prefix .cs. XAML files are preceded with the prefix .xaml.

It's not necessary for you to understand how these files work or understand what's in them to be productive with SketchFlow. However, just like good web developers can look at HTML, CSS, and JavaScript and know exactly what an application does, you'll find that over time, it might be to your advantage to learn more about XAML, C#, and what magic is occurring to make your applications work.

The next collection of files is actually all the elements that you create as part of your SketchFlow project. You'll see the same types of reference directories to DLLs and properties, plus a directory for fonts you use in the project. By default, SketchFlow uses a font called Buxton Sketch, named after Microsoft researcher and designer Bill Buxton.

In addition, you'll see any screens created here or other asset directories or files that you add to the project. Just as it is with Photoshop files or print production work, a modest amount of organization goes a long way here. Labeling and importing files consistently will help you be more productive as projects get more complex.

You'll also notice a search menu in this panel. This can enable you to quickly find project elements. Make sure you clear the search box when you are done looking for elements.

THE ASSETS PANEL

You can access all the assets available via the Tool menu, but in most cases, using the Assets panel will be more useful.

Figure 12.7   Here, we show the SketchStyles available in the Assets panel.

The Assets panel contains a number of elements, but not all of them are relevant or things you typically use in a SketchFlow project. For the most part, you'll confine yourself to using this tool to add SketchFlow styles to your project or see what assets are available in your project. Bear in mind that the asset manager is not an absolute filing system; some views in the Assets panel may duplicate items you'd see in other views:

- The Project section includes any project-specific assets that you've defined for the current project, such as screens.

- The SketchFlow category shows all the navigation screens, component screens, behaviors, and styles used in the project, including SketchFlow styles. Subcategories for navigation screens, component screens, and behaviors provide more specific views into your project.

The SketchStyles category contains all the controls in your project that use a SketchFlow style. In the Reference section, we detail both these controls and other controls available to you in Silverlight- and WPF-focused projects.

- The Controls category lists all the controls available for a given project and groups controls based on some different categories—such as basic, which are a collection of controls that are very easy to modify the appearance of, on to controls that are designed for data or layout. The controls you see here might vary a bit depending on the type of project you are working on or if a development team has created special categories of controls for you to use.

- The Styles category lists all the unique styles that you've created for your project. In the case of SketchFlow, you might not create styles at all or you might not do so until you get to a detailed design phase. Styles are basically anything that you make and convert to a control, or a control or style that you would actually apply to a control. In fact, the SketchFlow styles that you use in SketchFlow are a library of styles created specifically for SketchFlow.

- The Behaviors category is where you store all the specific behaviors used in your project. These include default behaviors that are included with SketchFlow, but they may also include behaviors that you download from the Expression Gallery that others have created or even behaviors that you or a developer on your team have created. If you're not quite sure you understand what behaviors are, don't worry—we discuss them in more detail in Chapter 15, "SketchFlow Behaviors."

- The Effects category includes any effects you might use in your project. Right now, Expression Blend 3 ships with two default effects (BlurEffect and DropShadowEffect). However, just like with behaviors, you may acquire different effects that can appear in your project that you download, create, or have provided to you by another team member.

- The Media category is where audio, 3D assets, or video in your project would display.

- The Categories and the Locations category contain the controls and assemblies that are specific to either Silverlight or WPF projects. This is basically another way of viewing the control options available to you. As a developer who understands the System.Windows.Controls Namespace for WPF and Silverlight in .NET, this might be an easier, or perhaps more familiar, way to find what you are looking for.

THE STATES PANEL

The States panel is where you create different states for screens in your SketchFlow project. You must create the states you want to use for a given screen; when you are not in a state for a screen, or you haven't created states for a screen, you are in the Base category. States can impact all elements on the screen or individual objects, and you can have multiple state groups and states for each screen in your project. We'll review the States panel in Chapter 14, "SketchFlow Animation and States."

Figure 12.8 *The States panel with the Base category selected.*

OBJECTS IN THE OBJECTS AND TIMELINE PANEL

The Objects and Timeline panel looks very similar to two types of interfaces you've seen in graphic design or animation programs.

By default the Objects and Timeline panel displays a list of all objects on a given screen in something called markup order—or a representation of how the items would appear if we looked at the code that makes up our interface and application.

We have the option, however, of also arranging objects in this panel by z-depth as well—which would arrange our items in a manner that may be more familiar to those of us used to how a graphics program would arrange elements.

The best way to understand this is to look at the following example.

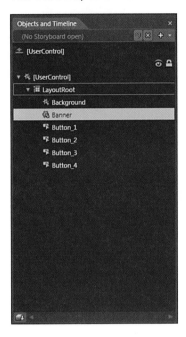

Figure 12.9   A sample screen showing objects arranged within layout elements, showing markup order.

We have drawn a primitive wireframe and made some simple groupings. If you look at the items, you'll notice they appear to be in the reverse order of how you'd see objects displayed in an application using layers. This is because SketchFlow by default displays item by markup order. An easy way to understand this is to look at the code view for this screen.

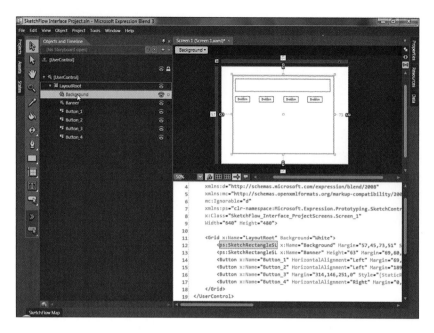

Figure 12.10 *A Split view that shows your Artboard and underlying XAML. Note the hierarchy of items in your Layout Root, which is a Grid object.*

Select an item. As you click through each item, you'll see the corresponding code view change, and you can see how the markup is arranged in your document.

Now if you decide that you don't want to see things in a markup view, you can select the following icon in the Objects and Timeline panel and choose to display items in Z order. This displays the items according to their z-depth, with the front-most items appearing before the items beneath them. For many items, it's important to understand the implications of markup order for your project and to understand which view you are looking at in the Objects and Timeline panel.

Figure 12.11 *Viewing items in Z-order in the Objects and Timeline panel. Note that this does not change the underlying code or layout; it's simply another way to represent objects in the Objects and Timeline panel.*

TIMELINES IN THE OBJECTS AND TIMELINE PANEL

In Chapters 4 through 11, you were exposed to SketchFlow animations and states, which are two ways to create interactions in SketchFlow. SketchFlow animations and states are both useful ways to create the interactions you need in SketchFlow projects. When you use these systems, SketchFlow does the hard work of interpreting the changes between your states, the transitions, for you. In advanced application design, more control is often needed, and for this, Expression Blend uses another animation model called storyboards.

In effect, the states and SketchFlow animations, and even the transitions you create, are storyboards as well, with SketchFlow doing the hard work of stringing together the different storyboards and wiring up the triggers and events that cause them to play. You can actually look at the Timeline view and add and remove keyframes and animate objects directly if needed. You'll get different results depending on if you are adding animations and keyframes to a Transition versus a State versus using SketchFlow animations. In general, we don't recommend mixing timeline animation with states and SketchFlow animations unless you're willing to learn more of the advanced options for application design that are available in Expression Blend. The User Guide and Online Communities are good places to get started with learning more about advanced animation techniques with Expression Blend.

To see the timeline for a state, select a state; then, in the Objects and Timeline Map, you should see a Description box at the top of the panel that lists your selected state. To the right of that description is an icon that opens up your storyboard.

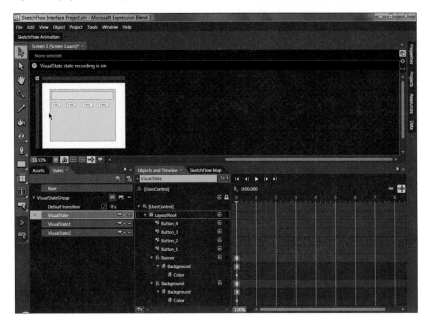

Figure 12.12 *The Timeline view of a state using the Animation Workspace that you can access from the Window menu.*

If you ever desire to see the timeline for a state or SketchFlow animation, you can select the Show or Hide Timeline icon again on the Objects and Timeline panel to hide your storyboard. In an advanced Expression Blend project, there is a drop-down that lets you selectively see all the storyboards you've created for a particular screen in your project.

Figure 12.13 *The Show and Hide Timeline icon when you'd like to see a Timeline view for states or SketchFlow animation.*

Figure 12.14   The storyboard selector, which is available in a project where you select and manipulate storyboards you've created for a project.

The Storyboard model and traditional animation system in Expression Blend gives you more control over how to do this, but it also requires more advanced knowledge of how to activate or trigger the storyboards you have created using behaviors. We'll show you some basic storyboards and behaviors in Chapter 14 and in Part IV of this book.

SKETCHFLOW ANIMATION PANEL

The SketchFlow Animation panel is an animation system designed for the type of interactions you typically use in a SketchFlow project; we cover it in detail in Chapter 14.

ARTBOARD PANEL

The Artboard is where the screens of your applications appear, and it's where you can directly manipulate items in your project. The Artboard tells you a number of useful things. Let's start with the tabs on the top of the panel.

Across the top of the panel, it shows via tabbed interface how many screens you have open for your SketchFlow project. Right below that, you see an indicator of any objects on the Artboard that you've selected; this breadcrumb feature provides shortcuts to advanced functionality when available, such as the editing of templates when controls are selected.

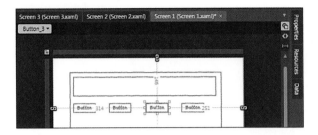

Figure 12.15   The tabbed interface and breadcrumb of the Artboard.

To the right of the Artboard are icons that let you select different views for the Artboard. In most cases, you'll opt for the Design view. But the XAML and Split views enable you to see the code that is generated as you create your SketchFlow project.

Figure 12.16   Icons to change your Artboard view.

On the lower portion of the Artboard, you see a number of other icons. From left to right, they are the following:

- The Zoom icon

- The Effects icon

- The Grid icon

- The Grid Snapping icon

- The Snapping to Snaplines icon

- The Annotation icon

The Zoom control enables you to adjust the size of the screen on your Artboard or resize the keyboard to selected items. You can also do this from your keyboard by using the Control and + and – keys or by using the scroll wheel on a mouse. Another useful trick is to select the space bar on your keyboard and use your mouse to drag the Artboard and reposition it.

The Effects icon turns on or off the display of real-time effects that you may have added to objects to improve performance of the interface. In many cases, you might not use many effects in a SketchFlow project unless you are working on higher-fidelity prototypes.

The Grid icon displays or hides a visual grid for your project. You control options for the grid by going to the Tools menu and selecting Options. The Artboard selection enables you to set the spacing for your grid and set other parameters for the Artboard.

The Grid Snapping icon allows objects to snap or auto-align to your grid.

The Snapping to Snaplines icon enables you to snap to snaplines that may exist in your document. Snaplines are created for grids and other layout structures, including the default Layout Root object that defines each screen in a SketchFlow project. You create snaplines by selecting a layout object. You should see a blue set of bars that surround the layout object that you can mouse over. As you do this, you'll see an orange snapline appear. If you click this line, you'll add a snapline to your canvas. You can reselect snaplines to move or delete them as needed. You find Snaplines are similar to Guides in tools like Adobe Photoshop.

- When you enable the **Snapping to gridlines** feature, every object that you drag on the Artboard snaps or pulls toward the closet horizontal and vertical gridlines. If you are using the **Snapping to snaplines** feature, any object you are dragging on the artboard snaps to:

  - Column and row dividers in a grid panel, which are the snaplines that you create

  - Default margins, which you can adjust in the Properties panel using the Layout category for the selected object

  - Baselines for text objects

  - Alignment boundaries

  - Default padding, which you can set in the Artboard Category in the Options panel accessed from the Tool menu

In advanced projects, how you enable detailed design snaplines is used to define the behavior for complicated layout containers, covered in detail in the Expression User Guide.

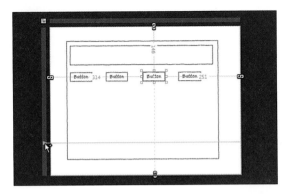

Figure 12.17   Adding snaplines to a layout object.

The final icon enables you to show annotations that you may add to your project. The annotations are always in your project but you may not want to see them all the time when you work on your project.

SKETCHFLOW MAP

The SketchFlow Map is where you create and edit the SketchFlow Map for your SketchFlow application. We cover how to use the SketchFlow Map and how to add screens to your project in Chapter 4, "Getting Started." There are some useful controls at the bottom of the SketchFlow Map panel that help you navigate through your SketchFlow Maps.

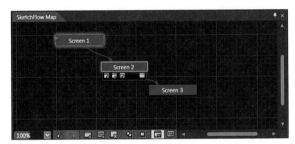

Figure 12.18   The SketchFlow Map.

The Zoom control enables you to adjust the size of your SketchFlow Map and works the same as the Zoom Control for your Artboard.

The Undo and Redo icons are specific to actions that you make with your SketchFlow Map. This is a quirk of SketchFlow in that if you remove a screen from a SketchFlow Map and want to undo that process, you'll need to use these controls versus the normal Redo or Undo commands in the Edit menu or via keyboard shortcuts.

The Create a Screen icon is used for creating new screens in your SketchFlow Map. You can, of course, create screens directly on the SketchFlow Map as well, as we did in Chapter 4.

The Create a Component icon enables you to add component screen to your project. Just as with normal screens, you can create component screens on the SketchFlow Map by simply dragging one out from an existing screen in your project.

The Delete a Selection icon removes selected items from your SketchFlow Maps. You can drag a marquee around items you'd like to use with your mouse in a SketchFlow Map; if you make a mistake, you simply use the Undo icon to correct it.

The Fit All icon fits your entire SketchFlow Map into the available real estate that you've allocated for your SketchFlow Map.

The Fit Selection icon fits whatever portion of your SketchFlow Map that you've selected into the available real estate that you've allocated for your SketchFlow Map.

The Show Navigation Connections Dimmed icon reduces the opacity of our navigation connectors. This is sometimes useful when your SketchFlow Maps become complex or you'd like to highlight where components would be used in your application.

The Show Component Connections Dimmed icon reduces the opacity of your component screen connections. This is useful when your SketchFlow Maps become complex or you'd like to highlight the navigation of your application.

THE RESULTS PANEL

The Results panel displays advanced information about your project when you compile and build it. It is also where errors are displayed when a build does not compete or has problems. Truly understanding the information in the Results panel requires advanced knowledge that is not required for using SketchFlow. If you find that you get an error when you build a

SketchFlow project, in most cases you simply need to shut down any earlier builds and simply attempt to rebuild your project again. Occasionally, if you get projects from other folks, they may forget to include certain libraries or assemblies that are needed for your project. The Results panel will tell you what's missing—much like the panels and palettes we see in graphic design programs when linked assets are missing.

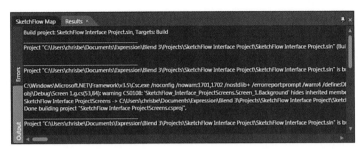

Figure 12.19   *The Results panel showing information from a build.*

THE PROPERTIES PANEL

The Properties panel is the most complex and intimidating panel in Expression Blend, and many of its functions aren't used in SketchFlow.

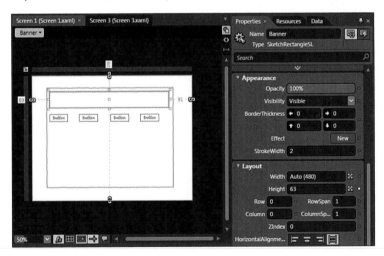

Figure 12.20   *The Properties panel as it would appear when you select an object.*

The Properties panel is contextual—it only shows you items that can be edited or altered for a given object. This means the panel may look very different when you've selected a behavior versus a control for example.

We discuss how some parts of the Properties panel that are germane to SketchFlow are used in the following chapters, and we also use it in Part IV of this book. Let's take a quick look at some of the categories that can appear in the Properties panel.

The Brushes category is where you control attributes like color, stroke, and alpha channels for elements. It's where you set gradients and apply advanced textures or tiled elements to different objects in your project. In SketchFlow, we usually use brushes for simple things, such as setting border and background colors and controlling the transparency of items with Alpha effects. With advanced or high-fidelity work, you may use gradients to add detail and richness to your objects. You'll also notice an opacity control that is accessible via an arrow at the bottom of the Brushes panel; it has the same name as an opacity control in the Appearance menu. Unless you have an advanced understanding of Expression Blend, we suggest you refrain from using this control because it may give you unexpected results.

Figure 12.21   *The Brushes category in the Properties panel.*

The Appearance category is most useful in SketchFlow for its Opacity control. In most cases, you'll want to use the Opacity control to make objects invisible versus the transparency features in the Brushes section. Opacity controls the visibility for the entire object, whereas Alpha controls the transparency differently for each component of an object, such as fill and stroke.

There are some neat tricks you can do with the appearance menu in SketchFlow, and we touch on that in Chapter 14.

If you wanted to, you could also use the appearance menu to add some simple effects, such as a blur or drop shadow, to individual objects— something we typically don't do until we're creating high-fidelity prototypes.

You may also notice little dots that appear next to many of the menu items in the Properties panel. These items link to advanced properties that are beyond the scope of this book. Occasionally some of these features may be set automatically by SketchFlow, but unless you're an advanced user of Expression Blend, you won't need to worry about how to use these functions now.

Figure 12.22   The Appearance category in the Properties panel.

The Layout category provides both basic and advanced details about your object. It tells you its size, placement, and alignment and margins within your canvas or any objects or elements you embedded it in. For objects you create in SketchFlow on the Artboard, it lets you control and refine the size and placement of things you added to the Artboard.

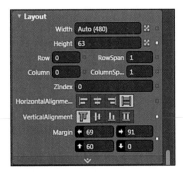

Figure 12.23   The Layout category in the Properties panel.

The Trigger panel appears when you're working with a behavior. Often, advanced behaviors may have parameters that you can set or edit.

Figure 12.24   The Trigger category in the Properties panel.

The Common Properties category has many advanced functions that aren't pertinent to SketchFlow; it's also contextual, so some properties will appear differently with different objects. There are a few parameters that are relevant to dynamic prototyping, however. You can add content that appears when someone mouses over an object via the ToolTip function, which is useful for application prototypes. You also can control what type of cursor appears over a given object when someone mouses over it, which is useful for different types of prototypes.

Figure 12.25   The Common Properties category in the Properties panel.

The Transform category contains all the usual controls designers would expect to have to transform objects. In most cases in SketchFlow, you'd probably make these changes directly on the Artboard, but you can also do them here. The Projection controls in the Transform panel enable you to manipulate your 2D objects in a 3D plane.

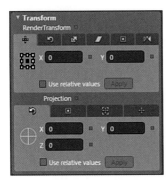

Figure 12.26   The Transform category in the Properties panel.

The Miscellaneous category is typically not used in SketchFlow projects unless you're an advanced user. It's a contextual panel, and properties that appear here are unusual ones that simply don't map to other categories in the Properties panel.

The Animation category is typically one that appears with specific behaviors and provides additional controls over how those behaviors drive different transitions. You may also see a panel that is similar in Silverlight-enabled SketchFlow projects that enable you to set easing functions.

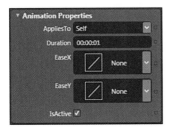

Figure 12.27   The Animation category in the Properties panel.

As you get more familiar with the typical functions that you use in the Properties panel, you'll quickly discover that removing some of the panels you don't need is helpful. One thing we've found that is most useful—once you're familiar with Expression Blend, is to use the Search box that appears at the top of the Properties panel. By typing in words like "Transform" or "Brushes," you can quickly cut down the clutter in this panel. Just remember to check and clear the Search box if you discover that you can't seem to find a panel.

THE RESOURCES PANEL

The Resources panel contains all the resources used on a given page in your project. It contains all the libraries and project data sources that you're using and any specific elements that you're using on your page. Much like the Assets panel, it can be used to add controls to your page or add styles to existing controls in a project.

Figure 12.28 *The Resources panel stores all the the styles and assets that are used in our project.*

THE DATA PANEL

The Data panel is where you work with live and simulated data sources. We took a good look at the Data panel in Chapter 10, "Working with Data," and we'll take a deeper look at this panel in Chapter 16, "Data," and in Part IV.

THE FEEDBACK PANEL

The Feedback panel is where you review and import feedback on your SketchFlow projects. We took a look at some of its features in Chapter 6, "Sharing Your Project and Getting Feedback," and explore it in more detail in Chapter 17, "Annotating Your Work, Getting Feedback, and Creating Documentation."

APPLICATION MENUS

Application menus duplicate most of the functionality found in the panel and icons that we've been looking at so far in SketchFlow. However, there are a few functions that can only be accessed via the File menu. As with other parts of the application, Application menus are contextual, so only the functions that are able to be used with an object will be available. Other items will appear in the menu but they will be disabled and you won't be able to select them. Let's take a look.

The File menu houses basic functions that enable you to open, save, and create new projects. It's also where you find functions to import assets from Photoshop, Illustrator, and PowerPoint, as well as to package up your projects for distribution and to export project specifications into a Microsoft Word format.

Figure 12.29   Options available from the File menu.

The Edit menu contains all the typical functions of any Edit menu. There are, however, some useful find and replace functions that can be helpful for large projects.

Figure 12.30   Options available from the Edit menu.

The View menu duplicates much of the functionality around different attributes that are visible on the Artboard. This menu controls various zoom and fit selections and the various visual aids that can appear on the Artboard.

Figure 12.31   Options available form the View menu.

The Object menu has some unique functions. If you think about applications like Adobe Illustrator, you'll find that many of the functions that you use around object clipping, merging, combing, or grouping reside here. There are also some duplicated links for editing controls or resources and attaching behaviors to objects. Many of the functions available for objects via right-clicking with your mouse when an object is selected are duplicated with this menu.

Figure 12.32   *Options available from the Objects menu.*

The Project menu enables you to add a variety of items to your project. This includes adding folders and items to an existing project, but it also includes importing existing or adding new projects directly to the one on which you're working. For example, you could merge multiple projects that are part of the same project but that were being worked on by different people on your team.

The Project menu is also where you add references to your projects, which are the DLLs that add additional controls or assemblies that might be needed for your project.

Figure 12.33   *Options available from the Project menu.*

The Project menu is also where you find the commands to build and run your project and control project settings. Project settings let you control which functions of the SketchFlow projects appear and change the colors that appear in your SketchFlow Map.

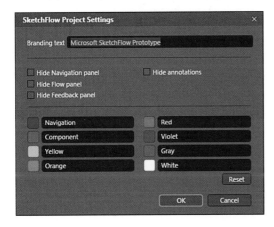

Figure 12.34   *Options available in SketchFlow Project settings.*

The Tools menu is where you can access advanced functions around the creation of user controls, states, and brushes. It's also where you can access options to embed fonts in your application and add annotations to your project. Finally, it's where you access the Options menu for Expression Blend. Most of the options are self explanatory.

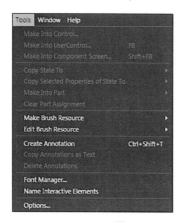

Figure 12.35   Options available from the Tools menu.

It's helpful to make sure your Artboard, Annotation, and SketchFlow settings are established and consistent across your team before you start big projects.

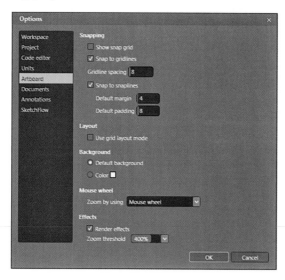

Figure 12.36   The Artboard category in the Options menu.

The Window menu is where you can save workspaces that you've customized for your projects and access all the panels and palettes that are available to you in Expression Blend.

Figure 12.37   Options available from the Window menu.

The Help menu gives you access to the User Guide and the Expression Blend SDK User Guide. It also contains links to external resources for SketchFlow and Expression Blend. Finally, this is where you enter your license key for Expression Blend and enroll in the customer improvement program for Expression Blend—which we encourage you to do, as it provides valuable feedback to the product team that is anonymous about how the tool is used.

Figure 12.38   Options available from the Help menu.

SUMMARY

The Expression Blend interface is complex. But the reality is that much of the interface is not needed for SketchFlow projects. Expression Blend has a very usable interface on monitor resolutions as low as 1280 by 800. However, larger monitors can enable you to keep more panels open and make panels easier to access. In Chapter 4, we detailed a quick way to simplify this workspace, and we encourage you to do so. Every panel in Expression Blend can also float, so you can create custom workspaces that are suited to your working style and that can even span multiple monitors.

In this chapter you learned about the key panels that you'll use in SketchFlow projects including the:

- Tools panel

- Projects panel

- Assets panel

- State panel

- Objects and Timelines panel

- SketchFlow Animation panel

- Artboard

- Sketchflow Map

13

ASSETS, STYLES, AND COMPONENTS

In this chapter we explain the assets, styles, and components that are available to you in SketchFlow Blend and the best ways to access them. We focus on a subset of all the controls that you use in a full Blend project and look at what you encounter in SketchFlow projects. We explain and segment these elements and give you examples of where you use them. By the end of this chapter, you should know how to access and use these elements in your proejcts.

We discussed how to access assets in Chapter 12, "The SketchFlow Interface." In this chapter, let's talk about the specific assets that are available in SketchFlow.

Figure 13.1 *The Assets panel shows a view of Controls that are available to us in our project.*

We prefer using the Assets panel to access styles, behaviors, and other resources you'll use in your SketchFlow projects, but you can also access Assets from the Tools panel as well by selecting the assets icon from the tools panel, which is the double arrow icon located at the bottom of the panel. Let's discuss the different categories that make up the Assets panel.

- **Navigation Screens**: As you create screens in your SketchFlow project, they'll be available in this section of the Assets panel. You can also see these screens in the Project panel as you create them and can also access them via your SketchFlow.

- **Component Screens**: As you create component screens in your SketchFlow project, they'll be available in this section of the Assets panel. Component screens were discussed in Chapter 11, "Bringing It All Together." Although you can also see them in your Projects panel and SketchFlow Map panel, you may find it's easiest to access them here in complex projects.

- **Behavior Assets**: There are many behaviors in Expression Blend. There are very specific ones that we use in SketchFlow and other behaviors that are typically used in more advanced projects. Finally, you may have other behaviors that you import into your project to use or that other folks have created for you. (We explore this in more detail in Part IV of the book.)

The behaviors that we use for SketchFlow are as follows:

- ActivateStateAction

- NavigateBackAction

- NavigateForwardAction

- NavigateToScreenAction

- PlaySketchFlowAnimationAction

We'll cover what these and other behaviors do in Chapter 15, "SketchFlow Behaviors."

SKETCHFLOW STYLE ASSETS

The SketchFlow category shows all the most important elements that you'll need in your SketchFlow project. This includes all the navigation and component screens you create, behaviors you use, and SketchStyles.

You may receive additional styles and behaviors from team members you collaborate with or via downloads from the Expression Community. You can import these libraries into your project as DLLs (Dynamic-Link Library) in the Project panel; the appropriate elements will then be listed in the Assets panel after you rebuild your project.

Sometimes it's helpful to use the search feature of the Asset menu when you're trying to find an item but not sure you know where to look.

In SketchFlow, you can use any of the controls and actions available to you in a WPF or Silverlight project; in most projects, however, you'll probably want to use SketchStyles. SketchStyles are available to you in SketchFlow projects and, in fact, they are actually just a special resource library that provides a sketch look to a subset of controls that you would use with your prototypes. SketchFlow Style Assets are useful as we progress from pure sketching to prototyping activities in SketchFlow as we iterate and slowly introduce more advanced functionality into the project.

What are some of the assets available to you? Expression Blend 3.0 ships with the following SketchStyles. These styles can generally be grouped into categories that are controls to interact with an application, house data, or allow for text input or descriptions. As you mouse over each tool, you should see a tooltip appear that describes exactly what each tool does.

Figure 13.2   A view of SketchFlow assets.

For simplicity, we've grouped these styles into logical categories.

Text-Focused SketchStyles

All the text-focused SketchStyles are based on a font called Buxton Sketch, after designer and Microsoft researcher Bill Buxton. The different SketchStyles can be used to easily create body copy, titles, and subtitles for your application. Sketch simply looks like a post-it style note and can be used in addition to annotations to call out details about your application. For items like Basic Text and Text Box versus Text Block and Text Box, the key difference is the default alignments. The Basic Text and Box styles default to a left-horizontal alignment and a top-vertical alignment, whereas the Text Block and Box styles default to a right-horizontal alignment and top-vertical alignment. Because it's easy to change the alignment of all these styles, you often find that you have a choice of text styles that work.

- BasicTextBlock-Sketch

- BasicTextBox-Sketch

- BodyCenter-Sketch

CHAPTER 13 | ASSETS, STYLES, AND COMPONENTS

- BodyLeft-Sketch

- BodyRight-Sketch

- Note-Sketch

- SubtitleCenter-Sketch

- SubtitleLeft-Sketch

- SubtitleRight-Sketch

- TextBlock-Sketch

- TextBox-Sketch

- TitleCenter-Sketch

- TitleLeft-Sketch

- TitleRight-Sketch

Control-Focused SketchStyles

Control-focused SketchStyles look simple, but they are actually quite powerful. They contain all the behaviors that you would expect them to have. So, buttons have multiple states and can be clicked; password boxes mask the data that is being entered into them; sliders slide; and so on.

- Button-Sketch

- CheckBox-Sketch

- ScrollBar-Sketch

- HyperlinkButton-Sketch

- PasswordBox-Sketch

- ProgressBar-Sketch

- RadioButton-Sketch

- Slider-Sketch

- TabControl-Sketch

- TabItem-Sketch

- Thumb-Sketch

Data-Focused SketchStyles

Data-focused SketchStyles don't look like much until you've added data to them. We cover this in Chapter 16, "Data."

- ComboBoxItem-Sketch

- ComboBox-Sketch

- ListBoxItem-Sketch

- ListBox-Sketch

- ScrollViewer-Sketch

- ScrollViewer-Sketch-List

Layout-Focused SketchStyles

Layout-focused SketchStyles are primitive rectangles and circles with the sketch style applied. In addition, as you get more advanced, you may use some of the Grid Layout elements we discussed in Chapter 12 for advanced or more complex prototyping and designs. Those additional layout contains don't have a SketchStyle applied to them and instead would be used to house other layout elements, such as Circle-Sketch, Rectangle Sketch, and the various Controls that you might add to an element.

- Circle-Sketch

- Rectangle-Sketch

WORKING WITH STYLES

SketchFlow styles look like the other standard controls that are available in Expression Blend for WPF and Silverlight projects. There's a reason for this. The sketchy look that you use with SketchStyles is really just a style that has been applied to these existing controls. Typically when prototyping, you'll use controls that are already available to you in SketchFlow or depend on your developer peers to provide you with resource libraries—much like SketchStyles that you can use in your projects. In some cases, the work you do in your prototypes informs how you create resource libraries that will be used in other projects.

You can access SketchFlow styles in three key ways, as follows:

1. You can open up an Assets panel from the Tools panel, navigate to SketchFlow styles, and drag them onto the screen. Or, you can load up individual styles in the Tools panel and add them to your Artboard by dragging or double-clicking on the SketchFlow icon in the Tools panel.

2. You can open up the standalone Assets panel from the Windows menu, navigate to SketchFlow styles, and drag them directly onto the Artboard.

3. You can access SketchFlow styles in your Resources panel and the SketchStyles.xaml library and drag them directly onto the Artboard.

When you look at styles in the Assets panel or Tools panel, you'll notice two icons to the right of the search screen. These icons let you toggle between an icon and list view for what appears in each panel.

Figure 13.3   *Here we are accessing Assets from the Tools panel. Note the two icons in the upper right corner that let you toggle between an icon or list view.*

Now the asset view in the Tools panel and the Assets panel look similar. The resource panel, however, looks very different. We prefer using the Assets panel in SketchFlow, but some advanced users prefer using the Resources panel and find that it's easier to sift through large collections of assets.

Figure 13.4   Accessing Assets from the Resources Panel.

UNDERSTANDING STYLES, TEMPLATES, AND RESOURCES

Even though we'll be working with styles versus creating them, quite often in SketchFlow, it's important to understand how Expression Blend enables you to create your own look and feel for controls. There are a number of ways to accomplish this. You can do the following:

- Edit or alter the style or template of existing controls.

- Import resources or create new or empty controls.

Editing or altering styles enables you to modify the default values of properties that make up a control—for example, a sketchy outline and the Buxton Sketch font versus the standard look and feel of a button. Sometimes you need to do more than simply modify existing properties, however. When you need to modify the structure of a control, you edit the template of a control. For example, a default button may need a new element—such as a background image for your project. In that case, you would need to alter the template.

Unless you're doing very advanced and high-fidelity prototypes, we don't recommend that you spend a lot of time with styles and templates until you get more comfortable with Expression Blend, Silverlight, and WPF. If you're part of large group in a company using SketchFlow and want to use SketchFlow with a common set of controls and styles, it probably makes sense to work closely with a developer to assist you in creating resource libraries that you can use just like SketchStyles. This is because the manner in which you work with styles and templates differs slightly in WPF and Silverlight and requires a more advanced understanding of that technology than is required for working in SketchFlow. We will, however, cover simple style and template editing in Chapter 14 "SketchFlow Animation and States," and Chapter 16 "Data" and Part IV.

If you are interested in understanding these differences, we recommend looking at the following sections in the Microsoft Expression Blend User Guide:

- Styling objects
- Styling a control that supports templates
- Create a resource
- Create a style
- Create or modify a template
- Styling tips for common Silverlight controls
- Styling tips for WPF simple styles

WORKING WITH COMPONENTS

Components are a way to take an existing object or group of objects and group them into an object that you can use elsewhere in your project. Components in SketchFlow are very similar to user controls that are used elsewhere in Expression Blend projects. In fact, a collection of user controls is what makes up a SketchFlow project in Expression Blend. The difference between a user control and component screen in SketchFlow is that a component screen is added to your SketchFlow Map as a reference.

There are two ways to create component screens.

You can select a group of objects on the Artboard, right-click, and select **Make Into Component Screen**. This takes all the selected objects, groups them into the component screen, and then links that component screen to where the control was created. It also adds that component screen to your SketchFlow Map, which makes it easy to add to other screens in your project.

Create a collection of objects and then go to the Tools menu and select **Make Into Component Screen**, or select **Shift + F8** on your keyboard.

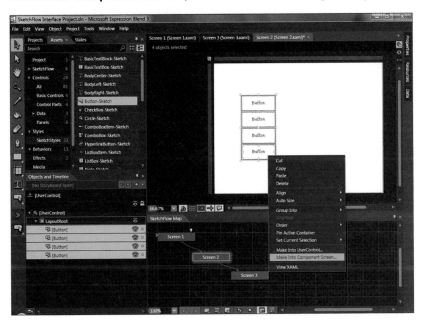

Figure 13.5   Making a component screen from the Artboard.

After you've made your component screen, you notice that it appears as a component screen in your Project panel, in the Objects and Timeline panel, and appears on the SketchFlow Map. After building your project, you also see that it appears in Asset panel and Resource panel views as well.

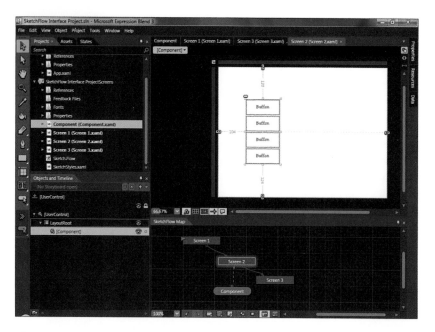

Figure 13.6 *A component screen in the Project panel, Artboard, and SketchFlow Map.*

In SketchFlow, components screens are a useful way to get out of the job of creating the same elements over and over again across different screens.

For example, you could create a user component that shows a banner and navigation elements for a user who is not signed into an application, create another for a user who is signed in, and then swap them out using different states. You can also create global navigation elements and application *chrome* and then only have to worry about updating those elements in one place if they need to change—your component screen.

The best way to take advantage of styles and components is to bring them to life with states and SketchFlow animation. We tackle that in the next chapter.

SUMMARY

In this chapter we've learned what Assets are and the different ways we can access them; what different types of SketchStyles are available; where to learn more about editing styles and templates; and how to work with components.

14

SKETCHFLOW ANIMATION AND STATES

In this chapter we learn about how animation works in SketchFlow. We explore the animation models that are available to us, which include SketchFlow Animation, States, Keyframe Animation, and Storyboards. We also explain why there are three models and make recommendations on how to take advantage of each of them. Finally, in the context of learning about these animation models, we work with a sample project that shows us some basic functions for editing and working with templates.

ANIMATION MODELS IN SKETCHFLOW AND EXPRESSION BLEND

In SketchFlow, you can create animation and interactivity with three different techniques. They are as follows:

1. SketchFlow animation

2. State animation

3. Keyframe animation using storyboards

These techniques are able to accomplish many of the same things. Each technique adds complexity, but also flexibility, in how you can add or demonstrate interactivity in a SketchFlow project.

Although all these models are available to you in SketchFlow, regardless of whether you are creating a project that uses Silverlight or WPF as a foundation, there are some minor differences in how these models work in Silverlight or WPF projects that are not SketchFlow based. We're going to focus on how you would employ these techniques in SketchFlow projects in Expression Blend that focus on dynamic prototyping, projects that start with sketching and then gradually move into prototyping. SketchFlow animation and states represent newer and simpler ways to create animation that are required for this type of work and are the core models that you'll use in SketchFlow.

Here are some general guidelines that can help you be successful:

1. SketchFlow animation is only available in SketchFlow projects. To create functionality where SketchFlow automatically interprets transitions that doesn't require or need a lot of user interaction this is often the easiest animation model to start with.

2. State animation allows for more control and complexity and the ability to provide actions that a user may trigger in the application.

3. Keyframe-based animation, where key start and endpoints are defined and smooth transitions are interpreted between those keyframes is the core animation system used in Expression Blend. It's available

to us in SketchFlow, but it is really useful for far more complex animations, interactions, and for individuals that have a deeper understanding of Expression Blend and animation concepts that are not a requirement to use SketchFlow. As you get more advanced in SketchFlow, you may find yourself using a combination of all three systems to get the desired results.

4. We recommend starting your education in SketchFlow with Silverlight Projects. In addition to making it easier to share your projects and get feedback, we feel the learning curve with animation models in Silverlight is a bit simpler than with WPF.

    You'll find that the methods for styling and templating controls are a bit easier to understand and work with in Silverlight versus WPF and that you'll have some additional functions around controlling your animations and transitions that will better support the design process.

    The Reference section of this book goes into detail about the differences between WPF and Silverlight. It's not necessary to understand these differences to be successful with SketchFlow, but it is useful if you are designing projects that target one platform or other other in production as your project progresses.

People make careers out of just learning how to animate things, and Expression Blend's animation system is as complex and as sophisticated as the most advanced motion design and 3D programs. You don't, however, need to be a master animator to be successful with using animation in SketchFlow.

SKETCHFLOW ANIMATION

SketchFlow Animation is the easiest way to add animation to your projects in SketchFlow. We recommend always starting with SketchFlow animation and moving on to States and Keyframe animation only when you find it necessary.

Create a new Silverlight-base SketchFlow project and see if you can follow some of the simple steps we go through here. After creating your project, you open the SketchFlow Animation panel by selecting it from the Window menu if it's not already visible.

If you look closely at the SketchFlow Animation panel, you see a Base category. This is the default for any screen in a SketchFlow project. In your new SketchFlow project, add a shape to your Base category.

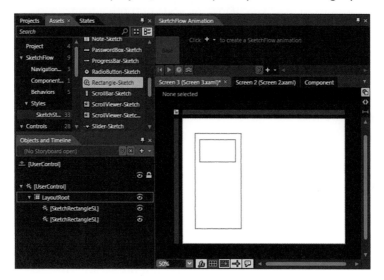

Figure 14.1   *A Base state with a few simple shapes we've created a using Buxton-Sketch style called Rectangle-Sketch.*

In the SketchFlow Animation panel, you should also notice a + control right next to this Base category, which you can use to create a SketchFlow animation. Click the +, and you should see a small icon appear that looks like a snapshot of your screen, which is a frame. Frames can be created by copying a Base screen or even other frames, which are now states in your animation.

As you do this, you should see a red outline appear around your Artboard, which indicates that SketchFlow is in a Record mode. This means that anything you do on this frame will be captured in SketchFlow. Move your geometric shape to the other side of the screen in Frame 1.

When you select the Play button in the SketchFlow Animation panel, you should see that the shape you've created moves across the screen.

Create one more frame. Do this by placing your mouse in Frame 1; you should see a + sign appear. You'll create a new frame by clicking the + sign. Alter the color and size of your shape in Frame 2.

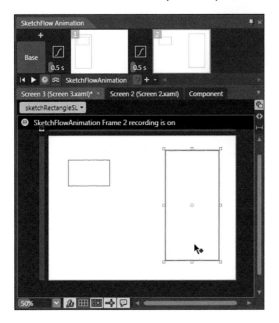

Figure 14.2   A SketchFlow animation with two frames.

Now, go back to your Base category and add a new shape. Notice that this new shape is automatically added to the other frames in your animation.

Now go to Frame 2 in your animation and add another shape. Play your animation again. When you add a shape, SketchFlow makes that object invisible in all other states, including the Base category of your screen. This is an important distinction that you should be aware of when working with Frames. SketchFlow assumes that you will want anything you add to a Base category to appear in any Frames that support that screen. However, when you add an element to a specific Frame for a screen, SketchFlow assumes you do not want that element to be visible in other Frames or your Base category.

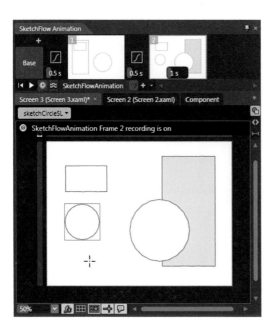

Figure 14.3   Your animation frames with objects added to the base and Frame 2.

If you go to the Objects and Timeline panel, you can see that items that are active in a given state have a red recording icon next to them. (You can see this by selecting different states and looking at the Objects and Timeline panel.) If you expand the twisty that is attached to each element, you can see that a RenderTransformation has been added to each item—which is a fancy way of saying you've moved items across the screen.

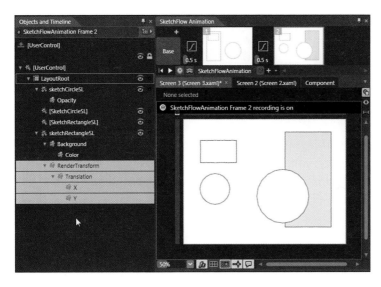

Figure 14.4   *Active objects as seen in the Objects and Timeline panel.*

SketchFlow determines automatically how to move the items across the screen when you create frames. If you've ever studied classic animation, you may see some similarities in how SketchFlow animation and classic animation works. In effect, each frame or state is a keyframe for all the items on a given screen.

In classic animation, the lead animator on a project was often in charge of establishing the keyframes in a project, and then production artists would do the work of creating all the art that would come between the keyframes, this work was called tweening. In SketchFlow projects, Expression Blend does all the tween work when you build an animation with SketchFlow animation. Another way to think about this is that SketchFlow is enabling you to create the transitions that occur between the different states of our animation—in this case frames.

So what's happening with the work we've just created? Let's take a close look at the SketchFlow Animation panel. See if you can find an icon on the lower-right portion of the panel next to the Play button that looks like a clock. Select it.

Figure 14.5   SketchFlow Animation panel with Time Editors pinned open.

You can notice a few things when you look at this panel. First, you should see your Base category; you should also see the two new frames you've created. In addition, you should see time indicators for your frames and the transition between each frame.

The time associated with each frame indicates how long a given frame will hold before moving to the next transition and frame in your SketchFlow animation. The timers between the frames indicate how long each transition will take, and it's here that SketchFlow interprets these transitions. So, going back to the first frame, what happens in the transition is that SketchFlow is moving your object across the screen in .5 seconds and then holding Frame 1 for 1 second before transitioning to Frame 2.

There is a feature that provides an extra level of control in SketchFlow projects that are based on Silverlight. If you look above the timer for your transition, you should notice a small box with a curved shape in it. This icon represents an easing function for your transition.

Easing functions, combined with thoughtful SketchFlow animation and states, let you create very polished and nuanced transitions. By default, all your transitions are set up with no easing functions supplied.

There are 11 default easing functions that you can access. It's best to experiment with them to truly understand how they work, but here are some brief descriptions:

- **BackEase:** Retracts the motion of an animation slightly before it begins to animate in the path indicated.

- **BounceEase:** Creates a bouncing effect.

- **CircleEase:** Creates an animation that accelerates and/or decelerates using a circular function.

- **CubicEase:** Creates an animation that accelerates and/or decelerates using the formula f(t) = t3.

- **ElasticEase:** Creates an animation that resembles a spring oscillating back and forth until it comes to rest.

- **ExponentialEase:** Creates an animation that accelerates and/or decelerates using an exponential formula.

- **PowerEase:** Creates an animation that accelerates and/or decelerates using the formula f(t) = tp, where p is equal to the Power property.

- **QuadraticEase:** Creates an animation that accelerates and/or decelerates using the formula f(t) = t2.

- **QuarticEase:** Creates an animation that accelerates and/or decelerates using the formula f(t) = t4.

- **QuinticEase:** Create an animation that accelerates and/or decelerates using a formula f(t) = t5.

- **SineEase:** Creates an animation that accelerates and/or decelerates using a sine formula.

Figure 14.6   A graphic representations of all easing functions that are available.

By now, the concept of Frames and what they can do should be clear to you. Frames only exist in the SketchFlow Animation player. In principal and practice, they let you do the exact same things that States let you do in the States panel, but in a way that's slightly more intuitive that States. Cognitively, it might be useful to understand that a Frame is just a State, even though it's not called out as one when we use SketchFlow Animation.

We've only designed one animation for this screen but each screen in your project can actually contain multiple collections of SketchFlow animations.

By using your mouse and placing it on the Base category or the frames you've created, you should see + and – signs appear that enable you to add or remove new Framesto your SketchFlow animation. A – sign appears only if you've added more than one frame to a SketchFlow animation.

If you've only created a single frame, it can be removed by selecting the arrow at the bottom of the SketchFlow Animation panel and selecting Remove; this action actually removes the entire SketchFlow animation. This is also where you can open and close SketchFlow animations for a given screen and create new SketchFlow animations.

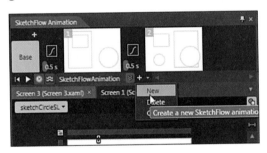

Figure 14.7 *Created a new SketchFlow Animation for a Screen. Screens can have multiple SketchFlow Animations that are independent of one another.*

Here, you can delete an individual frame in a SketchFlow animation and create new SketchFlow animations or close the one you are working on. The + sign to the left of the arrow also lets you create new SketchFlow animations and see the name of the current SketchFlow animation you are working on for a screen. The double arrow shows you all the SketchFlow animations you've selected for a screen.

Where you add new states *does* matter—it indicates to what state your screen will default. For example, adding a new frame from base creates a new state that is derivative of the Base or Stateless screen. Adding a new frame from Frame 2 creates a new frame that copies the state of Frame 2.

There's one final feature that is useful to understand. Next to the clock icon in the SketchFlow Animation panel is an icon that looks like two small wavy lines. This icon enables Fluid Layout. Fluid Layout is used when you change fixed properties from state to state in the Properties menu—such as Layout options like column spacing and margin properties. You can set these functions in the course of designing an application, but you may want to animate with SketchFlow animation to demonstrate an activity. If Fluid Layout is not enabled, you may notice that these items don't animate from state to state, regardless of what transitions and timing durations you've set. Fluid Layout allows for interpolation to be accounted for between these properties. In general, we recommend enabling it for most of the work you'll be doing in SketchFlow and then to disable it if it causes unexpected behavior—such as animations not playing smoothly or items appearing to jump around the screen.

STATES

States let you add both simple and advanced interactivity to your SketchFlow project, and they are an integral part of Expression Blend when you work with Silverlight and WPF, even though states work slightly differently in both platforms.

In SketchFlow, states are most often used at the screen level of a project; however, in reality, any object in a SketchFlow or Blend project can have different states, behaviors, or events that trigger them. In SketchFlow for Expression Blend, you can use states as a way to alter values for assets like forms, screens, objects, and user controls. You can edit or customize the appearance of existing states that might make up a series of buttons or controls, or create and define your own states.

If you have worked with the Web and CSS, or done other interactive design, you may be familiar with concepts that are similar to what states can do.

States in SketchFlow enable you to do three things, as follows:

- They enable you to alter the properties of objects in your SketchFlow project over time, such as visibility, color, scale, transforms, and so on (including properties that are generally fixed that couldn't change over time by enabling Fluid Layout).

- They enable you to create transitions between the states that can be simple or very complex.

- They enable you to add animation to the state itself that may occur after a transition.

As we discovered earlier when talking about SketchFlow animation, every screen in a SketchFlow project has a Base category.

When you add new states, you enter a different mode—which is basically one where you may move objects around the screen and perform operations that may transform their size, rotation, or visibility. You then enable SketchFlow to transition to these states when triggered via interactions in your project or the SketchFlow Player. A good analogy, introduced in Chapter 9, is that a given screen in SketchFlow is like the stage that is used during a play. Over the course of a play, you may rearrange or add objects to the stage as the play progresses through different acts.

When you are editing a state, some features of SketchFlow may not be available to you unless you revert to the Base category. In general, if you'll be working with a feature you wouldn't or couldn't animate—such as changing a type style or reordering items in the Objects and Timeline panel—you need to be on the Base screen that you want to edit. When you're in a state, SketchFlow will always want to animate or transition to whatever variables you are modifying.

A suggested best practice when working with states is to ensure that you always create a state that is a copy of your Base screen once you've configured and defined all the elements you need to create your states.

This can be useful for advanced animations and linking and can help set-up interactivity that you'll put into your dynamic prototypes. Basically, it provides a "default" state that you can easily transition back to from other states.

Both states and SketchFlow animation can be used to accomplish the same things. In general, we recommend using SketchFlow animation for demo mode where you need to quickly simulate complex interactions. We recommend using states for subtle or complex changes that occur through the use of the prototype—or where you want to wire up interactivity that a user of your prototype could trigger themselves and in effect use to states to enable them to interact with the application versus just seeing things happen.

Once you've created states, they are just like Navigate To functions. You can link objects and buttons to other screens of the application or to states that are available for the screen that you are on.

Let's take a deeper look at states and how integral they are to SketchFlow. Along the way, we're going introduce you to some advanced concepts around template editing and resource libraries as well. Finally, we'll show you how keyframes and the storyboard can support your work.

One of the best ways to truly understand how states work is to look at how to use states with a control (in this case, a button).

In our sample projects for Chapter 14 we've created a simple project for you to look at called Button. Open this project.

You should see a very simple project with one screen on the SketchFlow Map and one component screen. If you select your component screen, you have a collection of five buttons. Four of the buttons have a style applied to them, and one has the generic style of a button.

Figure 14.8   The ButtonComponents component screen.

Let's change the last generic button to the same style of the others. The easiest way to do this is to go the Resources panel. If you twist down the ButtonComponents.xaml, you can see that you've created a resource called MyButton.

Figure 14.9   A style we've created for our Button project called MyButton.

You can drag this resource onto your Artboard and onto the generic button. If you select the Template option, it applies the style of your button to the generic button.

CHAPTER 14 | SKETCHFLOW ANIMATION AND STATES

Figure 14.10   Dragging our Style to our button screen.

You could also simply right-click on the button and apply the resource directly.

Figure 14.11   Adding our Style by using a contextual menu.

Let's select the button labeled Disabled and make sure your Properties panel is visible. If you scroll down to the Common Properties window, you'll see a small arrow at the bottom of the window. If you select it, additional advanced properties are exposed. Unselect the IsEnabled box. You should see that the button changes color. What's actually happening is the button has inherited new properties from the style that we've created, which tells the button how it should appear when it's disabled.

Figure 14.12   A button in ButtonComponent Screen that has been disabled via our Properties Menu using features in the Common Properties category.

Let's go back to the Resources panel and find the MyButton resource. Select the Edit Resource icon.

Figure 14.13   The Edit Resource Icon is located next to the MyButton label that is highlighted.

You should now see that you have switched the scope of the Artboard to the style itself, versus your Component screen. In effect, you're editing the template of the control itself. Let's take a look at a few things. Ensure that you have your states panel visible.

The first thing you should notice is that your button is made up of a few generic shapes, and some text. You should also notice that states exist for your button as two state groups—one group details the CommonStates and the other group details the FocusStates. Click through each of these states and observe how the button changes subtly for each state. What you've actually done is slightly alter the color of the button for each state.

Figure 14.14   *States are used to control the different states our button would inherit if it's clicked, has focus, and so on.*

Let's look at some of the controls that are available for states in the State panel. Right above your Base category, you see icons that enable you to create state groups and turn on your transition preview. Because you are working with a button and it has a fixed set of states, the Create New State icon won't allow you to create new states in this particular instance. However, if you were working with states on a custom control or other object, you'd be able to create multiple state groups and states within those groups. Within a state group, only one state can be active at a given time. When you use multiple state groups, however, you can have different states in different state groups be active at the same time.

Figure 14.15   *The controls for creating Visual State Groups.*

If you examine some of the icons next to our state groups, such as the CommonStates group, you'll see an icon to the left that enables you to turn on Fluid Animation. The icon in the middle enables you to add new states to your state group, and the icon to the right enables you to remove the state group.

Below CommonStates, you see the Default Transition label; this area enables you to add time to the transition between each state. In a Silverlight-enabled SketchFlow project, you can also control the easing of the transition.

Figure 14.16 *Enabling the timing and easing functions of transitions between our states.*

When you look at each state within a state group, you'll see that you have options to remove the individual state and also apply custom transitions that override the default transition for a state group.

Silverlight's easing functions and these custom transitions enable you to create highly nuanced, subtle, and polished transitions.

With these transitions, there are three options:

- You can create a custom transition that overrides the default transition when coming from any state in the state group to this one. The "any state" is indicated by the *.

- You can dictate that the transition overrides the default transition from this state to any other state in the state group.

- You can dictate that the transition overrides the default transition from this state to other specific states in the state group.

Figure 14.17   Creating and defining custom transition settings for individual states.

Let's build this project and look at how your buttons behave in a prototype.

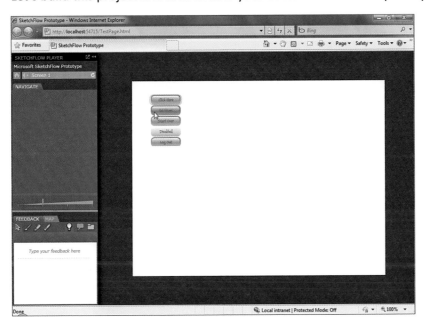

Figure 14.18   Looking at our project in the SketchFlow Player.

You should see that all the different states are working for your buttons. You should also see that a rather obnoxious animation begins to play on a button that has "focus." Let's see how to create that animation and look briefly at how you can use the timeline in SketchFlow.

If you look in the Objects and Timeline panel as you click through different states, you may notice that a timeline appears. If you don't see a timeline, make sure you are still in the Edit Template mode for your button. If you still don't see a timeline with different states, ensure that a state is selected and see if you can identify that state in the Objects and Timeline panel. Right next to the state name will be an icon that enables you to show the timeline.

Figure 14.19   *Activating a timeline view for our project.*

As you click through each state and state transition, you'll notice that this timeline appears. Within the duration of each transition and state itself, you can add and create animations by using the timeline. Go to the focused state and look at the timeline.

You should see that there are some keyframes present on the timeline. If you look closely at what changes are on those keyframes using the Property menu, you can see that you are animating the scale and transparency of the Focus_Stroke. You can use the Play buttons in the timeline to preview this.

You'll also see that right below the play controls, you have options for adding keyframes, seeing where you are in your timeline, and enabling snapping options to help you better select keyframes.

If you look at common properties for the specific items you're altering, Opacity and Render Transform, you can see that you have the ability to set easing functions for these keyframes as well.

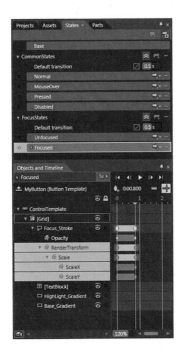

Figure 14.20   Looking at our timeline in detail

If you actually select your focused state and look at your common properties, you see some functions that you can set—in this case, by setting your RepeatBehavior to Forever versus just playing one time.

Notice that even though focused is a state, it's also in effect a storyboard.

Figure 14.21   Setting a repeat behavior for an animation.

Let's put the scope of your project back to Screen 1. You do that by selecting MyButton in the Objects and Timeline panel.

Figure 14.22   Moving our Scope from our button back to our screen.

If you look at your Objects and Timeline panel, notice that you don't have a storyboard open. You can use the plus + sign to the right of the panel to create a new storyboard that applies to the screen of your SketchFlow project. You then see a dialog appear where you can name your storyboard.

Figure 14.23   Creating a Storyboard for our screen.

You can have an unlimited number of storyboards to use in your project. You use your x sign in the Objects and Timeline panel to close storyboards for a screen.

Storyboards by themselves won't typically be as useful to you as SketchFlow animation or states because you must set up the events and triggers that actually cause a storyboard to play—and that requires a more in-depth knowledge of the steps you need to take to attach storyboards to the right objects and events that trigger them. In SketchFlow animation and states, Expression Blend does this for you automatically, but even in those models, you'll find that simple keyframe animation can add nuance and subtlety to your work.

SUMMARY

In this chapter we learned about the three animation models available to us in SketchFlow, including SketchFlow Animation, States, and Keyframe Animation with Storyboards; when to use which animation model; how to add nuance and subtlety to transitions with easing functions and custom transition settings; and basic template editing of a button control.

15

SKETCHFLOW BEHAVIORS

In this chapter we explore a power feature of SketchFlow and Expression Blend called Behaviors. Behaviors allow you to add complex interactivity to your prototypes without requiring the creation of code. You will learn the defintion of behaviors and their component parts and where you can find additional behaviors.

Behaviors were created as a part of Expression Blend 3 to make it easier to build and add interactivity to projects. Behaviors are a new concept that are not present in previous versions of Expression Blend, but instead build on previous concepts—triggers and actions—that enabled designers and developers to add interactivity to projects. With the addition of behaviors, Expression Blend makes it much easier to accomplish this.

HOW BEHAVIORS WORK

Behaviors are something that you use in SketchFlow, but the actual creation of behaviors requires the collaboration of a developer or your willingness to learn a bit about .NET and C# before you'll be able to create your own. We'll show you how to work with behaviors that have already been created by a developer including how to set properties, and add simple triggers and actions to existing behaviors. It's possible to be fantastically productive in SketchFlow without ever having to resort to creating your own behaviors and/or working with code.

One of the great things about behaviors is that it's pretty easy to explain to just about any .NET developer what you're trying accomplish and then be able to have that developer create the functionality that you desire in a behavior. Very rapidly, open source and community sites like CodePlex and Expression Gallery are seeing people create and share behaviors that you can use in your projects. We'll cover how to access these sites in the Reference section of this book.

The term "behavior" covers three different components, which include triggers and actions and also the collection of various code that sits under the behavior itself. When we refer to behaviors, we really mean the specific triggers, actions, and other functionality we've added via behaviors to create an encapsulated piece of functionality that we can add to objects in a project. Developers, and some designers, can easily write behaviors that encapsulate complex functionality that you can add to your SketchFlow projects. In fact, if you've linked screens and states in existing SketchFlow projects, you are using some of the behaviors included in SketchFlow in Expression Blend to accomplish this.

Figure 15.1 *You can see behaviors available to you in the Assets panel.*

TRIGGERS AND ACTIONS

If you've worked with interactivity, the concepts behind triggers and actions may be familiar to you. If not, we can quickly explain how they work by looking at the following sentence:

When *x* happens, do *y*.

This is basically saying that *x* is the trigger that causes *y*, the action, to occur. For example, turning the key in the ignition switch of a car is a trigger that starts the engine (an action). Setting a timer on a stove might set an alarm (a trigger) for you to take the action of removing a pot of boiling water off the stove. Triggers are the cause that tell you when something happens to effect or do something (the action itself).

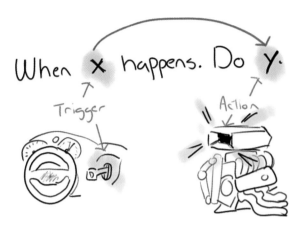

Figure 15.2 *Like starting a car, turning an ignition key is a trigger that starts an action.*

SketchFlow does a lot of work for you when you use behaviors. It makes assumptions about what the event will be to activate the behavior and also the action that will occur when that trigger occurs and makes assumptions about the target and source of those triggers and actions. When you use behaviors, you have the opportunity to specify or alter the triggers, actions, source, and target.

For example, a button might be a source; clicking the button might be a trigger that loads (the action) a new screen, which is a target. If this is still confusing, think of it this way:

When I *flick* the light switch, the light goes *on*.

Respectively, flicking the light switch is the trigger. The light going on is the action. If you think of this from a target and source perspective, we're adding detail and parameters:

When I *flick* the <u>kitchen light switch</u>, the <u>kitchen light</u> goes *on*.

Figure 15.3 *Sources and targets are just as important as triggers and actions.*

In this case, in addition to your trigger and actions, you also have the kitchen light switch (the source) and the kitchen light (the target).

Even though you might not be able to write your own behaviors from scratch, the ability to do even what was just outlined gives you powerful capabilities to creative sophisticated interactivity without having to resort to code.

BEHAVIOR

There is another part of a behavior that is powerful as well—the actual behavior itself, which can encapsulate code around triggers and behaviors in a form so that you can add complex interactions by simply dragging behaviors to a screen, or another object in a project. Behaviors inject their interactivity into the object they are assigned to and let you encapsulate multiple related and dependent activities, including states, into a reusable unit. Thus, the *behavior* part of a behavior enables you to do things that you can't do with just triggers and actions—or even require them.

This makes it easy for developers to create behaviors that can do the following:

- Open and close dialogs
- Run animation
- Set properties
- Validate input
- Navigate between screens or states
- Trigger animations

However, behaviors can also be used for much more complex interactions, such as the following:

- Making objects drag-able
- Simulating physics
- Enabling on-the-fly scripting

Because these behaviors contain encapsulated functionality, it's easy for you to add these behaviors to objects in your SketchFlow project.

ADDING BEHAVIORS AND SETTING PROPERTIES

If you spent time in Part II of this book, you've already worked with behaviors when you added navigation to your project or triggered states.

In fact, there are specific behaviors designed just for SketchFlow, which are as follows:

- **ActivateStateAction:** Navigates to a specific state in your SketchFlow project.
- **NavigateBackAction:** Navigates back to the previous screen in your navigation history.

- **NavigateForwardAction:** Navigates to the next screen in your navigation history.

- **NavigateToScreenAction:** Navigates to a specific screen in your SketchFlow project.

- **PlaySketchFlow Animation:** Triggers a SketchFlow animation to play in your SketchFlow project.

For example, let's presume you had a small SketchFlow project with a collection of five screens. You may have a sixth screen in the project which is a component that houses global navigation for the prototype. You can open this project in the Chapter 15 projects folder as well to follow along.

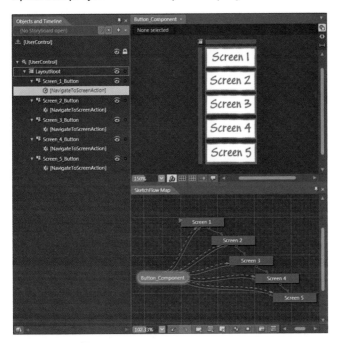

Figure 15.4 *A project with five screens and a component screen that is linked to each one.*

For each button that is wired-up, you are using a NavigateToScreenAction.

If you take a close look at the properties of those buttons in our component screen, you notice the following. One, you see the name of the specific behavior. (You could also tag it with your own reference name if you chose to.) You'll see two icons to the right of that naming field as well. The left most icon is the Properties icon, and you want to make sure in this case that it's selected for what we want to accomplish. The other icon called the Events icon is for advanced functions that aren't relevant to what we're doing here.

In the case of NavigateToScreenAction, you should see two categories: Trigger and Common Properties.

Figure 15.5 *Editing behavior properties in the Properties panel.*

Look at the SourceName and EventName categories. You'll notice the SourceName is set to Parent. What this means is that the source is the parent object—in this case, a button. You'll also see that an EventName is already set, namely that your trigger occurs when the button is clicked. You could change these defaults if it's not the behavior you wanted.

You could also create a new TriggerType by clicking the New button.

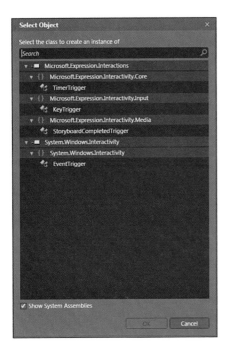

Figure 15.6   Adding a new TriggerType.

This presents a dialog of all the types of triggers available to you (and these might vary between WPF and Silverlight projects and may also be influenced by any custom triggers that were designed for you by your development team). In general, this panel may be difficult for you to understand until you spend a bit more time learning the fundamentals of interactivity in Silverlight and WPF, but with a little practice, you'll find that you can modify behaviors without having to look at or work with code fairly easily.

For example, a KeyTrigger would enable you to assign an event trigger that was based on keyboard input, such as using arrow keys to navigate or tab through an application. It's worth spending time experimenting with different triggers and understanding the different events that you can have control over with behaviors.

If you look at the next category of properties for behaviors for NavigateToScreenAction, you'll see that we can set your Target screen, or more generically, whatever object would be the target of our action—which, in this case, is the actual navigation to that screen.

Figure 15.7   Editing behavior properties.

Let's take a look at two more simple behaviors. On screen 5 in your project, you should see the series of rectangles you've created. Next navigate to behaviors in the Assets panel and find the MouseDragElementBehavior. Make sure you are looking at Behaviors in the top of the Assets hierarchy and not at the ones that are nested in the SketchFlow category or you will not find it. If you still have difficulty finding it, simply enter the word mouse in the search box in the Assets panel. After you've done this, your screen should look like Figure 15.8.

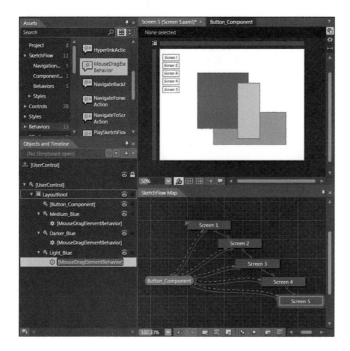

Figure 15.8   Our three rectangles with the MouseDragElementBehavior attached.

Next, build your project and navigate to screen 5. Click and drag on the rectangles. You should note that all the code required for that complex interactivity was encapsulated in that MouseDragElementBehavior.

If we look in the properties for this Behavior we see there is very little we can access or control regarding this behavior—in this case it simply works.

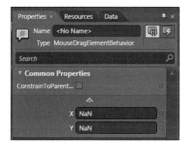

Figure 15.9   There are not many properties we can configure for the Mouse-DragElementBehavior.

But let's add another behavior to our rectangles. Use the search function in the Asset panel to find the behavior called PlaySoundAction. Add that behavior to each of the rectangles. If you look at the Properties for the PlaySoundAction behavior, you see some relevant attributes in the Common Property category that you can alter, like the file that you'll play and the volume for it. We've included some sound files you can attach to each rectangle.

Figure 15.10   *Editing behavior properties for the PlaySoundAction behavior.*

If you build and play this project, you'll see we've easily added sound to your interface. Play with some of the event names here to see if you can alter the effect.

It's likely as you get more familiar with behaviors that you'll want to experiment with other behaviors that ship by default with Blend. In addition, it's likely that you'll find many useful behaviors in the Expression Community and on sites like CodePlex that will enhance your productivity. Finally, you'll find that you'll often work with developers on your own team that may create behaviors for you to take advantage of. In Part IV, "Applied Knowledge," we'll show you how to work with custom behaviors in your project.

SUMMARY

In this chapter we learned what behaviors are and how they work; how to apply behaviors in our project; and how to alter parameters on behaviors that are available to us.

16

DATA

In this chapter we are going to show how you can use data in your SketchFlow prototypes. We look at the data panel, cover its functions, and show you how to create sample data that can be used in your prototypes with user controls available in Expression Blend.

In SketchFlow, the ability to work with data can bring your projects closer to reality in demonstrating key interactive concepts. Expression Blend has always had the ability to take different controls and objects and bind them to data. In the past, a designer would need a pre-existing data source to link to, or they would need to have someone create a special type of file that would mimic how a data source would work—typically an XML file. In SketchFlow in Expression Blend 3, the product enables designers to easily create sample data collections that you can use with SketchStyle controls in your project in addition to being able to link to other data resources.

Working with data and binding is a slightly more complex task that requires more knowledge of Expression Blend and .NET than you'd typically need to know to use SketchFlow. Before we cover the basics that you'll use in SketchFlow, let's learn some basic concepts around data and binding for Expression Blend. This foundation will serve you well as you begin to learn more about Expression Blend and move beyond just the capabilities of SketchFlow.

UNDERSTANDING DATA AND BINDING

One of the most powerful features of Expression Blend is that you can bind virtually any object to any type of data. What this means is that through the act of binding, you can create relationships between different entities or objects (and those objects could be just about anything—input from a device, a color value, or a data source).

For example, let's take a look at the following slider control and text block, which is something you should be able to create quickly in a sample project.

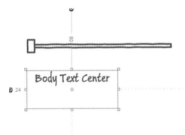

Figure 16.1   *A simple slider control and text block.*

Let's select the text block and look for its text properties in the Properties panel. Note the options we have for not only layout but also the Text category.

Figure 16.2   Properties for our text block in the Properties panel.

Let's select a feature that you probably haven't noticed so far. In the Text category if you can select the Text tab, which should be selected by default, find the area where you set the size of type for the text block. Do you see a small gray box to the immediate right of that drop down menu? If you select the gray dot you'll get access to Advanced Property Options. Advanced data properties exist for virtually every property in Expression Blend. Like other parts of Blend, they are contextual, so these are only selectable when there's an actual property that can be set. In some cases, you see these boxes are white; that is because a style resource is controlling some of the characteristics of that property.

Select the Data Binding element.

Figure 16.3   Selecting Data Binding in Advanced properties options in the Text tab of the Text category in the Properties panel.

After you have selected the Data Binding option you should now see the Create Data Binding panel. There are three tabs for this panel. The first tab is for a data field; if you were binding data to a particular element, you could select here, and all the data elements that were available to you in the project would appear here.

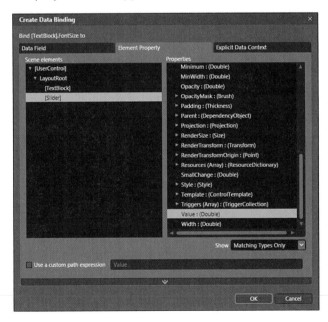

Figure 16.4   The Data Binding panel with the Element Property tag selected.

The second tab is for an element property. Let's take a look at that tab now. By default, the element property highlights the currently selected element: the TextBlock. Select the slider you've created in the Scene Elements window; then in the Properties window, mouse all the way down to the Value property and select it. If you click OK, you should be able to return to your screen.

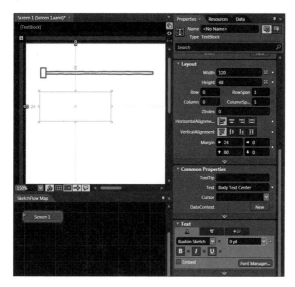

Figure 16.5 *Our workspace after using advanced properties to bind our slider control to a TextBlock.*

You should notice a few things. Your Text Size selector now has a yellow outline around it; this shows that you are binding this property to something else. Select your slider, and then make the following changes to the common properties for the slider. In the Maximum field enter a value of 36. In the Minimum field enter a value of 20.

Figure 16.6 *Editing common properties for our slider.*

Now build your project. The slider control now controls the size of the text on your screen. In a nutshell, this is what binding is. As you learn more about Expression Blend, the trick is learning more about WPF and Silverlight to understand what properties you have available for binding.

But even without this knowledge of WPF and Silverlight, you can do powerful things with data within SketchFlow. Let's learn more about the Data panel, how to create data resources, and how you can work with data and binding on the Artboard.

We covered the Data panel and creating data resources in Chapter 10, "Working with Data." It's worth reviewing that chapter for a basic overview of functionality as we'll cover more advanced topics here.

THE DATA PANEL

A data set is typically a collection of properties or values that you can define and use in different controls in SketchFlow in Expression Blend. When a data collection is created, you can use it by simply dragging it on to the Artboard.

There are two basic ways to do this: by a List Mode or a Details Mode.

The List Mode takes an entire data collection and creates a control that can be used to view it on the canvas.

Figure 16.7   The List Mode icon in the Data panel.

When the Detail Mode is selected, what you typically do is select one data element in your collection and drag that to your artboard. For example, if you had a data collection with prices, model numbers, and images, you might select only the image for an addition using Detail Mode. You can actually use both of these settings to quickly create what are called List and

Detail views, where one control that contains data elements can be bound to another one that shows a detail view—something we'll show you how to do in a moment.

Figure 16.8   The Detail Mode icon in the Data Panel.

If you are an advanced user of Expression Blend, you may consume a data source directly. Many people use Expression Blend to work with live data, and the Add live data source icon lets you do exactly that. In some scenarios, you might work with a developer that would enable you to use a feature such as this to bind to data that might be exposed via an API. An example of this might be a Twitter feed, RSS feed, and so on.

Figure 16.9   Linking to a live data source with the Add live data source icon.

Sometimes a developer may give you a template data schema that you would import into your project. But often for prototyping, you want to leverage a sample data set that you create directly in SketchFlow. In our case let's explore how to create a master and detail data view. First you need to create a sample data set.

CREATING DATA RESOURCES FOR SKETCH-FLOW PROJECTS

When you create data sources in SketchFlow, you created your own data set versus linking to a live data solution. Although your data set can be representative of a real schema that perhaps hasn't been constructed or created by your development team, how you create and use a data resource depends on what stage you are in during your project. Earlier stages might just use data for design, and later stages might use data that represents database schema to ensure a design team doesn't create a solution that a development team can't support from a data context.

We begin this process by selecting the icon for Add sample data source.

Figure 16.10   Creating data for your project using Add sample data source.

We then determine if we'd like to Define New Sample Data or use a feature that allows us to Import Same Data from XML. You may use the later process if your development team would like to you to be confined by a data schema that has been defined by a development team but is not yet live.

Figure 16.11   You have two options for creating sample data.

You'll then be asked to define a new data source and give it a name. Default data collections have two properties that you can configure initially but it's easy for us to add more as needed.

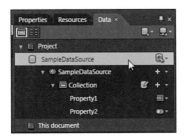

Figure 16.12   A default data collection with two properties.

You can easily add more properties to this data collection by simply selecting the arrow icon next to the + sign in a collection. There are three types of properties that you'd typically add, as follows:

- Simple property

- Complex property

- Collection property

A *simple property* is an option to add a string, number, boolean, or image to a data set. You can then edit the parameters of each of these to customize your data.

A string is a set of auto-generated content; by default, SketchFlow can generate strings for the following:

- Lorem ipsum or "greeked" or placeholder text

- Addresses

- Colors

- Company names

- Dates

- Email addresses

- Names

- Phone numbers

- Prices

- Times

- Website URLs

Number and Image properties work as you would expect, and the Boolean property creates a selection toggle for a data element.

A *complex property* is an option that can contain child properties. An example of a type of data set that might do this would include RSS feeds or an API from a social networking service that may represent a channel using a complex property that includes child properties that would contain a user name, user status, and collection of posts or activities from that individual or *collections* of individuals.

A *collection property* is used to create collections of records where each record may contain multiple items of data. For example, a news-based RSS feed may be delivered this way—where news items are a part of a collection and where each record in that collection may include the title of a news item, the description, and other related information.

What you most often find as you work with more advanced data samples is that your sample data sets will often be a collection of simple, complex, and collection properties. In addition, you find that you can nest these objects to create a hierarchal or tree view data set.

By default, you'll see that when a new property is generated, a flat collection of data with no hierarchy is created. It's easy to convert flat data sets to a hierarchal data or tree view data set by selecting the Convert to Hierarchal Collection option.

Figure 16.13   Converted a flat data set to a hierarchal or tree view.

You can select the following icon to edit the parameters of that collection, such as changing what type of data you want to use and adding additional properties, like specifing the strings, numbers, Booleans, or images that appear in your sample data set.

Figure 16.14   Editing the values of your data set.

The edit view for your data set is a grid that looks similar to a spreadsheet.

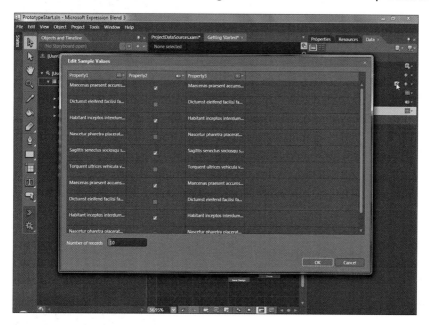

Figure 16.15   *The Edit Sample Values view.*

You can modify the values for each property by selecting the data type and format for each property. SketchFlow makes it easy to auto-generate this data, and with smaller data sets, you can enter specific values easily. To get an idea of how this works, select the parameters option for your first category and explore the different settings available to you.

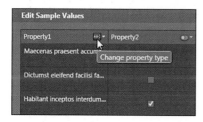

Figure 16.16   *Selecting parameters for the first category in a sample data set.*

WORKING WITH DATA IN SKETCHFLOW

Once you have a data set, you need to create a control to bind it to. There are a number of ways to do this, as follows:

- You can drag a data source onto your Artboard and have Expression Blend create a control for you.

- You can add a control to the Artboard and can manually drag data elements to the control.

- You can manually bind data from the Context menu on the Artboard or via the Properties panel. (This is an advanced concept that we won't cover here as it requires a more advanced understanding of how Silverlight and WPF work.)

What you will typically do in SketchFlow is one of the first two options. This allows your project to use your data at runtime. Normally, to create such a complex interaction, you'd need the assistance of a developer, but in this case, SketchFlow makes it easy for you to create these interactions yourself with drag-and-drop editing.

Let's demonstrate that by creating a simple master-list relationship that builds on what you explored in Chapter 7, "Basic Animation with SketchFlow Animation."

First, let's create a sample data set that uses a photo, a name, a price, and a stock category. We can use our lorem impsum string for the name and stock categories.

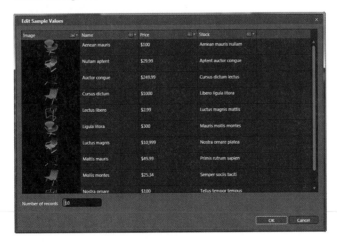

Figure 16.17   A sample data set.

Let's select the first three items of that data collection and drag it to your Artboard and look at what happens.

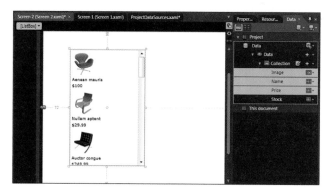

Figure 16.18   Dragging a sample data collection to the Artboard with our List View enabled.

You should see that you have a list box with your image, a product name, and a price. Now let's go back to your Data panel and switch your Data panel from List mode to Details mode. Drag your image data onto the Artboard and also drag your stock data to the Artboard. See if you can get your Artboard to look like Figure 16.19.

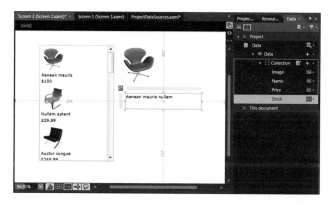

Figure 16.19   Dragging a sample data collection to the artboard with your Detail View enabled.

Build your project and look at it. You can see very quickly that you've created a nice data binding and master list detail with very minimal work. You could easily expand this data collection to include more information and create a detailed data-driven experience in a prototype.

But this probably doesn't look quite how you want it to. If you want this to match the look of the rest of your prototype, you can do that simply as well. You can rearrange and resize the grids that make up your image and stock indicator. You can change the type style and size of your type to Buxton Sketch. You can even add a sketch border with the SketchStyles Rectangle.

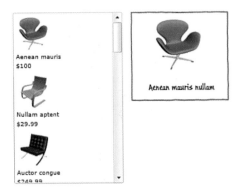

Figure 16.20 *Here we have added a border to our detail image and changed the type on our stock category of content.*

You can easily change the look of your ListBox as well. Simply select it, and then select Edit Resource and Apply Resource. You should see that your SketchStyle for a ListBox can be easily applied.

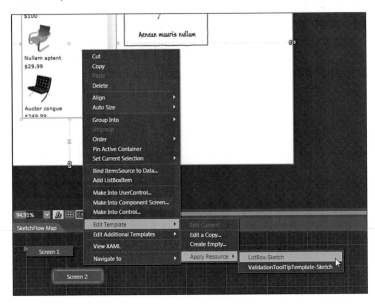

Figure 16.21 *Here we are selecting our list box to have the SketchFlow style that we want to use in our prototype.*

The order and structure of elements in the ListBox still doesn't look right, however. Let's select and right-click the ListBox again. This time, select Edit Additional Templates/Edit Generated Items (Item Template)/Edit Current.

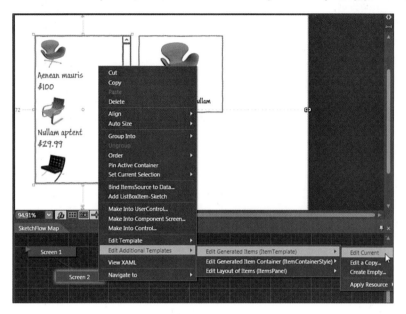

Figure 16.22   Here we are editing the template of our List Box control.

You can now make some simple edits. First, select the StackPanel in your Objects and Timeline panel. This is the layout control that holds all the elements of your List Control.

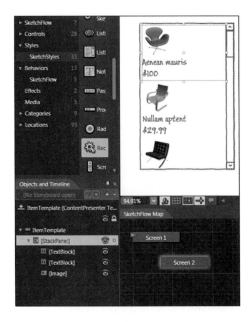

Figure 16.23   Selecting the StackPanel in our List Box control.

Then, find the Layout window in your Properties panel. Change the orientation from vertical to horizontal.

Figure 16.24   Altering the layout of our StackPanel from Horizontal to Vertical.

Spend some time playing with the sizing and margins of the other elements so you get something that looks similar to the next image. (Margin controls will be in the Layout window of the Properties panel.)

Once you've got this to a place where you're happy and the template looks good, go to the Objects and Timeline panel and select the item template to return your scope to the Artboard.

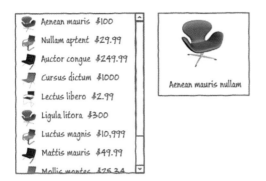

Figure 16.25   How our List Box looks after we've competed altering its template.

You can adjust the sizing of your ListBox and see with a few quick steps that you've been able to style all of your data quickly, even though you may not necessarily understand all the underpinnings of Expression Blend. If you run your project and look at it now, you can see that you've created a nice piece of interactivity with just a few minutes worth of work.

The more you play with templates and data, the more likely you're going to want to develop a better understanding of how Silverlight and WPF let you bind and use data to drive just about any interaction you can imagine. You'll also find that working with data and applying a designer's sensibility to data models and understanding how data structures work will make you a more effective designer.

SUMMARY

In this chapter we learned what data binding is and how to take advantage of it using the advanced properties menu; how to create new data collections and the types of collections available to us in the Data panel; how to create a sample data collection and the different types of properties we can have in our data collections; how to create a master detail view with a sample data collection; and how to alter the appearance of our data collection by using SketchFlow styles and editing User Control templates.

17

ANNOTATING YOUR WORK, GETTING FEEDBACK, AND CREATING DOCUMENTATION

We covered sharing projects and getting feedback in Chapter 6, "Sharing Your Project and Getting Feedback." In Chapter 11, "Bringing It All Together," we covered annotations and generating documents. We'll review that information here.

ADDING ANNOTATIONS TO YOUR PROJECT

Sometimes you need to provide guidance to people who will be looking at and reviewing your application that may not be obvious. You can also insert annotations directly into your SketchFlow project on each screen. Both you and stakeholders have the ability to show or hide these annotations.

To begin adding annotations, you need to ensure that they are visible. You do this by first ensuring that annotations are visible on the Artboard and enabling them by selecting the following icon on the lower-left quadrant of the Artboard (see Figure 17.1).

Figure 17.1   *Activating annotations on the artboard.*

You can then select any portion of any screen and use a keyboard shortcut or the Tools menu to insert a comment.

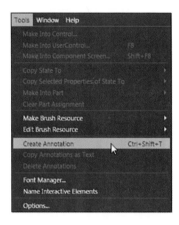

Figure 17.2   *Creating an annotation from the Tools menu.*

One of the things you'll notice is that feedback and annotations also appear in the SketchFlow Map itself, with a lightbulb for stakeholder feedback and with a comment balloon for annotations that you've added. In the SketchFlow Player, stakeholders can also view your annotations.

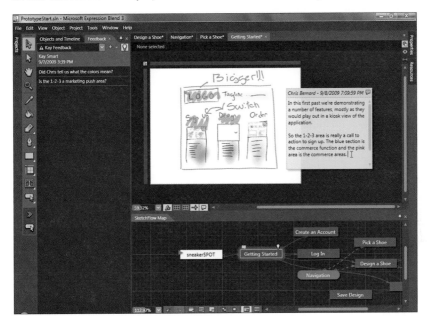

Figure 17.3 *Looking at how feeback and annotations appear in the Feedback panel, the Artboard, and the SketchFlow Map.*

GETTING FEEDBACK WITH THE SKETCHFLOW PLAYER

SketchFlow makes it extremely easy to share your dynamic prototypes and get feedback on them. The first step is to actually run your application. You do this by going to the Project menu and selecting Run Project or, the easier way, by simply hitting F5 on your keyboard.

When you build a project, you are actually compiling all the code to run your project—and updating certain files and assemblies based on changes you are making in your project. Occasionally, you might get an error when trying to build your project in SketchFlow after significant project editing, something that will be displayed via the Results window. Typically, rebuilding your project again should allow it to compile successfully if you encounter this.

Figure 17.4   Building a project from the Project menu.

If you're using a SketchFlow project in WPF, this creates an instance of the application that will open and present the SketchFlow Player application, which is the interface that allows people to see your project. If you're building the SketchFlow project in Silverlight, Expression Blend will create an instance of the SketchFlow Player that is hosted in a browser. Like any Silverlight application, you'll be able to share this application with anyone who can view it in a web browser and operating system that supports Silverlight.

You can take these files and distribute them in a number of ways. You can go to the File menu and select Package SketchFlowProject, which will create a directory with all the files that are required for playback.

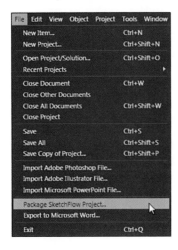

Figure 17.5 *Packaging a SketchFlow project.*

You can also do the following:

- Email the files.

- Host the file on a computer or server where stakeholders can access them.

- Distribute the WPF application via the Web as a click-once application for download.

- Host SketchFlow projects created in Silverlight in a browser that the stakeholder can view on the browser and platform of his or her choice.

- Distribute or host the WPF SketchFlow Player on a server or website.

The SketchFlow Player looks the same regardless of whether it's in WPF or Silverlight; the exception is that a SketchFlow application built in Silverlight will be surrounded by the browser chrome—which you can, of course, remove in browsers that have a full-screen capability.

Figure 17.6 shows how an application looks in a browser with the SketchFlow Player in the browser.

Figure 17.6   The SketchFlow Player running in a browser.

NAVIGATION IN THE SKETCHFLOW PLAYER

There are four ways to navigate in the SketchFlow Player, as follows:

1. By using the Navigation panel.

2. By using the Map panel.

3. By overlaying the map on the Artboard.

4. By activating interactivity within the application itself.

Notice that, by default, the SketchFlow Player displays your Start screen. In effect, this screen is the Home, or what we call the Default, screen of your

SketchFlow project. In the Navigation panel, however, you should see a link to the Getting Started screen.

Figure 17.7   The SketchFlow Navigation panel allows you to click on each screen in your application according to the flow that is determined for your project by the SketchFlow Map.

You may notice a zoom bar at the bottom of that screen. This zoom bar enables you to zoom in and out of the screen to look at details or resize the application for the screen you're viewing it on.

Figure 17.8   The zoom bar allows you to resize your interface for different screen resolutions.

You can link to other screens in your application if you want to return to the Home screen of your prototype; you merely need to hit your home icon.

Sometimes this linear navigation can mask what's available in a prototype. Take a look at the Feedback panel in the SketchFlow Player.

Figure 17.9   The Feedback panel.

By default, you should see a Feedback panel selection; select the Map panel. You should now see that the actual SketchFlow Map is available to a reviewer as well.

Figure 17.10   The Map panel.

You can actually put your cursor on this panel and drag around the SketchFlow Map. In addition, you can use the Zoom control to increase the size of the SketchFlow Map or even to pop an overlay of the map onto the Artboard. You'll notice that the Map panels will auto-update as you navigate through your prototype in overlay mode.

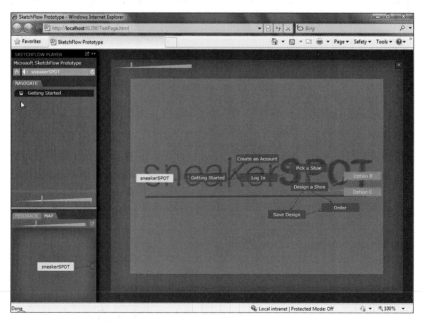

Figure 17.11   The Map panel in overlay mode.

You can also either close or break out the SketchFlow Player panel using these controls.

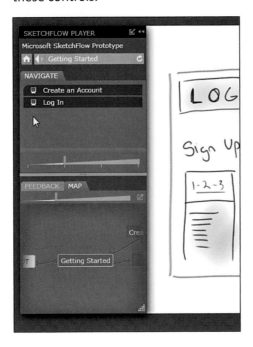

Figure 17.12   *The SketchFlow navigation undocked and floating in the SketchFlow Player interface.*

Now let's look at how we can use the SketchFlow Player to easily leave or create feedback. Make sure you can see the SketchFlow Player panel. Find the Feedback panel again and select it.

This panel lets a stakeholder provide a variety of feedback in a number of ways, starting with the ability to insert type directly into the feedback text entry box. Every screen in an application gets its own instance of this feedback area. To enter feedback, simply start typing. Once you're done, you must click the small + sign to save the feedback. Let's investigate the feedback functions in more detail.

Figure 17.13   The Feedback panel.

Here are the controls available to you when you provide feedback.

The arrow lets you select a text box for direct text entry into the feedback text entry box.

The pen lets you add feedback directly on the Artboard, as does the highlighter.

The eraser lets you edit or remove feedback from the Artboard. The next set of controls actually controls what feedback is visible.

The lightbulb lets you show or hide inked feedback (from the pen or highlighter). When the lightbulb is on, this feedback will appear.

The quote bubble actually displays annotations inserted into the prototype in SketchFlow. When the quote bubble is on, the annotations will appear.

Feedback wouldn't be very useful if you couldn't do something with it. Here, you can reset all the feedback, which removes it from the application, or you can export a copy of it, which can be emailed. When you export information, it asks you for your name or initials and prompts you for a place to save the feedback. You can then email or post this feedback file, and it can be incorporated into your SketchFlow project.

Figure 17.14 An example of feedback being exported.

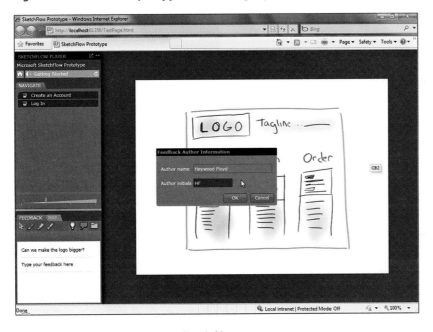

Figure 17.15 Naming our Feedback file.

IMPORTING FEEDBACK INTO YOUR PROJECT

When you need to look at feedback in Expression Blend, you can simply load that feedback file into your SketchFlow project.

The best way to do this is to go to your Window menu and select Feedback. This will open up the Feedback panel in the SketchFlow project.

Figure 17.16   The Window menu lets you enable your Feedback panel.

Once that panel is loaded, you should see the Feedback panel and you can load information into it. (If you have previous feedback loaded into your project, it will also be displayed in this panel.)

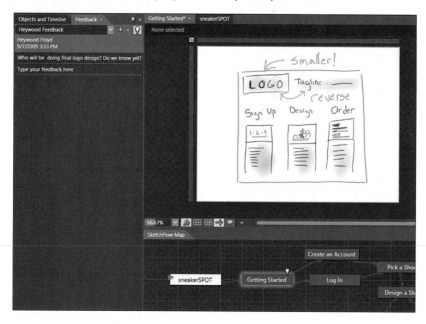

Figure 17.17   The Feedback panel in the SketchFlow workspace.

You'll use the following controls to load feedback. Load some sample feedback that you've created.

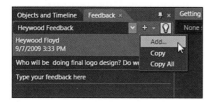

Figure 17.18   Loading new feedback into your Feedback panel.

You can load multiple sets of feedback but only view feedback from one person at a time. You'll see their text-based comments and any input they provide on-screen. You'll also notice in the SketchFlow Map that little icons will appear on screens where there's been feedback from a stakeholder.

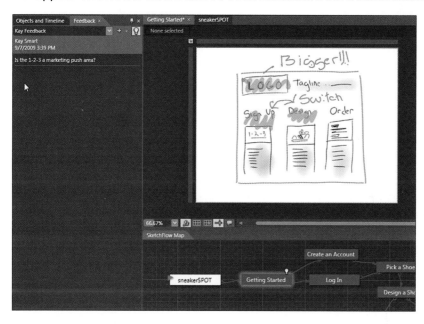

Figure 17.19   Feedback appears on your Artboard but is also noted in your SketchFlow Map panel.

When you're done with feedback, you can turn off the lightbulb to hide feedback that appears on the Artboard and then close the Feedback panel. You also can remove feedback from the project by deleting feedback files that appear in the Project menu.

In version 3.0 of SketchFlow in Expression Blend, the process for exporting feedback out of the SketchFlow player so that it can be incorporated into the designer's or developer's workspace is a manual one that requires exporting and loading as we've demonstrated here and in Chapter 6. We expect to see automation and round trip workflow features added to the feedback features in future versions of Expression Blend.

CREATING DOCUMENTATION

Documentation is still a critical part of the design and development process. Often we must create vision documents, design specifications, and other artifacts to support the design process. SketchFlow in Expression Blend gives you great features to automate the document creation process by exporting the flow of an application and all of its figures and annotations into a Microsoft Word document. These documents serve as an excellent foundation for additional information that might need to be added to your documents and eliminate much of the busy work that goes into making these documents. With careful planning and annotation, these documents can live with the project as it progresses and can be easily updated.

With your project completed—or in a state where you'd like to document what you have—you simply need to go the File menu to export your work to Microsoft Word.

After you select Export to Microsoft Word, you'll be presented with a dialog. If you have a standard template that you use for documentation, you can choose to leverage that as a starting point for your document. You'll be asked to name and save the file you are creating. After that process is complete, you'll see you have a document that has been created out of all the assets you created in SketchFlow.

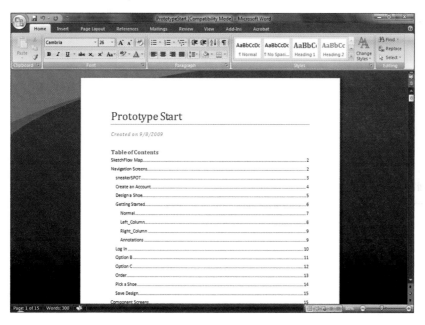

Figure 17.20   A Word document created from your SketchFlow project.

As you explore this document, you'll see the comments and annotations that are present in the project appear in the document as well. Carefully looking at your workflow and how you collaborate with others can maximize the effectiveness of the documentation function of SketchFlow. With clear design and workflow processes in place and clever use of annotations, your SketchFlow project can become a living design specification that is never out of date.

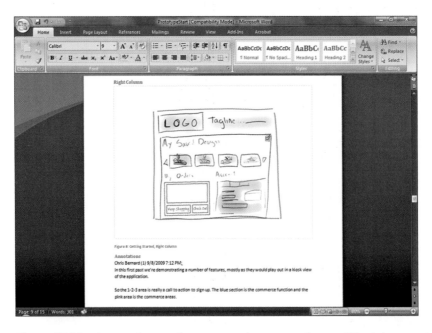

Figure 17.21   *Annotations and comments that appear in your Word document.*

An important consideration for SketchFlow is to establish plans for how you want to use feedback and annotations in your project. For example, do you want to use annotations to respond to feedback as you iterate through the project? Does Feedback live in the project for its duration? Do you want to use feedback not just among stakeholders but other members of the design team? Pondering and having answers to these questions that drive consistent usage with your team can enable you to be more productive. It's likely that feedback and commenting will be one of the first areas of SketchFlow in Expression Blend to get new features. If you're using a version of Expression Blend that is beyond Chapter 4, "Getting Started," check the User's Guide for new features and remember to check www. dynamic-prototyping.com for any late-breaking changes.

SUMMARY

In this chapter you learned how to add annotations to your project in SketchFlow; how to create feedback using the SketchFlow player; how to use the SketchFlow player; how to import feedback in SketchFlow; and how to create documentation from SketchFlow.

PART IV

APPLIED KNOWLEDGE

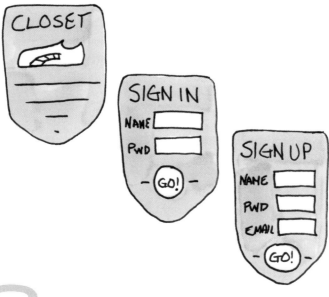

18

PROJECT BRIEF
AND SKETCHES

The next chapters, 18 to 29, will focus on a specific client project and tasks. We will walk through a tested design process, step by step. We will use everything learned thus far and apply it with an in-depth exploration. Starting with a view of not only the materials we will be using in the coming chapters, but all the ideation, sketches, collaboration, email communication, and research that was done to get us here.

Our hope is that this tutorial will be relevant to your daily life as a designer—quick ways to add interactivity, component fidelity advancement, and opportunities for tangible productivity. The overarching intention is for you to take sketches and easily evolve them into a *real* working product. Along with teamwork, collaboration, and a bit of planning, the practices outlined here will prove to be a very successful path to cutting down the redundancy of project work so you can increase the time spent dreaming up the best innovative ideas.

In keeping with the context of how client work typically flows, we will walk through changes in not just visual solutions but also the overall direction and scope of the product. As you dive into the tutorial section, keep a few things in mind:

1. Changes in prototypes and direction *drive* innovation in your process.

2. *How* your team prototypes predicts not just the culture of the product you create but also the culture of your company.

3. Prototyping is not just a tool or a means to an end; it shows you where you are going and the right road to get there.

4. True innovation is a social act.

During the initial stages of prototyping, remember that the time spent here is not just about ideas and refinement; it is about observation. Great companies pay close attention to the patterns and idiosyncrasies of their teams, clients, and the people using the product. Keeping record of what is said, sketched, expressed in email, or offered as annotative feedback is critical for several reasons, as follows:

1. You may forget the justification or validation for the choices you have made. If it is all collated chronologically, it can be recalled within moments.

2. It allows you to track and maintain focus on the project goals and themes.

3. It helps answer new questions or concerns with previous insights. "This seems a bit fuzzy." or "What happened to idea X?" become much easier to resolve when you can reference the support material quickly.

4. Afterward, you can analyze and synthesize the process for reflection on what worked and what needs improvement for the next project. You are creating your own patterns of success that could be handy in winning new clients and keeping the ones you have.

You can track and examine process in many ways, such as digital, paper, and otherwise. We suggest dedicated wall space with butcher paper, pens, markers, and sticky notes nearby. Everyone should have access to the projects' progression and be able to join in the conversation. Other teams and people outside the project should be able to see what you're thinking about, how you're working through problems, and participating in the conversation. Even if you only have a small common space to post and share the process, utilize what you have. An amazing book on visual organization and problem solving is *Rapid Problem Solving with Post-it Notes* by David Straker. This is a must-have book for the design team.

PROJECT BRIEF

```
-----Original Message-----
From: Team SneakerSpot
Sent: Monday, August 11, 2009 11:02 AM
To: Awesome Agency Team
Subject: RE: New ideas for SneakerSpot

Greetings team!
SneakerSpot needs some fresh thinking around our
online experience. We need to have way to
customize a unique shoe design, a clever way to
show details of a specific shoe, possibly a
social component (sign up/login is required) and
a way to save or store shoes to purchase later.
Any other neat thoughts or ideas would be great
as well.

When do you think you will have something we can
look at?

Thanks,
Team SneakerSpot
```

Figure 18.1   Email from our client

With the client's email in hand, and after a bit of user research with the "loyal customer" survey, our team began sketching and brainstorming ideas. Some were experience concepts that seemed to meet client requests; others added pleasure and an addictive quality to the solution. Specifically, SneakerSpot wants us to prototype an engaging custom shoe experience that speaks to their dedication to the avid shoe consumer, who likes to have individual control and creativity with the shoes they purchase.

The following pages are a visual field trip of the ideation process and the things that we iterated on along the way. Our hope is that this will be not only fun to look at, but compelling to use in the practice of the tutorial. Enjoy!

LOYAL CUSTOMER SURVEY

Tell us what you want!

What do you like about the SneakerSpot experience?
(a few adjectives is great, other thoughts are super also)

    a. *unique*

    b. *colorful*

    c. *I get compliments on the shoes I buy*

If you could add or change the features to design the shoe you want what would that be?
(a couple words is perfect, if you have big ideas, you are awesome)

    a. *more choices*

    b. *rare or special designs*

    c. *different fabrics*

Say you are designing a custom shoe, would it be fun to see similar shoes that others have made?

    a. Yes, I want to be sure I am designing something original

    b. Yes, it would be fun to get ideas from other people

    c. No, I don't care about anyone else

If you could share your designs with other people on the site, would you do it?

    a. No, I would not want anyone to see my secret recipe

    b. Yes, but I wouldn't want anyone else to be able to purchase what I designed

    c. Yes, and it would be even cooler if others could buy my design and SneakerSpot informed me about it

If SneakerSpot picked famous graffiti or other artists to design custom shoes, and let you vote on who you wanted to design the coming seasons styles would you participate?

    a. Yes, please

    b. Maybe, if they picked really cool artists

    c. No, I could care less about what new artists are designing shoes

Would you like to have your shoe closet on line, to share and keep track of your sneakers?

    a. Yes

    b. No, that sounds like work

I would probably go broke buying sneakers if I could only *get a few one of a kind pairs.*

Figure 18.2   *The survey sent to SneakerSpot's most vocal, pro users.*

SKETCHING IDEAS

SARA'S SKETCHES

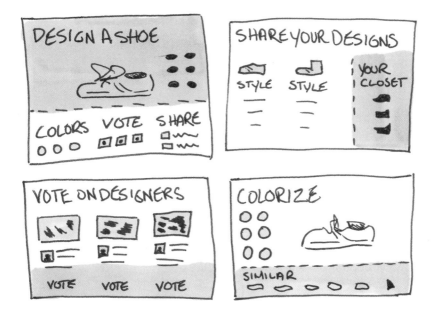

Figure 18.3   Initial sketch concepts.

HAL'S SKETCHES

Figure 18.4   Initial sketch concepts.

CHAPTER 18 | PROJECT BRIEF AND SKETCHES

LEE'S SKETCHES

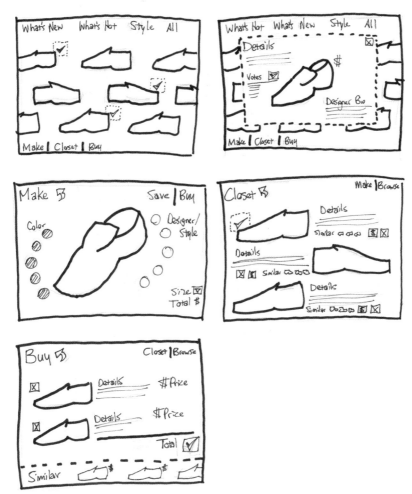

Figure 18.5   Initial sketch concepts.

REFINEMENT AND MASTER SKETCHES

With everyone's ideas laid out before us, it is time to hone in on what we want to move forward with and which concepts will be critical to explore and show to the client.

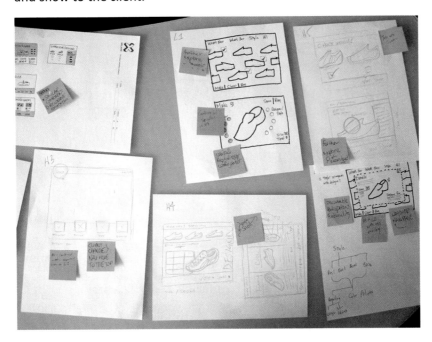

Figure 18.6   Sticky organization and brainstorming session.

Here, we stickied in pink all the screens on which we want to work; in green, we called out everything we should pull out and combine with our pink-labeled screens. Because we identified that the shoe customizer, "design a shoe" page, was likely to be the most important pivot of the entire application, we agreed to spend the most time thinking and sketching around it. Once everyone agreed on a viable visual and interaction direction, it was back to the sketching table to create a series of master sketches to be used in SketchFlow. These sketches will be componentized in some cases, like a long series of shoes for a scrolling animation, or simply a clean and defined way of representing our concepts. Following are a few of the master sketches we will be using to craft our prototype.

Figure 18.7   Initial login screen.

Figure 18.8   Main page.

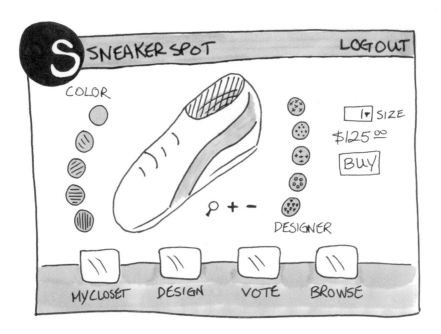

Figure 18.9   Shoe customizer.

Figure 18.10   Checkout screen.

Figure 18.11   Closet screen.

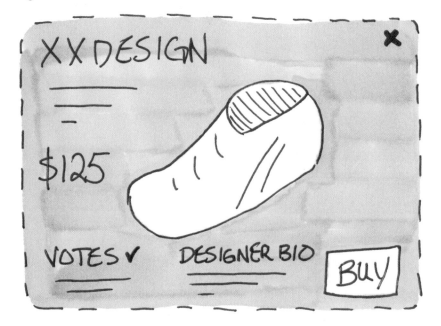

Figure 18.12   Shoe detail pop-up.

SUMMARY

All the work done here will instruct and inform the decisions and conversations we will do in the next 10 chapters. The following tutorials are a reflection of the visual journey of this chapter and help create a flow to the client and design process. The beauty of working as a team and the simple brilliance of the scientific method is that all accept variation and impermanence. Your team collaboration could bare different fruit with the same input as we have here.

19

NAVIGATION VIA COMPONENT SCREENS

In this chapter we'll show you how using a component screen can simplfy navigation in your project and empower users to navigate through your project without using the SketchFlow Player animation.

REAL WORLD ROUND 1

Now that you have had a sneak peek at the sketches, let's dive in and breathe some life into them for your client meeting. In the next few pages, we will walk through how to add global navigation to your project by utilizing the power of component screens. Any reused or multi-page asset can benefit from this feature. Components are also helpful when changes are required or when advancing the fidelity of the project, which we cover in Round 2 of the tutorial (in Chapter 28, "Advanced Fidelity with Templates and States").

You can download the project files and assets for this chapter from www.dynamic-prototypes.com. Open Expression Blend 3 and then open the Silverlight SketchFlow file called SneakerSpot_A. Import your "master sketches" from the Images folder by right-clicking on the project file, adding a new folder called "Sketches," and adding in all of the existing sketch files. You should have something that looks like Figure 19.1.

Figure 19.1   *Our workspace after we've added our sketches.*

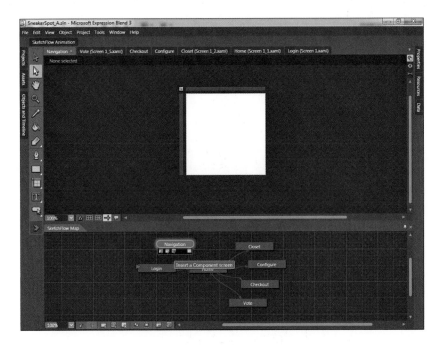

Figure 19.2   *Our SketchFlow Map with our Component Screen.*

Let's take a look at the screens in the SketchFlow Map. We want to include the global navigation to be reused throughout all the pages, so right-click in the SketchFlow Map and create a Component screen. Select "Layout Root" in the Objects and Timeline panel. In the Properties panel, set the Background to No Brush; then set the width to 800 and the height to 600 in the right side under Layout.

From the Sketches folder, place the image, navigation_component.png, in the Navigation screen. Drag connections from your Component screen to all the screens except the Login page. When you are finished, your SketchFlow Map should look like the one in Figure 19.3. You can test your progress by hitting F5 and then clicking through the screens to see the global navigation on each page.

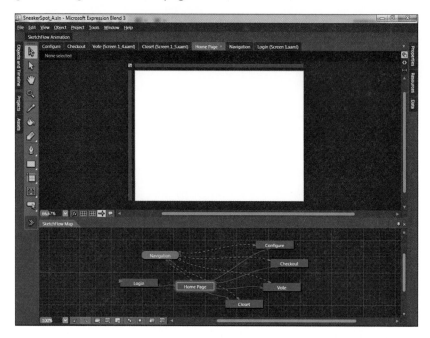

Figure 19.3   Linking our Component screen to other screens in our project.

SUMMARY

In this chapter you learned how to make your prototypes more realistic by using a Component screen to add global navigation. This makes your application more useful when testing and collecting feedback from stakeholders, and it makes it easy to make global changes in your application without having to make changes to individual screens that need global navigation. Instead, you can simply edit the Component screen that contains your global navigation and the updates permeate through your project after you've rebuilt it.

20

ADDING ANIMATION

Animations, transitions, the events, and actions between each screen or click don't always get the undivided attention they deserve. Historically, designers are pressed for time and have lacked the tools necessary to prototype real interactions. Animated gifs, hand waving, and strings of adjectives are used, instead, to convey the magic of our dynamic experiences. But our best efforts leave a lot to the imagination, which leads to inevitable miscommunication, frustration, and becomes expensive to fix later.

Prototyping the true *how* of interaction between screens and states becomes a powerful method of effectively communicating and selling experience design. One of the most potent uses of Sketchflow is the ability to quickly and easily begin describing, testing, and sharing the *journey* of the application. Guiding your team and stakeholders through the behavior and personality of the product gives the entire process a successful edge.

Other important animation and interaction uses include

- Developing relationships between user action and the reaction of the application

- Interactive constancy in common behaviors and users tasks

- Empathic and rewarding actions for daily and/or mundane user tasks

- Control of the more emotional aspects of pacing, impressions, interactive cuing, and reassurance

In this chapter we concentrate on a few simple ways to create a compelling, enjoyable interactive event. With the Sketchflow animation panel and the built-in easing and transition options, prototyping discrete functionality takes just a few minutes. The animation panel is also a great place to test, validate, and feel interactive ideas.

Create a new component screen, from the home page, and label it "Details Overlay," change the color to orange, and repeat the size and brush steps you took for the navigation component. Place the image, details_overlay_component.png, and center it on the screen.

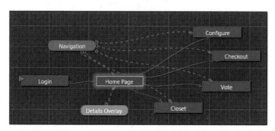

Figure 20.1   *Details overlay component screen.*

Let's animate the Details Overlay component you've created. In the
Sketchflow Map, click on the Home screen. Under Window, select
SketchFlow Animation; if there is already a check next to it, click on the
tab of the same name on the top left. Click on the Plus icon to initialize the
animation. To ensure that you are working on the Base state, select it on
the left to ensure that it is highlighted. This will be your "before" stage.

In the Properties panel under Transform, select the Scale icon tab, and set
the X and Y to .7. Then, under Appearance, set the Opacity to 0.

Figure 20.2   Properties panel adjustments.

Back in the SketchFlow Animation panel, change the name of the animation to ViewDetailsOverlay by clicking inside the text field at the right of the Play button. Now, select the first stage, labeled 1. The red recording light will turn on. Set the Hold time to 2 seconds; then, in the Properties panel, set the Opacity back to 100%, and in Transform, under the Scale tab, set X and Y to 1.

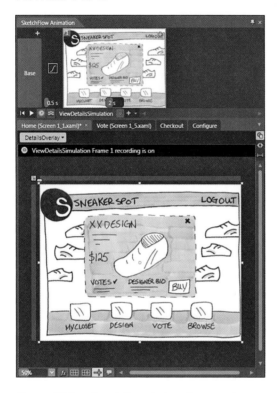

Figure 20.3   SketchFlow Animation panel.

You're nearly there now. Click on the Easing Function icon and select BackOut.

Figure 20.4   Easing Function transitions.

All that is left now is to make your detail component disappear in the same way it appeared. Click on the Plus icon on screen 1, adding a new state to the animation. Set the Opacity to 0 and the X and Y back to .7 in the Transform panel. Make the Hold time 1 second. Update the Easing Function to BackIn. To test, hit F5 and click on the ViewDetailsOverlay animation to see what you have just created.

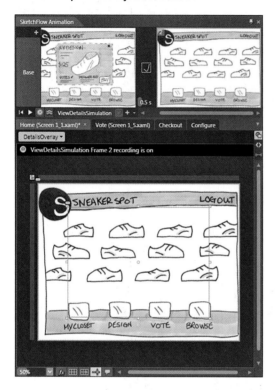

Figure 20.5 *SketchFlow animation progress.*

You are close to sending your concept off to the client. Let's take a moment to wire up the sketches a little more so the stakeholders can interact directly with them.

Similar to what you did in Chapter 4, "Getting Started," place a button from the toolbar on top of your sketch, set the Opacity to 0 and right-click, select Navigate To, and then select Closet, for example. Now copy and paste the transparent button and change the navigation location accordingly.

Under Project, select Build Project and then F5 to see the results. Now, all you have to do is package up your results under File, Package SketchFlow Project, and send off the folder to the client to see what they think.

The SneakerSpot team has sent you feedback using the SketchFlow Player. You drop the file into the project folder and load the feedback file into Blend, via the Feedback panel under Window, to see what they thought. According to the light bulb icons, there are three screens that have annotations.

SUMMARY

In this chapter we used a sketch to describe a pop up detail page, but once the interactivity is approved, the application will need to advance toward the final product. Because we used a component screen for the Details screen, we can remove the sketch and begin adding real assets, while still taking advantage of the animation work we already created.

21

CLIENT FEEDBACK

In this chapter we will review the feedback sent by our client and examine
what notes and direction provided. Here we start to appreciate the role
of changes and constraints on the design process. As designers we are
focused on solving problems, working with and reworking changes, and
finding the most graceful path around obstacles. How well we interpret
and synthesis feedback and guidance from the client can determine the
success of the product. Project changes and constraints often remove the
bindings to our own creative problem solving. So remember to use critique
and feedback time with clients as the ultimate opportunity to discover
something meaningful and innovative.

The SneakerSpot team has sent us feedback using the SketchFlow player. We dropped the file into the project folder and loaded the feedback file into Blend via the Feedback panel under Window to see what they thought. According to the lightbulb icons, there are three screens that have annotations.

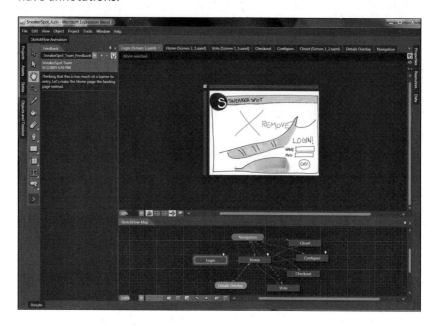

Figure 21.1 *Looking at our application in SketchFlow with Feedback loaded into our project.*

Figure 21.2   On the first screen, we see a more detailed view showing feedback from our client.

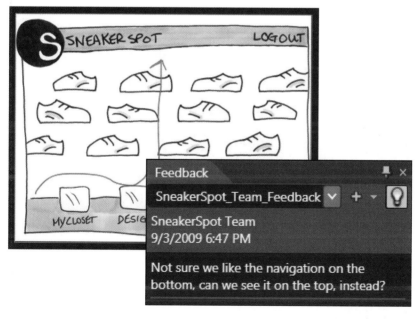

Figure 21.3   On the second screen, our client has a navigation suggestion.

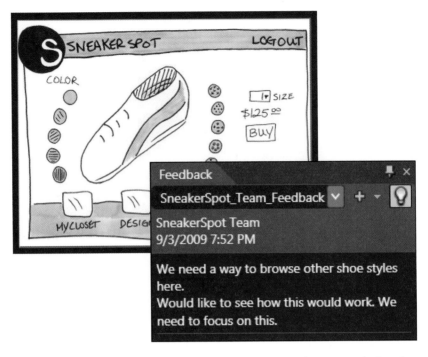

Figure 21.4 *On the third screen, we have a question about our solution that we need to address.*

Our mission is clear—we need to redesign the global navigation and fully explore the custom shoe design experience. After we sketch out the new nav, the biggest challenge will lie ahead: actualizing a compelling and enjoyable solution that is both well designed and technically sensible.

PRO TIP:
Project documentation and tagging is another great use of the annotation and feedback features. If you want to mark and take notes for each benchmark or date change for you and your team, using the **SketchFlow Player** is a nice solution. To try it, change the name of your project to reflect that you will be using it as a document repository; then mark up and annotate as desired. Keeping a separate file allows you to create internal documentation by exporting it to a Word document. So, if you need to update your boss or brief the team on what changes have been made in the last week, it drastically cuts down the busy work.

Design of products and applications continue to require much adaptation and iteration. The complexity of user testing and prototyping for ethnography, usability, and cognition means repeated exploration and conversation. Using the SketchFlow Player for collecting and reviewing feedback can be a powerful means to do all these tasks well. When we think about prototyping in the same medium as the end result or communicating in the language of the interface, the value and quality of the process become much greater. All the feedback and changes benefit from sharing concepts and ideas with the SketchFlow Player.

SUMMARY

In previous chapters we learned how feedback tools work. This chapter introduced how to use these features in our design process for:

- Collecting team comments or ideas

- Project critiques anonymous or named

- User testing (with tasks or questions on Note-Sketch stickies)

- Tracking and cataloging project benchmarks or findings

22

SET UP FOR BEHAVIORS

This chapter lays the ground work for how we craft a dynamic user experience for the magnifying glass functionality. Then, in the next two chapters, we add interactivity and advance the complexity using states and triggers. First, we need to make the navigation changes represented in the feedback the client gave us in Chapter 21, "Client Feedback." By putting the pieces in place here, we can then create full functioning behaviors with ease.

Now, we break out the big guns, testing interaction and technique with our master sketches, then adding custom, reusable animation. Because the shoe customizer page is such a pivotal part of the whole application, we focus on it almost exclusively. Perfecting the experience design of this page will better inform the decisions we make throughout.

REAL WORLD ROUND 2

Download and open up project SneakerSpot3, in the folder SneakerSpot3, from www.dynamic-prototypes.com (if you haven't already). There are updated sketches, so import the new images into the Sketches folder. Refresh the Configure, Closet, and home pages with the latest art.

Then, do the same for the new navigation sketch, and remove the old one from the navigation component screen. Place the new sketch, labeled navigation_component_v2.png, from the Sketches folder. Now, move the transparent nav buttons to the top and align the hotspots to fit the updated button placement. With all the nav buttons selected, go to Object, Order, Bring to Front, and Build the project to see the changes globally.

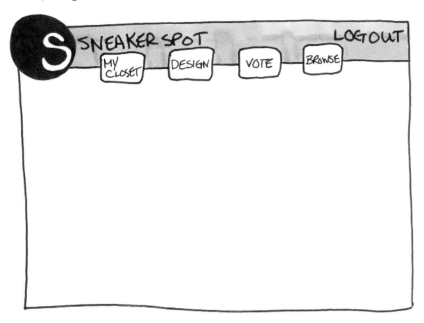

Figure 22.1   New master sketch with top global nav.

In the SketchFlow Map, right-click on the login screen and select Remove from the drop-down menu. Notice that the home page becomes the default start screen, designated by the green carrot.

> PRO TIP:
> You can change any screen to be the start screen at any point in the project, by right-clicking on the desired page in the SketchFlow Map and selecting Set as Start.

INTERACTION GROUND WORK

The terms *actions*, *triggers*, and *behaviors* all denote different types of behaviors. Often, the distinction may only be relevant to developers who write custom interactions or animations for a number of separate situations. For the duration of this chapter, we will refer to them as simply behaviors, for clarity's sake.

> QUICK NOTE:
> As a designer using Blend, you can choose from a selection of available built-in behaviors.
>
> However, if you come across a situation that requires a custom solution to get the desired interaction, collaborate with your developer teammates.

We are going to begin focusing on the Configure screen. To start, you'll make the Zoom control into a working, interactive function, using the real behaviors that will, if approved by the client, carry through to the final version of the application. Following is the list of things we would like the Zoom control to do:

1. The lens or zoom viewer appear when the user mouses down on the magnifying glass icon.

2. The zoom viewer disappears when the user mouses up on the magnifying glass.

3. The magnifying glass and zoom viewer both follow the mouse when the user drags them.

4. The magnifying glass returns to its "home" or default location when the user finishes using the control.

In the Projects panel, right-click on the Sketches folder and Add Existing Item, configure_page_zoom_controller.png (the magnifying glass icon) and configure_page_zoom_viewer.png (the viewer), from the Project Images folder.

Then, create a new component Screen in the SketchFlow Map and name it *ZoomViewer*.

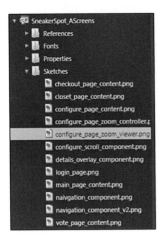

Figure 22.2   Zoom Viewer image in the Sketches folder.

Under the Objects and Timeline panel, select Layout Root; then open the Properties panel. In Brushes, set the Background property to No Brush by clicking the icon below on the left.

Figure 22.3   No brush selected in the Properties panel.

Back in the Objects and Timeline panel, select UserControl; then, back in the Properties panel, under Layout, set the width to 225 and the height to 235.

Figure 22.4   Width and Height adjustments under Layout.

Place the configure_page_zoom_viewer.png (viewer) on the component Artboard. Drag to align it at the top-left corner of the board.

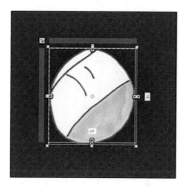

Figure 22.5   The zoom viewer placed in the component screen.

Rename the image "ZoomView," in the Objects and Timeline panel.

Figure 22.6   Renamed image.

Now, place the configure_page_zoom_controller.png (magnifying glass) on the component board and drag to align it at the bottom-right corner.

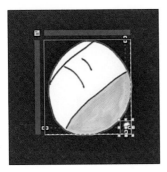

Figure 22.7 The magnifying glass placed in the component screen.

Back in the Objects and Timeline panel, name the image "MagnifyingGlass."

Figure 22.8 Renamed image.

SUMMARY

With the magnifying glass ground work in place and the global navigation swapped out, we can start to focus on the functionality list from above. In the next two chapters, we check off each item and gain a deeper understanding of behaviors in Blend. From this moment on, our prototype seems less like a hopeful idea and much more like a real, working application.

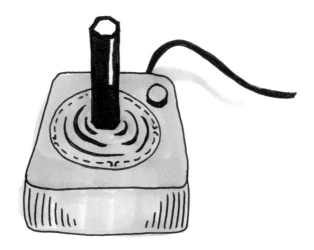

23

REFINING STATES

Let's build on the foundation we just laid out in the previous chapter. To truly customize a few unique experience moments, we must further explore the features of the States panel. We can think of states several ways; the more direct, straightforward view, like a button has a MouseOver state and animated, motion-based actions over time activities. Both allow for discrete, customizable control over the users interaction within the application.

Here we are going to use states to simply reveal our zoom lens and design its transitions. Here are some other powerful ways to utilize states:

- Control the visual transition between states or objects

- Create assets and motion within individual states

- Align elements easily within and from state to state with FluidLayout

Like a lot of other graphic applications you use, order *is* important. Make sure you have the ZoomView sketch on top of the magnifying glass (this enables the mouse properties), which allows the images to work properly.

Now that your images are in place, let's begin adding functionality using the States panel on the left. Here, you will be pairing up your two images to work together: on mouseover, mousedown, and mouseup.

To create a new state, click on the Add State Group icon on the top of the States panel.

Figure 23.1   Base state name changed.

Change the name to VisibilityStates.

In the Objects and Timeline panel, select the ZoomView sketch. Then, go to the Properties panel, under Appearance, and set the Opacity to 0. Under Transform, Scale tab, set the X and Y properties to 0.7.

In Blend, the Base state is created automatically for you, so once you initialize states by creating your first state group, you've now set what the application will look like before any action takes place.

Back in the States panel, click the Add State button and name the state *Show*.

Figure 23.2   New state button on the right.

Figure 23.3 *Click the Add transition button and choose *→ Show as the transition type.*

Figure 23.4 *Adding the "Show" transition.*

Think of the *→ Show as "Any other state to the Show state."

Here, you've chosen to create a transition that will be played any time you enter the component's Show state.

Next, set the EasingFunction to BackOut and the TransitionDuration to 0.25.

Figure 23.5 *EasingFunction choices.*

Figure 23.6   Changing the transition duration.

Double-check that the ZoomView image is still selected in the Objects and Timeline panel.

The finishing touch for the Show state is to return the Opacity to 100 and the X and Y values to 1 in the Properties panel.

Back in the States panel, click the Add State button to create another state under Show; name this state *Hide*.

Click Add transition, and choose *➔ Hide.

Set the EasingFunction to BackIn and the TransitionDuration to 0.25.

Figure 23.7   Adding and updating the "Hide" transition.

In the Properties panel, click on the Advanced property options for Opacity (the small square icon on the right). Select the last option, Record Current Value.

Do the same for each X and Y value, under Transform, Scale tab.

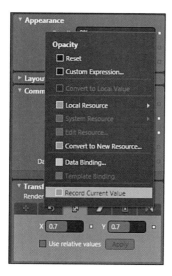

Figure 23.8   Advanced options for Opacity.

QUICK NOTE:
Because your settings for the Hidden state exactly match those of the Base state, you have to explicitly tell Blend what you are intending. In other words, you just explained, "I am not telling you to do nothing for this state, scout's honor!"

SUMMARY

Now that we have set our show and hide states, we can begin to see how much more can be done with the States panel. Making image modifications within the Properties panel and refining the timing and user driven actions are just a couple of the quick ways to enhance the application. With this new layer of functionality, we can begin to add more complex interaction—nuances that define compelling experience.

24

REFINING ANIMATION
AND INTERACTIVITY

This chapter puts the finishing touches on the magnifying glass function, which completes our work on it. We start by taking advantage of the built in behaviors that Blend provides, import a custom drag and drop behavior, and edit its properties to perfect the experience. Then, if you're up to the challenge, there is a do-it-yourself (DIY) exercise using the States panel. There are some powerful trigger and properties tricks in this chapter, so stay tuned!

In this section, you now begin to take advantage of the power of Blend and check off your project goals from Round 2, in Chapter 22, "Set Up for Behaviors." Some of the steps here may seem like "heavy-lifting," but remember: Most everything you do now can be carried through to the final result. In the cases where things cannot be brought all the way through to the end, you are still showcasing exactly how the functionality will work and act. So, you can get accurate, confident client approval and avoid the often-lengthy post-launch troubleshooting.

The majority of work is in the left panel, for this section. Set up the panel layout as shown next, by selecting the Assets tab and then turning off AutoHide with the pushpin icon. Do the same for the Objects and Timeline tab.

Figure 24.1   Assets panel set up.

In order to use the foundation previously established with states, you must wire up the sketch images to the coordinating behaviors.

Remember your goals for the zoom viewer from the beginning of this section? You are going to bring each of these to life right now:

Goal 1: The lens or zoom viewer appears when the user mouses down on the magnifying glass icon.

Goal 2: The zoom viewer disappears when the user mouses up on the magnifying glass.

Goal 3: The magnifying glass and zoom viewer both follow the mouse when the user drags them.

Goal 4: The magnifying glass returns to its "home" or default location when the user finishes using the control.

Goal 1 specifies that mousing down on the magnifying glass should cause the zoom viewer to appear. You already created a state called *Visible* to support this; now you need to add a behavior to the magnifying glass image to initiate it.

Select the MagnifyingGlass image in the Objects and Timeline panel.

In the Assets tab, click on Behaviors, select GoToStateAction from the behaviors list, drop it onto MagnifyingGlass in the Objects and Timeline panel, and then name it *ShowAction*.

Figure 24.2   Rename behavior to ShowAction.

In the Properties panel, under Common Properties, set the StateName to Visible.

Take note of the settings under Trigger; the EventName defaults to MouseLeftButtonDown, so you won't need to change that this time.

Figure 24.3   Reference the default events under Trigger.

Now you are ready to tackle Goal 2:

> **Goal 2:** The zoom viewer disappears when the user mouses up on the magnifying glass.

Drag another GoToStateAction onto MagnifyingGlass and rename it *HideAction*.

In the Properties panel, under Triggers, set the EventName to MouseLeftButtonUp.

Under Common Properties, set the StateName to HideAction.

Figure 24.4   Changing the StateName in the Common Properties.

Let's connect the ZoomViewer component up to the Configure screen in the SketchFlow Map, so you can test out your progress.

Once connected, navigate to the Configure screen and rename the component to ZoomViewer, in the Objects and Timeline panel.

Position the ZoomViewer to its correct location.

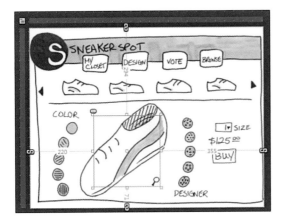

Figure 24.5   *ZoomViewer placement in the customizer page.*

Hit F5 to run the project and take a look at what you've made so far.

CUSTOMIZING FOR COMPLEX INTERACTIVITY

Goals 3 and **4** require a degree of interactive difficulty that is more complex than the preexisting behaviors in Blend. A custom solution is needed, and thankfully, our talented development team created just that:

> **Goal 3:** The magnifying glass and zoom viewer both follow the mouse when the user drags them.

> **Goal 4:** The magnifying glass returns to its "home" or default location when the user finishes using the control.

To start, import the .dll file that contains the custom behavior into the project. Click on Projects panel; then right-click on the References folder under the SneakerSpot_Screens file.

Figure 24.6   Add a reference to the SneakerSpot_Screens file.

Within the Add Reference dialog box, select DragAndReturnTargetedAction.
dll file from the SneakerSpot3 folder.

Once imported, open the Project menu and choose Rebuild Project.

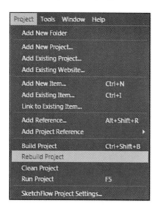

Figure 24.7   Rebuild project.

Rebuilding the project loads the custom behavior into the Assets tab under
Behaviors; check to be sure it is there.

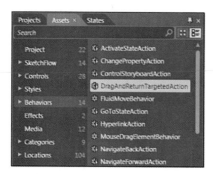

Figure 24.8   *Custom behavior is available in the Assets panel.*

Drag the new behavior onto the MagnifyingGlass and rename it
DragAndReturnAction.

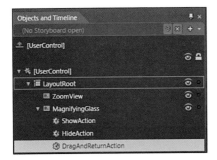

Figure 24.9 *Add and rename the behavior to the MagnifyingGlass.*

In the Properties panel, under Common Properties, select the Artboard
Element Picker icon next to TargetName.

Figure 24.10 *Select the Artboard Element Picker "bull's eye."*

This gives you a bull's eye icon attached to the cursor. Use the cursor to
select the LayoutRoot object in the Objects and Timeline panel.

> PRO TIP:
> Because you want both the magnifying glass and the viewer
> to move in tandem, selecting the LayoutRoot object was the
> more accurate way to grab both. Using the Objects and Timeline
> panel, versus the Artboard, is faster and reduces the guesswork
> associated with a busy screen filled with images.

Now you need to adjust the settings of the DragAndReturnAction to perfect interaction experience.

In the Objects and Timeline panel, under Return On Release Properties, change the duration to 0.4 seconds. This describes the time it will take for the magnifying glass to return back to its original location after the mouse is released. Set Pause to 0.3 seconds so that it will briefly pause before returning. Finally, change the ReturnEasingFunction to Bounce Out and the Bounciness to 3.5.

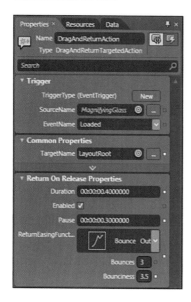

Figure 24.11   *Set Bounce Out and Bounciness properties.*

Now run the project and test out your handiwork.

DIY REFINEMENTS

There are just a few subtle interactions missing from your application. Give it a shot—using what you've learned so far, try improving the Zoom control.

Here is what you want to do:

1. On mouseover, the magnifying glass should grow slightly. On mouseout, it should return to its original size.

2. Create a new state group with two states: one where the magnifying glass grows, and one where it returns to its original size.

3. Assign two GoToStateAction behaviors to the MagnifyingGlass image that trigger the visual states you have created.

Figure 24.12 gives you a hint to what the final setup should look like.

Figure 24.12 *Visual hint as to what the States should look like after the DIY changes.*

SUMMARY

The magnifying glass is complete. The behaviors we added and the extra fine tuning made the user experience enjoyable and unique. A few fancy tweaks can make all the difference. This type of advanced prototyping hasn't been possible with the tools we have traditionally worked with. The next chapter continues to showcase how to use Blend to produce high impact results, focusing on the color selector function and data sourcing.

25

INCORPORATING DATA

Using and working with data has typically been difficult for designers. This chapter details how to work with custom data and edit and define a collection of connected data elements. The following details the prep steps we need to take to make the color picker a reality and the goals for how we would like it to function. After we create a new data set we can dive in, edit and wire the customizer shoe swatches within the interface.

REAL WORLD ROUND 3

We have spent some time with state- and behavior-based interaction. It's time now to focus on examining interaction that depends upon dynamic, customizable, and often-changing information. Through data binding, you can intelligently and powerfully marry information with design and experience. In this chapter, we describe the scope and goals of how we will explore these concepts in this section.

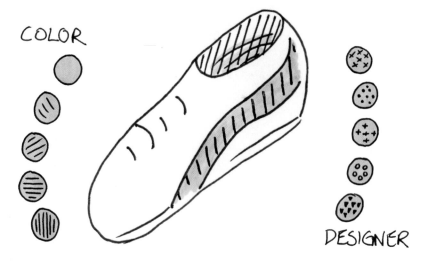

Figure 25.1 *The color picker visual design.*

Preparing the ColorPicker prototype for dynamic interaction:

- Creating a test data source and then populating it with custom content.

- Linking the test data and modifying its display to match our design.

- Applying custom code to custom visual layouts.

The goals for our ColorPicker control are as follows:

> **Goal 1:** Display a list of five color swatch images.

> **Goal 2:** On mouseover, for each swatch, the color name appears.

> **Goal 3:** Once a color swatch is selected, the shoe image updates accordingly.

> **Goal 4:** The color picker needs a custom ListBox (standard ListBox layouts are either vertical or horizontal) that curves as our sketch does.

Let's download and open the project SneakerSpot4 in the folder SneakerSpot4 from www.dynamic-prototypes.com. Even though your shoe customizer solution is not quite ready to send to the client, we consider this to be a new round because the subject matter is a sizable departure from everything you've learned to this point.

Most of your efforts in this chapter will be to reach **Goal 1**. To do this, you will create a color palette data set that contains a color name, a swatch image, and the coordinating shoe stripe image.

Goal 1: Display a list of five color swatch images.

Select the Data panel on the right and click the Add Sample Data Source icon and then Define New Sample Data.

Figure 25.2 *Add new sample data set.*

In the pop-up, name the data source *ColorPaletteDataSource* and make sure the Enable Sample Data When Application Is Running box is checked.

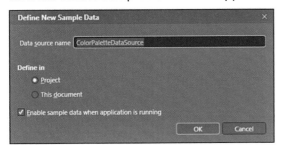

Figure 25.3 *Name new sample data.*

Next, using the default data source, Collection, you want to edit its two properties, Property1 (by default, a string) and Property2 (a Boolean), and create a third. Needed in this collection are a color name, a color swatch image, and a shoe stripe overlay image.

Rename Collection to "ColorSwatch" by double-clicking inside the Name field.

Property1 is already a string, which just so happens to be perfect for supporting the name of your color. Change its name to *Name*.

Figure 25.4 *Change Property1 to "Name."*

Change Property2 to *SwatchImage*.

SwatchImage's data type is currently Boolean (a true/false value). Change it to an image data type by clicking the Change Property Type drop-down and choose Image.

Figure 25.5 *Choose Image under property type.*

Location is blank by default (when left as default, Blend uses a set of its own "dummy" images), but you want to use your custom swatch images. Click the Browse button; then select the SwatchImages folder, which is located in the Sketches folder within the SneakerSpot_AScreens project folder.

Now, you need to add one more property to your data source for the stripe overlay image. Click the Add Simple Property button on your ColorSwatch collection and rename it *StripeOverlay*.

CHAPTER 25 | INCORPORATING DATA

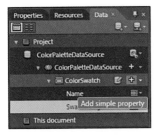

Figure 25.6 *Add sample property to the ColorSwatch set.*

Change its property type to Image, as you did before, and set the Location to the ShoeOverlay folder, which is also in the Sketches folder.

Let's take a look at the data sets you just made; click the Edit sample values icon.

Figure 25.7 *View the sample data just created.*

There are five swatch sketches to display. Let's update the number of records to 5, at the bottom left, to reflect this.

Figure 25.8 *The sample data values should look like this.*

The current sample text in the Name field is too long. Click the Change Property Type icon; then, under Format, change the name to Lorum ipsum. Set the max word count to 1. Click OK.

In order to display the color palette, you need a ListBox for the dataset. Click on the Configure screen in the SketchFlow Map, if you're not already there.

Open the Assets panel, click the Styles carrot, and then click SketchStyles. Out of the list, select ListBox-Sketch.

Figure 25.9 *Select the ListBox-Sketch.*

Drag and drop a ListBox-Sketch control onto the Artboard. Approximate the relative size and position of the original sketch; then rename the ListBox to *ColorPicker* in the Objects and Timeline panel.

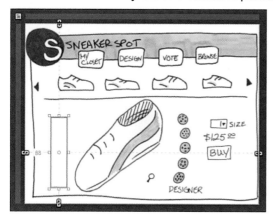

Figure 25.10 *Place the ListBox-Sketch on the Artboard.*

Back in the Assets panel, find TextBlock-Sketch; then drag and drop it onto the Artboard. Position it above the ListBox and change the text to read *COLORS*. Increase the font size as desired.

From the Data panel, drag and drop the ColorSwatch collection onto the ListBox on the Artboard.

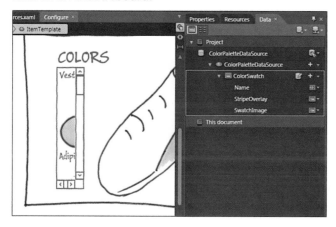

Figure 25.11 *Drop the ColorSwatch data set into the ListBox.*

SUMMARY

After examining the stages for developing the interaction and the goals for the color picker, we created and edited a data collection using text and our custom images. With the ListBox in place and the data dropped inside, we now can start thinking about the appearance of the container and elements. In the next chapter we do just that and end with a full-functioning control for the client to try out.

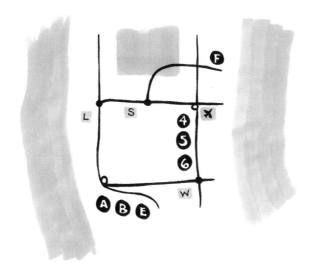

26

REFINING DATA

This chapter takes you through how to edit control templates to achieve the desired visual look, how to tweak the images globally within the templates, and work with some of the more advanced aspects of the Properties panel. We are again building on the data collection created in the last chapter, taking it all the way to an operational color picker with the correct appearance. After we walk through the steps of this section, we will have a prototype fit to send to our client for feedback. By the end you will have the knowledge to edit and modify any sample data collections to act and look the way you desire.

To start, let's focus on improving the visual look of your data in the ListBox by editing its ItemsTemplate.

Select the ListBox on the Artboard. Under the document tabs along the top of the Artboard, click on the ColorPicker breadcrumb and select Edit Additional Templates, Edit Generated Items (ItemsTemplate), Edit Current.

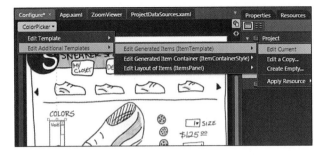

Figure 26.1   Edit Items using the ColorPicker breadcrumb.

The breadcrumb updates to reflect that you are indeed in the ItemTemplate. The same information is mirrored in the Objects and Timeline panel, which also shows all of the images that lie within ItemTemplate.

Figure 26.2   The ItemTemplate breadcrumb.

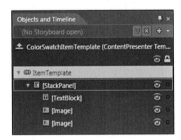

Figure 26.3   All the items within the ItemTemplate.

> **Quick Note:** Because we included all of the items associated with the color swatch list, you can see that the shoe overlay and the text is also included in your ListBox. Drag out a corner of it to see for yourself. You will edit the template now, to make visible only what was originally intended for the list: the color swatches.

To update the contents of the ItemTemplate to display the swatches alone, delete the TextBlock control and the Image control that contains the stripe overlay image (when you select the image, it will be visibly selected on the Artboard, so you can verify which you have picked) from the Objects and Timeline panel.

Let's make a few more tweaks, before you exit the ItemTemplate. First, let's match the size of the swatch images in the ListBox to the Designer swatches on the other side. Set the Width and Height properties to 39 in the Properties panel under Layout and change the bottom margin to 4.

Because you are making changes inside the template, the adjustments are global across all the items.

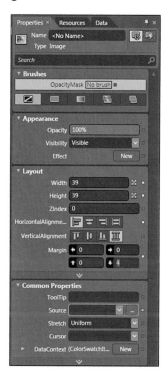

Figure 26.4   Changes to the Properties of the ItemTemplate should look like this.

Finally, you will use one more data-binding trick within the template to display the name of the color on mouseover.

Be sure you have the Image control selected in the Objects and Timeline panel; then in the Properties panel, select the Advanced Properties Options icon next to Tooltip under Common properties and then choose Data Binding.

Figure 26.5   *Select Data Binding from the Advanced properties option.*

Choose the Explicit Data Context tab at the right. Expand the ColorSwatch option (this will look familiar, because it's the data set you created earlier) and select Name: (String). Click OK.

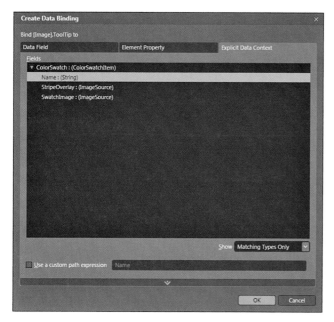

Figure 26.6   Binding the Tooltip to our data set.

Click on the ColorPicker breadcrumb to exit the ItemTemplate and return
to the Artboard. Because you don't really need the scrollbars on the
ListBox, adjust the size with the handles to achieve the look shown in
Figures 26.7 and 26.8.

Figure 26.7   Select the ColorPicker from the breadcrumb.

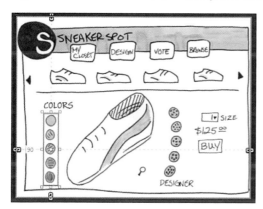

Figure 26.8   Adjust the ListBox to get the effect above.

To bring all the work you have done full circle, you need to wire up the ColorPicker to its coordinating shoe stripe. You already associated the images together when you bound the data. Let's utilize it—when a swatch color is clicked, the overlay image appears on the shoe.

In the Assets panel, type **Image** in the Search field. Select the Image control.

Figure 26.9   Choose the image control.

Drag and drop an Image control onto the Artboard and rename it *CurrentColor* in the Objects and Timeline panel.

Figure 26.10   Rename the image CurrentColor.

In the Properties panel under Layout, set the width to 190 and the height to 230. Change the horizontal alignment to left and the vertical alignment to top. Finally, set the left margin to 282 and the top margin to 286.

Figure 26.11   *Adjustments in the Properties panel will look like this.*

With the CurrentColor image still selected, in Common Properties, click the
Advanced Property Options icon next to Source. Select Data Binding.

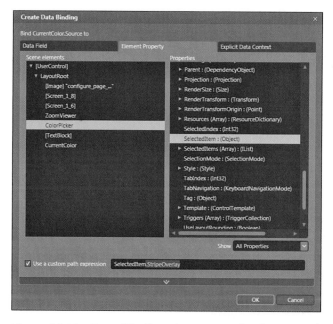

Figure 26.12   *Data Binding changes to the CurrentColor.*

Then, select the Element Property tab. Scene Elements matches the
contents of the Objects and Timeline panel. Select ColorPicker (our ListBox
data source). Change the Show option from Matching Types Only to All
Properties. In Properties, select the SelectedItem: (Object). Check the Use
a Custom Path Expression checkbox and add .StripeOverlay in the text field
at the right. Click OK.

Run the project to test your results.

Finally, to reach Goal 4, you need some advanced functionality. We have enlisted the help of our developer teammate to create a custom panel that displays your color swatches on a curve, as you had originally designed.

Goal 4: The color picker needs a custom ListBox (standard ListBox layouts are either vertical or horizontal) that curves as your sketch does.

Our developer pal has set up a folder called ArcPanelAssets, which contains everything you need to finish out your ListBox.

In the Projects panel, right-click on the Resources folder under the SneakerSpot_AScreens project and select Add Reference.

In the ArcPanelAssets folder, choose the file called ArcPanel.dll. Then, click Rebuild Project in the Project menu, to update the new file.

Next, you want to import the accompanying resource dictionary by right-clicking on the SneakerSpot_AScreens project in the Projects panel and selecting Add Existing Item.

Figure 26.13   Add Existing Item to the project file.

In the ArcPanelAssets folder, choose the file ArcListBoxStyle.xaml, which will appear in the Resources panel as an available resource dictionary.

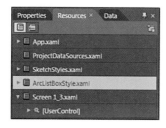

Figure 26.14   Select the ArcListBoxStyle.xaml from the Resources panel.

You can now connect your new custom layout to the Color Picker ListBox. Select ColorPicker from the Objects and Timeline panel. In the Properties panel, under Brushes, set the BorderBrush to None.

At the bottom, expand Miscellaneous and click the Advanced Property Options icon next to ItemsPanel.

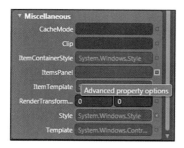

Figure 26.15   Click on Advanced Property Option icon.

The Local Resource list now includes the option we uploaded: ArcListBoxItemsPanelTemplate.

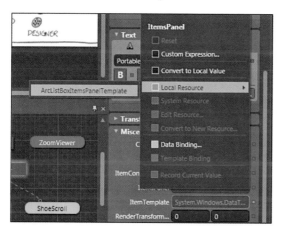

Figure 26.16   Select Local Resource in the ItemsPanel.

Once selected, you'll see the ColorPicker ListBox update on the Artboard to use the new custom layout. Update the position of the ListBox so that it mirrors the swatches on the other side.

Run the project to see all that hard work—we are done!

SUMMARY

You have just used some fancy foot work to edit, customize, and visually improve the color picker data and its container. When prototyping, it may not always be necessary to create something this in-depth, but for selling your concept to clients or stakeholders, it's often worth it. Our work here now showcases the joy and functionality of the application, which will surely garnish great feedback and renewed excitement. Where we take the project in the next chapter is significant. Adding design fidelity is a critical step in the design process and will utilize the hard work we did here.

27

ADVANCING FIDELITY

This chapter focuses exclusively on how to work in Blend to advance
your application toward the final product. After we examine the client
feedback, we can then begin to create universal styles and templates for
the frequently used elements, like buttons and fonts. Here you define style
resources that make changing the appearance of the assets quick and easy
for the whole team. Then you discover the tricks for modifying templates
in Blend, which gives us yet another way to progress the project from
prototype to reality. What we learn here carries through to the following
chapter where we will continue building a process for productivity when it
really matters and give you the tools to make guides and cheat sheets for
the team to make "heads down" time smooth and less chaotic.

REAL WORLD ROUND 4

There are several smart things we have done behind the scenes to ensure
that this part of the process goes smoothly. Because SneakerSpot already

had a visual style that the client liked, we were able to use what they had, make some improvements to it, and then get approval on the adjustments. We wanted to do this ahead of needing to skin the functional prototype that wasn't complete or client approved. This way, by the time we were ready to add it to our functional application, we could ideally do it once.

By separating the interaction and the visual style, the team gains two important advantages. First, you can narrow the conversation to the client. You can have a simple, lo-fi discussion around the experience and another focused on the look and feel of the visual skin. Breaking down these conversations keeps things easier for SneakerSpot to grasp and understand. Second, the separation gives the team an advantage when you move into the production phase of your process. Each person can now do his or her job with reduced revision repetition and confusion.

We sent off our functional shoe customizer to the client, and it looks like they really liked it.

```
-----Original Message-----
From: Team SneakerSpot
Sent: Monday, August 15, 2009 10:46 AM
To: Awesome Agency Team
Subject: RE: New Shoe Customizer Functionality

Hello Team!
The SneakerSpot team enjoyed using the shoe
designer page and we think that it will fit the
needs of our picky customers.

We think we are ready to see the visual skin, we
approved last week applied to this page.

Hopefully that won't take too long, we are very
excited.

Thanks,
Team SneakerSpot
```

Figure 27.1 *Feedback email from the client.*

The first step is to use the existing sketchy style as a starting point for our final style. This is the best way to get up-and-running quickly as you can leverage work that's already been done. Open up the project, SneakerSpot5, in the folder, SneakerSpot5, from www.dynamic-prototypes. com.

In the Objects and Timeline panel, expand the StackPanel element to reveal the nested navigation buttons.

We want to create a copy of the existing sketchy style to use as your starting point. Right-click on the Closet radio button and choose Edit Template, Edit a Copy.

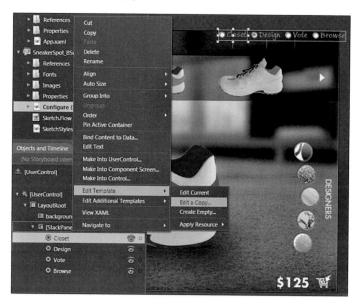

Figure 27.2 *Edit Template for the Closet radio button.*

Name the style NavigationButton, and under Define in, select Resource dictionary and click New. Name it "NavigationButtonStyles." Blend will automatically place you inside the template for the new style you just created.

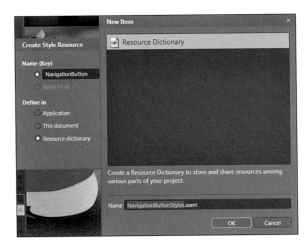

Figure 27.3 *Change the new item name to "NavigationButtonStyles."*

As you head into style creation, think of a style as simply a set of values
that determine the appearance on a control, such as a background color
or font. A template, on the other hand, is used to *change* the visual
appearance of a control (it is also where you add state changes and
animations).

Using the breadcrumb trail above the Artboard, step out of the template
and into the root style by clicking the palette icon so that you can modify
the basic properties.

Figure 27.4 *Select the root Style icon on the breadcrumb.*

Update the following style settings in the Brushes section of the Properties
panel: Change Background and BorderBrush to no brush and Foreground
to a white solid color brush.

Figure 27.5 *Adjustments to the Brushes in the Properties panel will look like this.*

Now let's make sure your font is set up correctly so that anyone visiting the site will see the intended design. Under Text in the Properties panel, click on the Advanced Properties icon next to FontFamily. Choose Reset, which will remove the current sketchy style font association. Select Microsoft Sans Serif as the font family.

Figure 27.6 *Reset font style association.*

> **Quick Note:** Feel free to set the font family to any typeface you like. The original design for SneakerSpot used a Futura font. Here, we opted for the default, Microsoft Sans Serif, because we knew you would have it on your machine.

Set the font size to 15px. Blend will then convert the pixel value into the appropriate font size for you.

Next to the Bold option, select the Advanced Properties icon and choose Reset.

Figure 27.7 *Advanced properties for Bold.*

Now click the Font Manager button and select Microsoft Sans Serif (or whichever typeface you previously selected) to be embedded. Embedding default system fonts isn't always necessary, but for custom, non-standard typefaces, it is.

TEMPLATE MODIFICATIONS

The template is where the real power of Blend (with WPF and Silverlight) is harvested. It will enable you to alter the standard appearance of your radio buttons and turn them into something completely your own.

Modifying the template may occasionally seem a bit complex, but you are, in essence, following the same steps you had before—changing states and UI elements, but this time, from the *inside*.

Using the breadcrumb above the Artboard, select Template to drill into the NavigationButton style. There, you'll see that your template is composed of a root grid that holds a contentPresenter and another grid that contains a number of elements that make up the radio part of the radio button.

Figure 27.8 *Template contents in the Objects and Timeline panel.*

The contentPresenter is a special control that knows how to automatically display your content. For example, the text you assigned to the first radio button is Closet. It's the contentPresenter that actually communicates that to you. When working on the style, this control will display the specific name, which is why it says RadioButton and not Closet.

You don't want any of the default elements that make up the radio button, so right-click on the grid that contains them and select Delete. You should end up with the Template contents, like the image in Figure 27.8. Blend informs you that it has removed some state animations because you deleted the elements they relied on. This is a nice perk; Blend has done some automatic housekeeping for you.

Figure 27.9 *RadioButton contents after deletion.*

The root grid is split into two columns, which we don't need. Check to be sure Grid is selected in the Objects and Timeline panel; then click Show Advanced Properties under Layout of the Properties panel. Then click the Advanced property options next to ColumnDefinitions and choose Reset.

In the Properties panel under Brushes, set the root grid's Background to no brush.

Now, select the contentPresenter in the Objects and Timeline panel and, under Layout in the Properties panel, set its horizontal and vertical alignment to Center.

Next, we are going to be adding an image for the selected state of the button that is much larger than the surface area designated for mouse input. In order to specify how much of the control's real estate gets treated as "live," you'll need to wrap the contentPresenter in a border element.

From the Assets panel, enter "Border" as the search term. Drag and drop the Border element into the root grid of the template (either onto the Artboard or the Objects and Timeline panel); then nest the content Presenter inside the border.

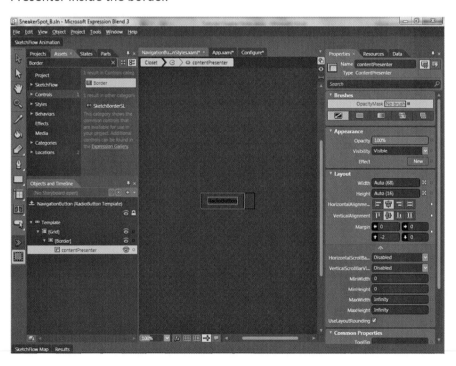

Figure 27.10 *ContentPresenter should look like above.*

Select Border in the Objects and Timeline panel; then in the Properties panel, set the Background to transparent solid color brush, the BorderBrush to no brush, and the horizontal and vertical layout to Center.

Make sure the margin is set to 0 and the padding to 5 for all sides.

Finally, under Common Properties, set the cursor to Hand.

SUMMARY

Now we have walked through several ways in which to move and advance styles and templates into the last stage of the design process. We have edited the sketch style template, created a resource dictionary for global assets, and updated root Styles to make it easy for the team to be productive. In the next chapter, we take what we have done here even further to explore other tools to aid in the production process. The lessons to come are designed to help you evolve how you work and cut down on confusion and frustration that often accompany the last stages of product development.

28

ADVANCED FIDELITY WITH TEMPLATES AND STYLES

This chapter introduces some tangible ways to enhance how you and your team work. First we examine a visual guide for mapping lo-fi to hi-fi, which can remove some of the pains of productions. Then we dive into how to update visual states and root user interface templates and styles within our color picker data source. Lastly, you finish the visual upgrade by taking what you have learned to do-it-yourself (DIY) the remaining combo box element.

Working with and mastering templates and styles is one of the key methods to truly evolve a prototype into the actual product. There are a few tricks and a bit of effort involved, but the benefit and time savings is tremendous. In the previous pages and the ones to come, you have begun to transform your simple sketch, test, and approval environment into the real thing. Creating these hi-fi assets outside of the prototype is *the* best practice we want to share with you. The style guide that you might normally create after the project is completed is what we recommend you create after the visual skin is approved but before production begins. It's a working file, with the styles, behaviors, and visual direction displayed, and it's built so that all the assets can be shared with the team.

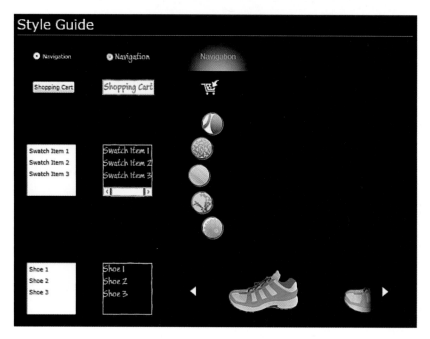

Figure 28.1 *The style guide for the project.*

Now we can begin to add new elements to support the requirements of the full fidelity design. First, add the "shine" image; from the Images folder in the Project panel, drag nav_selected.png onto the Artboard.

In the Objects and Timeline panel, rename it "shine," and make sure it is located above the contentPresenter.

Figure 28.2 *Rename image to "shine" in the Objects and Timeline panel.*

In the Properties panel, under Layout, explicitly set the width to 148 and height to 56; set the horizontal and vertical layout to Center.

Reset the margin by clicking the Advanced Property Options icon and selecting Reset.

Set the Opacity to 0, under Appearance.

In Common Properties, click on Show Advanced Properties and then deselect IsHitTestVisible. You don't want this element to respond to mouse input; its only purpose is visual. So, you're instructing Blend to ignore the logic.

Now, let's add two TextBlock elements to support mouseover and on-click appearance. Select the root grid in the template. From the Assets panel, search for "Textblock" and double-click the TextBlock control to automatically add it to the Artboard. Rename it to "TextHover."

Set the foreground color to #FF12BFF7, and horizontal and vertical alignment to Center. Change the opacity to 0, and the bottom margin to 1.

You will use binding to make it look exactly like the contentPresenter: Under the Common Properties section, click Advanced Property Options and then Data Binding.

In the Create Data Binding screen, select the Element Property tab, and choose the contentPresenter from the Scene Elements and Content from Properties to bind to.

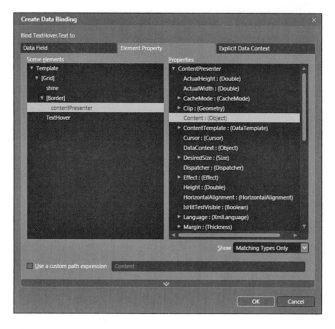

Figure 28.3   Create Data Binding screen should look like above.

Under Text, click Advanced Property Options next to the Font Family drop-down; choose Template Binding and Font Family.

Figure 28.4 *Select FontFamily from the Advanced properties icon.*

Repeat this same process for the Font Size and Font Weight properties; then, deselect IsHitTestVisible under Common Properties. From the Objects and Timeline panel, copy and paste the TextHover TextBlock and rename the new one "TextSelected."

ADDING VISUAL STATES

You now have all the elements needed for your new navigation style. Here, you'll alter their appearance for various interaction states.

Expand the States panel. You'll see a number of states already defined for you, from the existing sketchy style. Let's focus on the MouseOver and Checked states.

Select the MouseOver state to initiate record mode and change the opacity for the TextHover element to 30.

Figure 28.5 *States panel, MouseOver with record mode on.*

Select the Checked state to enter record mode and change the opacity for both shine and TextSelected elements to 100. Set the opacity for the contentPresenter to 0.

Set the Default transition time for both the CommonStates group and the CheckStates group to 0.2.

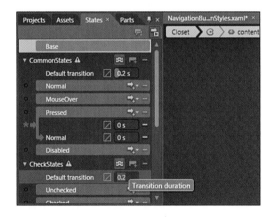

Figure 28.6 *Adjust the default transition durations.*

UPDATES TO THE ROOT UI

In these last few steps, you will apply the new style to the rest of the buttons and update their layout so that it looks like the intended design.

Then you can update the Style Guide with the latest visual elements. Using the breadcrumb above the Artboard, click the Closet element to return to the root project.

For the rest of the navigation buttons, right-click and choose Edit Template and Apply Resource; then select the NavigationButton.

Figure 28.7 *In the root project, apply the NavigationButton resource.*

Set the right margin for the Closet button to -75; then change the right margin to -80 for both Design and Vote. Run your project to take a peek.

In the SketchFlow Map, update the Style Guide to use this style.

Apply the style to the third navigation radio button as you did before, by applying the resource style.

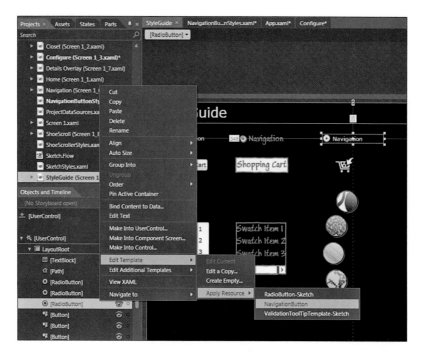

Figure 28.8 *Apply the NavigationButton resource to the third radio button.*

APPLYING HI-FI STYLES

Navigate back to the Configure screen and choose the ColorPicker ListBox from the Objects and Timeline panel. In Miscellaneous under Properties, make these changes:

- Click on Advanced Property Options next to ItemContainerStyle; then, in Local Resources, choose ArcListBoxItemStyleFinal.

- Click on Advanced Property Options next to ItemTemplate; then, in Local Resources, choose ColorSwatchesItemTemplateFinal.

Now let's update the sketch images to the finished style by editing the sample data.

In the Data panel, expand each, starting with the Project carrot, then the ConfigureDataSource, and last, ColorSwatches. Select the ColorSwatch item and click the Change Property Type icon on the right.

Figure 28.9 *Change the property type in the Data panel.*

Click Browse and choose the FinalColorSwatches folder from the Assets folder within this project.

DIY IT

You left one control un-styled: the combo box. Use the following steps to style it yourself:

- Right-click the SizePicker combo box and choose Edit Template and then Edit a Copy. Create a new resource dictionary in which to put your combo box styles, just like you did for the navigation button styles.

- The combo box is composed of several sub-controls. You'll need to create styles for those controls as well:

  In the ComboBox style, there is a pop-up control. It contains a ScrollViewer that needs a style.

  The ScrollViewer has a Horizontal and Vertical ScrollBar control. You can create one style and apply it to both of them. Inside the ScrollBar control, you'll need to create styles for the scrollbar buttons.

SUMMARY

Taking the application to this stage with template, state, and style updates is no small feat. Reimagining the design and development process with the potential and possibilities in Blend can improve how you work and what you can do together as a team. SketchFlow and Blend were created for this purpose: to begin to dissolve the siloed nature of how we work and take advantage of a powerful platform that allows for products to live on the Web and as stand-alone software. Changing our workflow for the better also carries into the next chapter, where you will examine the process and project as a whole and look for ways to improve how you work for and with the next client.

29

POST-MORTEM

It's done, feature and project complete—your creation is out there for the world to see. But how did it go? What went well, and what didn't? The post-mortem wrap meeting is the best way for the entire team to divulge the victories and the pain. Your primary goal for this funeral is simple: This is *the* moment to exercise your team's ability to DEFEAT habit and to grow. To combat stagnation and frustration with the documented reality of the project is the most powerful opportunity to engage and empower the team.

Here is a list of some of the highest-value questions to be covered during a post-mortem.

PROCESS

Your project process discussion should include conversation about the length of time given to the project, how accurate the initial scope was to what was actually done, where the pain points were along the way. The concept that everything could be improved or bettered in some fashion is helpful when focusing on project process. When the *how* of what we do becomes rigid, we very often miss out on opportunities to evolve and grow. Here is a starter list of process questions:

- Did you try something new during the course of the project? Did it work? Could it be carried through to the next effort?

- Were there process ideas that didn't get utilized? Are they worth experimenting with for next time?

- Are there residual points of frustration in the current process that should be examined and bettered? What are some ideas for fixing them?

- Could you have used more time during any section of the process? Did you have extra time at any point? If so, what were the contributing factor(s)?

MEASUREMENT

The fear of drowning can seem tolerable next to the terror surrounding the idea of being measured or using metrics in the creative process. The main reason: It is difficult to take accurate readings on new and innovative ideas. One solution is one-on-one interviewing with team members or with customers. Testing for relevance, cognition, cultural meaning, or value with prototypes or interviews may be the only way to gather real exact measurement. With that said, the post mortem should air out concerns around how metrics are taken and adhered to, what the true value or benefit is, how the information was used and what could be improved in the future. The following list of questions is a good place to begin:

- Are there limitations in how much the team and especially management relies on predictability and measurement?

- If there are measurement constraints in place, do they help or hurt the team and the workflow?

- Is there a better way to gauge progress or results?

- Do current measurement tools embody the foundation of scientific method? Or could you learn more by augmenting some of the predictability testing by adopting a scientific approach?

TEAM

Most great products were not created by a singular entity. A collaborative, team environment produces award winning results. Shared goals and vision for the client and what you design and develop for them isn't possible without management support and open communication. The post mortem should ensure teammates feel heard and their ideas are given thought or consideration and that the team is granted the environment and permission to wade into the project and problem solve together. These questions get you started; but because teams and personalities can vary greatly, we encourage you to come up with some of your own as well:

- Did each individual feel like his or her ideas were heard? Did someone's idea get canned that could have been useful? If so, describe what transpired.

- Were there missed opportunities to work together?

- Were there times where you had to reengage someone? Did that help the morale or fix the communication gap?

GENERAL

The overall success of the project, the flow and transfer of information, and any issues or problems should be addressed. Treat part of the post mortem as a "customer service hotline" to give everyone an opportunity to air concerns or offer general feedback. Also, it is important to examine if the team members are proud of the final result and what they would do if they could change it in a perfect world. Here are a few suggestions to begin the conversation:

- Is the client as excited about the finished product as they were in the initial meetings? Is your team happy with the output? This is a fantastic opportunity for brutal honesty. Ask everyone if this is something they would put in their portfolio or show off to their peers. If not, why? If so, explain what makes this such a compelling accomplishment.

- Are there snafus that could have been avoided? Prototyped out? Discovered in advance?

FINAL THOUGHTS

With all of this feedback from the team, decide on some actionable changes and vote on which will be amended and tested for the next project. You don't want to lose this valuable information and opportunity to improve and evolve team practices. This exercise is the most agile, innovative, and beneficial thing you can do for your team, the value of the work you produce, and the culture of prototyping within your company. Your output increases the net worth of everyone on the team and dramatically improves individual job satisfaction.

As designers, technologists, and developers, our founding challenge that brings us the most reward is problem solving. But this cannot begin with client work; it must start within the team, the workflow, and discovering the problems that are most worthy of being solved together. What we deliver will always change, but defining and evolving the things essential to our discipline can earnestly better you; your perception, intention, and building repeatable and measureable value are all critical for success. Feel empowered to push forward the practices of the industry; don't wait for someone else to do it for you.

PART V

REFERENCE

WHAT IS .NET?

Most of the fundamental ideas of science are essentially simple, and may, as a rule, be expressed in a language comprehensible to everyone.
—Albert Einstein

INTRODUCTION

As the great Albert Einstein states in the preceding quote, certain fundamental concepts and ideas should transcend any specific language and be expressed in a way in which everyone can understand and benefit from them. Although Einstein was referring specifically to scientific ideas, this same principle can also be applied to creating great software.

Ultimately, programmers, designers, web developers, and information architects strive to express an idea or create a service that is useful and available to anyone regardless of browser, platform, and hardware. On the flip side of that coin, developers (and designers) should have a common set of tools that allows them to create great applications regardless of what language they prefer to work in. With so many language options available like C#, Visual Basic, C++, and more, the need for a "universal translator" and common set of tools is essential.

WHAT IS .NET?

The .NET framework is a software framework that gives developers access to a common set of essential tools, methods, and code libraries for building software for the Web, desktop, mobile devices, and even gaming systems, such as the Xbox 360. The .NET framework enables developers to work with several different programming languages such as C# and Visual Basic

(VB), and the code libraries included with the .NET framework provide developers with out-of-the-box solutions to many common programming tasks. This can include the creation of user interfaces, website development, database connectivity, and work with media files.

The .NET framework (with version 4.0 shipping with Visual Studio 2010) comes installed with a variety of Microsoft applications and operating systems, including Windows 7, and Server editions. You can also download the .NET framework directly from the Microsoft website for installation on additional operating systems, such as Windows XP.

Because you can build applications for the .NET framework with a variety of languages and approaches, .NET provides the Common Language Runtime (CLR). The CLR acts in a sense as a *universal translator* as well as a separate layer that manages the ground-level tasks of an application during runtime (when the application is active).

.NET AND SILVERLIGHT

Silverlight applications and the languages used to develop them, such as XAML and C#, are derived from or utilize coded solutions and libraries from the .NET framework. It is important to understand, however, that Silverlight uses a smaller portion (subset) of the .NET framework, so libraries that may be available when developing desktop applications may not be available to Silverlight developers. Nevertheless Microsoft has taken all the libraries that make sense to have in Silverlight and even created some new ones (DeepZoom, Pixel Manipulation, Effects, Visual State Manager) to help developers and designers build Silverlight rich applications.

DEVELOPMENT TOOLS

There are a few choices when it comes to development tools and environments for building, testing, and deploying applications built on the .NET framework. Beginning with Expression Blend and upcoming versions, Expression Blend provides a stripped-down .NET environment specific to Silverlight and WPF application development. This is why developers can work in the language of their choice and share common .NET and

Silverlight-specific libraries. Blend 3's integrated Code Editor window provides some basic yet key features for working with code, building applications, and testing your work (see Figure A.1).

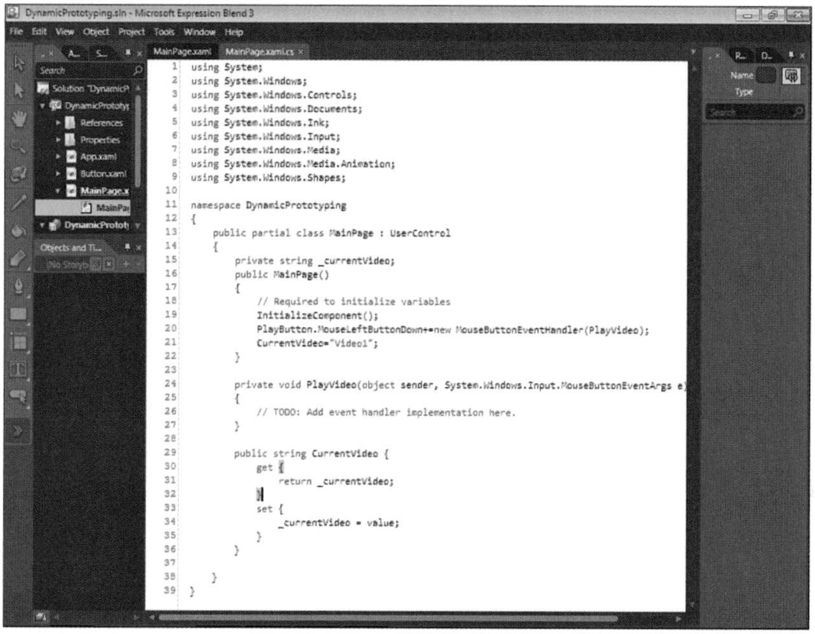

Figure A.1 *The Expression Blend Code Editor window provides a stripped-down environment for working with code and .NET libraries and techniques.*

For more heavy-duty coding tasks, such as building desktop applications, websites, and web applications, many developers utilize Microsoft's Visual Studio, which is a fully integrated development environment that gives programmers access to a full gamut of development and debugging features, .NET framework languages, and libraries. Visual Studio can also be used to develop Silverlight and WPF applications from the ground up, although many designers or design-centric web developers may tend to prefer the more visual and tool-driven environment of Blend.

Visual Studio, like Expression Blend, provides a number of views (such as a Design and Code view) for application building, but its uses extend far beyond the world of Silverlight development (see Figure A.2).

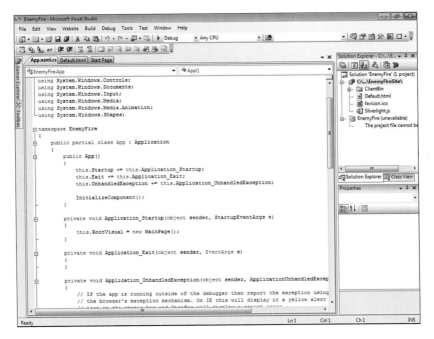

Figure A.2 *Visual Studio 2008 (shown) can build and publish Silverlight and WPF applications, as well as any project that uses the .NET framework and its languages.*

THE COMMON LANGUAGE RUNTIME (CLR)

.NET's versatility comes from its ability to work with several languages that all share a common set of tools, and the Common Language Runtime (CLR) is a core component of .NET that, in part, makes this possible. The CLR goes into action at *runtime*, or the point in time in which an application is active and running, and provides a central point of interpretation from CIL code (which is compiled from the languages in the .NET family such as C#) to native machine code. In addition, the CLR serves as an abstract layer that manages the core tasks of an application's lifecycle, such as memory management and security (see Figure A.3).

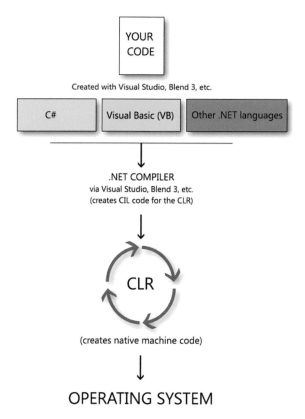

Figure A.3 *The .NET flow of code from development to deployment.*

The Silverlight runtime and CLR is similar to the .NET CLR, but is a compacted, optimized version that utilizes a smaller portion of the .NET CLR. Although the CLR for .NET is typically Windows-specific, the Silverlight runtime brings the CLR cross-platform, as it can run on other operating systems, such as Apple's Mac OS X and run in multiple browsers including Internet Explore, Safari, and Firefox.

WHO USES .NET?

.NET is at the heart of countless applications that we use each and every day across a wide variety of devices and mediums. Whether it's an e-commerce site, mobile application, or desktop application you rely on, the .NET framework is used by a large number of organizations—big and small, public and private, online or offline.

DESKTOP APPLICATIONS

Alongside established programming languages such as C++ and JAVA, C# and other .NET languages have become a prominent method of developing desktop applications for business, entertainment, media production, and workflow tools to name a few.

Like the rapid and intuitive process of developing Silverlight applications, .NET gives software developers a way to build applications in a variety of languages, and features access to a core set of Windows interface components (referred to as Windows Forms or *WinForms*) for building the front-end of an application.

As an alternative and potential successor to traditional Windows Forms applications, Windows Presentation Foundation (WPF) applications harness the power of .NET but utilize a richer and modern graphical interface similar to those seen in Silverlight applications. WPF has gained tremendous traction, and shining examples of WPF in action are the Expression Studio applications themselves, including Expression Design and Expression Blend (see Figure A.4).

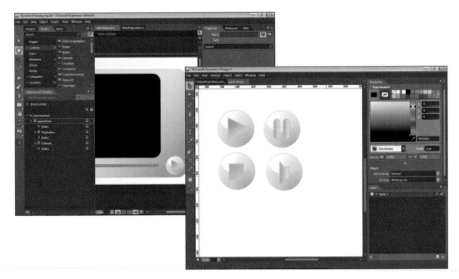

Figure A.4   The Expression Studio applications are a key example of WPF at work; these applications are developed using WPF's rich interface capabilities and the power of .NET.

WEBSITES AND WEB APPLICATIONS

Microsoft has long been in the website development game since the release of Active Server Pages (ASP), allowing otherwise static HTML-based web pages to display dynamic content, interact with databases, and automate other web-based functions. With the release of the .NET Framework 1.0 and ASP.NET, developers can use a variety of languages (such as C# and VB) along with standard HTML-based interfaces to create database-driven websites.

ASP.NET server controls allow for rapid web page and application development by using "server tags" to create dynamic interface elements on a page right within an HTML-driven interface (often referred to in this context as WebForms), as shown in Figure A.5.

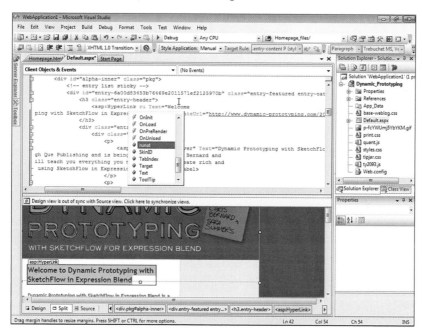

Figure A.5   *Visual Studio 2008 is used to build dynamic web applications on the .NET framework.*

RICH INTERNET APPLICATIONS WITH SILVERLIGHT

Silverlight provides a platform on which designers, developers, and anyone in between can build and deliver sophisticated and attractive web-based applications, or Rich Internet Applications (RIAs). Similar to other web technologies such as Adobe Flash or AJAX-enabled applications, Silverlight RIAs typically combine a graphically rich user interface, integrated audio and video, and real-time data.

Silverlight applications utilize a subset of the .NET framework that provides essential libraries, as well as additional tools necessary for building user interfaces, retrieving real-time data, streaming video, and creating complex logic for game development (see Figure A.6).

Figure A.6   The Microsoft Silverlight showcase utilizes a sleek Silverlight gallery that enables users to navigate through and visit cutting-edge Silverlight 3 applications.

Tools such as Expression Blendand SketchFlow enable designers and interactive professionals to conceive, prototype, and evolve an application, whereas developers can evolve an application using C# or VB and many of the same core libraries and techniques they are familiar with in traditional .NET environments. Silverlight applications now feature the ability to install and run out of the browser, providing a unique, more integrated experience. It's important to note that Silverlight applications, similar to Flash, require the installation of a plug-in to work properly and that AJAX capabilities that require no plug-ins still require a modern browser for applications to function correctly.

MOBILE APPLICATIONS

The .NET Compact Framework, as the name states, is a smaller subset of the .NET framework utilized for mobile application development and deployment. The Compact Framework is optimized for resource-limited environment of mobile devices, and is hardware independent for devices running the Windows Mobile OS.

B

WHAT IS XAML?

Wouldn't it be great if we had a simple, easy-to-interpret language to represent the most complex tasks in life? Whether it's fixing a car, doing taxes, or performing minor rocket science, the skills and concepts behind some tasks are only within reach for a select few.

Fortunately, in the world of Silverlight, we do have such a language—one that's intuitive enough to read and understand right out of the box, and to enable designers, information architects, and developers to all work in the same space and be a part of the process. Xtensible Application Markup Language, more commonly known as XAML (pronounced zam-el), is the foundation of a Silverlight or WPF application. XAML represents the user interface of an application from a structural, hierarchical, and in some cases, behavioral point of view.

XTENSIBLE APPLICATION MARKUP LANGUAGE (XAML)

XAML is an XML-based markup language, visualized as a series of bracketed tags and keywords. If you've seen or worked with XML or XHTML before, you'll notice that they are very similar to XAML in appearance and approach. Each XAML element represents some object in your Silverlight application, such as a shape, canvas, custom control, or storyboard.

To Silverlight, XAML gives instructions on what, how, and where to render an element on the screen, and in some cases how that element will behave in response to events. Expression Blend renders XAML in the Design view so that you have a visual preview of your application and are able to work with things in a more tactile way (see Figure B.1).

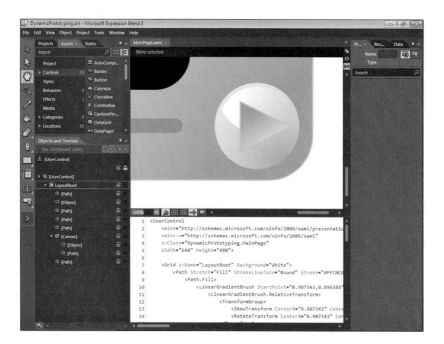

Figure B.1 A split view in Expression Blend showing both code and rendered XAML.

For designers, XAML is a friendly representation of the user interface of a Silverlight application that provides a way to create and adjust the user interface without the need to dive into complex programming code. This can be achieved in either Code (XAML) view or Design view through the use of the Expression Blend tools and panels.

ANATOMY OF A XAML ELEMENT

XAML elements (sometimes referred to as "tags," borrowed from the HTML nomenclature) create the user interface of a Silverlight application. This includes graphics, media files, storyboards, and animation. A XAML element is constructed as shown in Figure B.2.

```
<Ellipse x:Name="myEllipse" Height="31" HorizontalAlignment="Left"/>
```

Figure B.2 Looking at the Element Type, Property, and Value for a XAML element.

XAML elements define (create) objects and through a series of properties (referred to as *attributes* in the context of XAML syntax) and values that enable you to tune the object's appearance and behavior. Let's take a look at a XAML element that defines an Ellipse on the screen:

```
        <Ellipse Height="60" HorizontalAlignment="Right"
Margin="0,0,175,7" VerticalAlignment="Bottom" Width="60"
Fill="#FFCC0000"/>
```

Here, an Ellipse object is created, set with a red fill color, and set with a width and height of 60 (in pixels). You could probably figure that out just by looking at the element—the language is very human, and it's clear what's being created and where. The HorizontalAlignment, VerticalAlignment, and Margin attributes help position the Ellipse relative to its container.

Let's look at another sample that reflects some structure, as follows:

```
<Canvas Height="75" HorizontalAlignment="Right" Margin="0,0,144,6"
VerticalAlignment="Bottom" Width="75">
<Ellipse Height="10" Width="60" Fill="#FFCC0000" Canvas.Left="10"
Canvas.Top="10"/>
            </Canvas>
```

Here, the last example was extended, and a Canvas has been created as a container for the Ellipse. Because the Ellipse is shown within the opening and closing Canvas tags, it's clear that the Ellipse is a child element of the Canvas. The hierarchy and relationship between the two objects can be easily visualized without even needing to see them on the screen. You'll also notice that the Ellipse now uses some different positioning attributes, Canvas.Left and Canvas.Top, which are unique to elements contained within a Canvas.

MORE THAN JUST GRAPHICS

XAML can create and represent much more than just graphics in an application—it is the foundation for the entire interface seen in a Silverlight application, including media (such as video or audio), layout, and animation.

As storyboards and animation are created, interactivity (such as clicks and rollovers) is assigned to controls, and new graphics are created, you will see lots of additional XAML added to your application to create and control these elements.

Let's look at an example of a document that contains a simple, single storyboard with some animation and a button that starts the animation (see Figure B.3).

Figure B.3   The source XAML view for a basic application.

It may look a bit complicated at first, but ultimately XAML tells the story of your application; as your eye becomes more trained, you'll be able to decipher what's going on without relying completely on Expression Blend's Design view. This also means that you have more control in certain situations where adjustments or troubleshooting are necessary.

VIEWING AND EDITING XAML

Expression Blend gives you the tools necessary to create XAML and build your application with little to no understanding of coding or XAML itself. The design tools and panels in the Expression Blend workspace all share a common task: They write XAML in the background as you drag, drop, type, and build your application from the ground up in Design view. Each tool is responsible for creating the necessary tags in your XAML document, whether it is a shape, layout container, media file, or storyboard.

The tool panels found on the bottom and right side of your workspace fine-tune the elements you add; for that reason, they are almost always contextual to whatever you have selected in the Design view. As shown in Figure B.4, a Canvas drawn to contain other elements on the screen can be selected and further fine-tuned using the Properties panel.

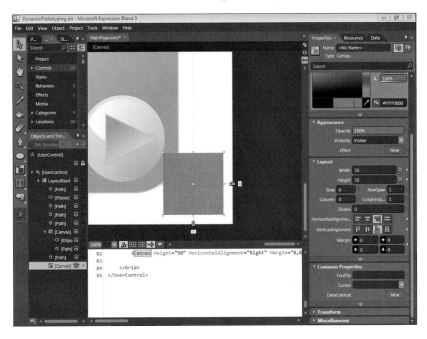

Figure B.4   *We can fine tune XAML using the Properties panel in Expression Blend.*

THE XAML VIEW

Expression Blend gives you a way to look at and work with the XAML code you've generated in the XAML view. The XAML view is essentially a built-in text editor just for XAML. As you build your application, you can see the code being created, and for those who are comfortable writing and working with XAML directly, it can be edited and arranged in this view. Similarly, the Split view enables you to view XAML and preview the interface at the same time.

You can switch into XAML or Split views using the icons shown in the upper-right corner of the document window (see Figure B.5).

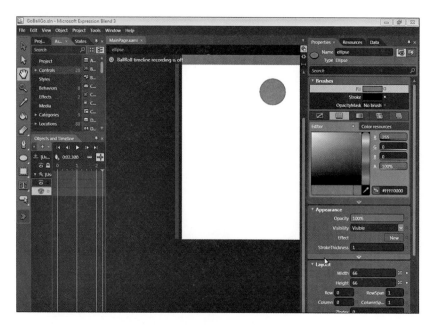

Figure B.5 *View and edit XAML in either the XAML or Split views.*

For novices, the Split view can be a great way to learn and understand XAML while building applications using the Expression Blend tools.

Let's take a look at an example of Split view. In Figure B.6, a piece of artwork pasted from Expression Design is shown in Split view, revealing the XAML that recreates and represents the artwork on the screen while simultaneously previewing the artwork as it will be seen on the screen.

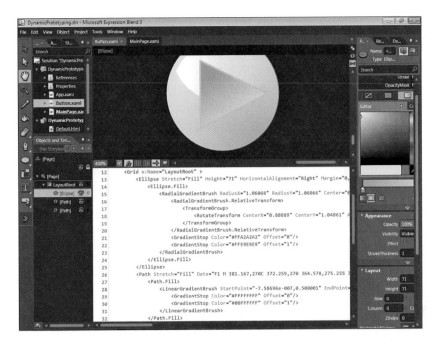

Figure B.6 *Split view can show us how the XAML creates the elements that are displayed in our rendered view.*

QUICK NOTE:

If you have ever worked with any visual web development or application-building program such as Expression Web, Adobe Dreamweaver, Microsoft FrontPage, or Visual Studio, you are already familiar with the concept of a Design and Code view. Expression Blend works in very much the same way, writing and displaying XAML code that represents your Silverlight application.

CREATING LAYOUTS WITH XAML

XAML provides us with a number of tags that are used to build and lay out the interface of an application. Each one of these tags creates a container in which other elements can be placed and positioned, and each has a unique behavior or characteristic that makes it suited for different layout tasks.

THE LAYOUTROOT

The top-level container in any Silverlight application is the LayoutRoot, which holds all other elements and is created by default in your application's primary XAML file (MainPage.xaml). When you begin work on a brand-new Silverlight application, the LayoutRoot is represented by the white work area in the middle of the Design view. By default, the LayoutRoot is a Grid container, which is one of several containers you can work with in Silverlight. The Grid is described in more detail later in the appendix. Although the LayoutRoot's container type can be switched, the LayoutRoot itself should never be removed or forcibly renamed in XAML.

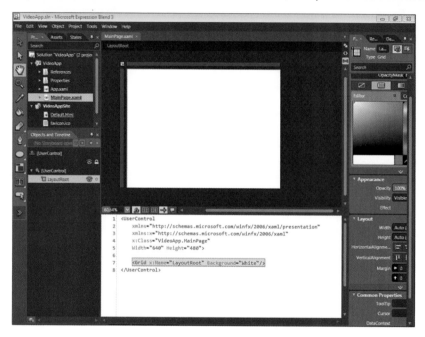

Figure B.7   Looking at the Layout Root.

NAMING OBJECTS

Every XAML element can be named in either XAML itself, or using the Properties panel in the Blend workspace. This includes individual elements such as a single TextBox or Ellipse, or a layout control such as a Canvas, which contains several elements.

To name an element, you can add the x:Name property to a XAML tag, as follows:

```
<Ellipse x:Name="myEllipse" Width="80" Height="80" />
```

Select an element in Design view, and use the Properties panel (see Figure B.8).

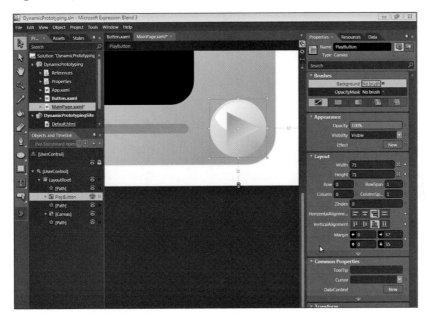

Figure B.8   *Selecting an element and using the Properties panel.*

Or, double-click the element in the Objects and Timeline panel and rename it, as shown in Figure B.9.

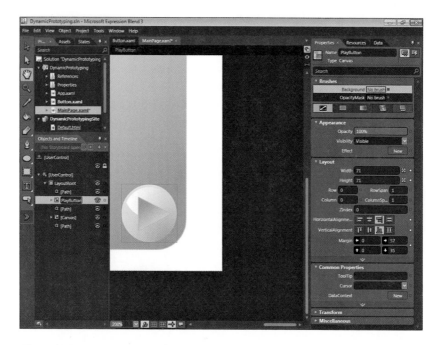

Figure B.9   Renaming an element in Objects and Timelines.

We name elements for two primary purposes. First, it's a great way to organize objects in an application and make it easy for others (and yourself) to figure out where crucial elements of an application are. Second, it enables you to target those objects from your code-behind file. In order for C# to work with an element you've defined in XAML, it must have a Name defined.

XAML LAYOUT CONTAINERS

Each of the six layout containers available in a Silverlight application can be placed and drawn using the containers from the Expression Blend tools panel. In addition, you can create these containers using XAML code. Each of these containers has a unique type of behavior that makes it suitable for positioning and arranging elements a certain way.

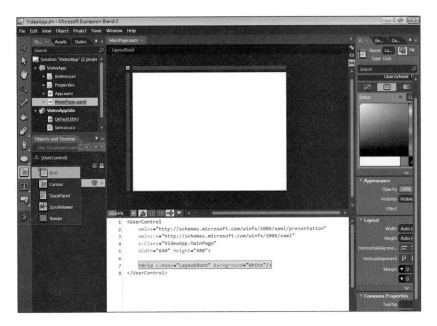

Figure B.10   *Adding a Grid layout container.*

GRID

```
<Grid x:Name="Grid1"></Grid>
```

The Grid container can contain several child elements of most any type, and as the name states, can divide its area into a virtual grid that allows items to be individually scaled and anchored to certain areas of the Grid.

In addition, a Grid uses "relative" style positioning, which means that the position of a child element will change on screen as the Grid scales (proportionally or non-proportionally) but can be set to either scale or simply reposition itself the same distance from the corners and sides of the Grid itself. Here's an example of how several elements will scale within a Grid when the "star-sized" option is set for all sides (see Figure B.11).

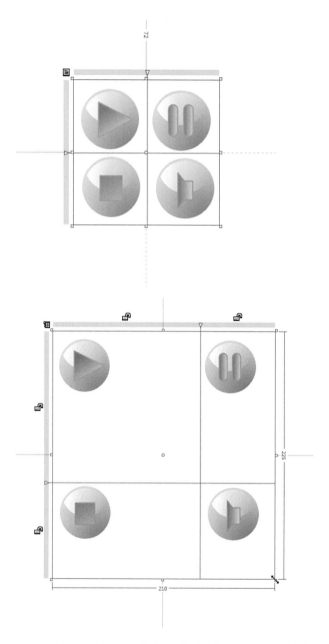

Figure B.11 Using Grid's "relative" type positioning to alter the position of child elements as a Grid scales.

APPENDIX B I WHAT IS XAML?

CANVAS

```
<Canvas x:Name="Canvas1"></Canvas>
```

Like the Grid, the Canvas can contain multiple child elements of different types. The key difference is that elements within a Canvas are absolutely positioned, fixed at a specific set of coordinates. Scaling a Canvas has no effect on the position of its child elements, and in certain cases, the boundaries of a Canvas can actually be smaller than the area occupied by its children. The advantage of working with a Canvas is knowing that elements within it will remain at a fixed position, unaffected by other elements in the same Canvas or by the behavior of the Canvas itself.

> TIP:
> If you have experience working with absolute positioning in Cascading Style Sheets (CSS), the positioning behavior of elements in a Canvas will be familiar to you.

STACKPANEL

```
<StackPanel x:Name="StackPanel1"></StackPanel>
```

Unlike the Grid or Canvas, child elements in a StackPanel do not have a specific position, but instead fall in line behind each other. Removing an element causes the other elements to collapse in and occupy the free space, and transforming the StackPanel itself rearranges the child elements based on the available space and orientation. Much like text flowing in a box, child elements conform to the shape and area of the StackPanel that contains them, flowing either horizontally or vertically.

In Figure B.12, we see the four player buttons shown in a StackPanel. Notice that removing or hiding the Stop button causes the other buttons (especially the Mute button) to collapse in and occupy the free space.

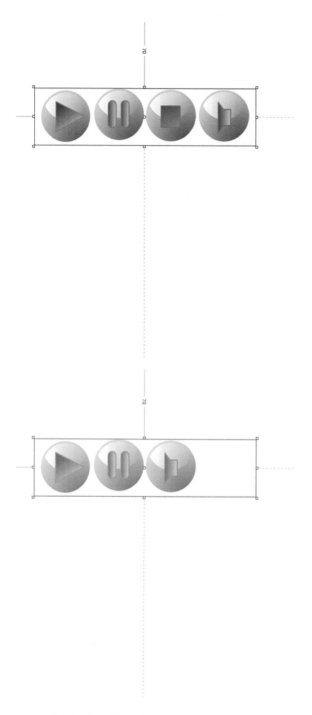

Figure B.12   *StackPanels compensate for objects that are added or removed.*

SCROLLPANEL

```
<ScrollPanel x:name="ScrollPane1"></ScrollPanel>
```

The ScrollPanel container lets you scroll a single child element within the viewable area set by the size of the ScrollPanel. This is ideal if you want to confine a large amount of content to a smaller area within your application, and allow users to scroll vertically through that content. Unlike the Grid, Canvas, or StackPanel, the ScrollPanel can only contain a single child element. However, you can still have the ScrollPanel include several elements by grouping them into a single container, such as a Grid or Canvas.

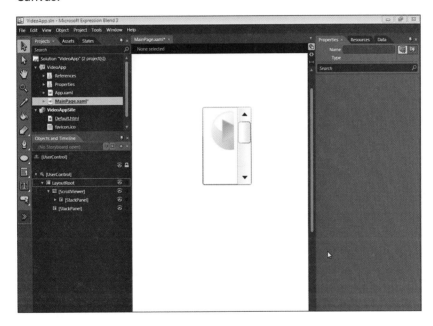

Figure B.13 *Grouping elements in a Scroll Viewer.*

BORDER

The Border control, like the ScrollPanel, can only contain a single child element. However, that is where the similarity ends. The Border control has the unique ability to apply different values for all four corner radiuses and border widths on all four sides. This makes it ideal for creating items such as content panels and navigation tabs without having to create and merge shapes from Expression Design or other design applications (see Figure B.14).

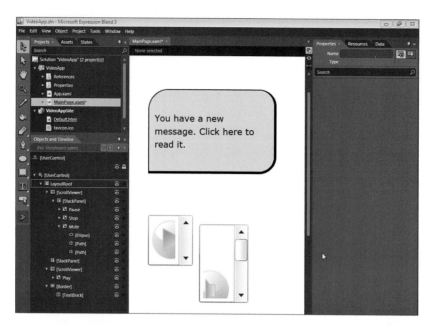

Figure B.14 *The Border control in action. Note the varying border widths and corner radiuses that create the alert box's shape.*

XAML AND CODE-BEHIND FILES

You may wonder why each XAML document in your application (as seen in the Project explorer) has a companion code file. More importantly, what does this code-behind file do that XAML can't? Where does one begin and the other end?

NOT-SO-DISTANT COUSINS

You may be surprised to know that C# and XAML ultimately can represent many of the same things in a Silverlight application. You can create a canvas, shape, or storyboard (to name a few) in XAML by using the tools and panels in Expression Blend, or using pure C# in the Code Editor.

The same Ellipse, for instance, can be created in XAML or in C#, and the XAML and C# code excerpts shown next will both create the same thing when the application is compiled.

XAML:

```
<Ellipse x:Name="myEllipse" Width="80" Height="80" />
```

C#:

```
Ellipse myEllipse = new Ellipse();
myEllipse.Width=80;
myEllipse.Height=80;
```

You can also further manipulate, duplicate, or control an object (such as a graphic or custom control) drawn with one of the tools using code in your code-behind file. Similarly, if you create certain structures in a code-behind file (such as a property that sets speed or color for a custom control) in C#, you can often manipulate these custom properties using the panels in the Expression Blend workspace.

Truth be told, C# and XAML elements become the same things when you build your application. So, why can't we just do everything in XAML, or along the same lines, why not just do everything in XAML or in C#? It comes down to three things: Who, What, and When:

- **Who:** What type of person is building the application? The beauty of the Silverlight workflow is that designers, developers, and every skill set in between can contribute to the process. Designers may feel more comfortable working visually or using a markup-based language such as XAML to build an application, whereas a developer or programmer will be more used to working in pure code (such as C#). There is also the skill set in between (affectionately referred to as the "dev-igner") who may utilize both methods in Silverlight development.

  The Design view, XAML, and C# offer building blocks for nearly every type of contributor in the prototyping, setup, and completion of a Silverlight application.

- **What:** What design or development task are you trying to achieve? Although XAML can do many things, there are certain tasks that are either exclusive to or better left to C#. This includes connecting to databases and web services, adding scoring logic for a game, or enabling a series of buttons to control a video stream. Similarly, there are certain things that are just faster and clearer when done with Blend/XAML.

- **When:** XAML and the Blend tools are most effective at what we call "design-time." Design time is the process of building and setting up an application and all of its various pieces before it is built and deployed in a browser. However, if you are creating a game in which the action will be different for each player and each level, this is impossible to do completely at design time.

With code, however, we can manipulate, add to, and control the application at *run-time*, the point at which the application has already been built, deployed, and is in use. Code can add things to the screen, control user interactivity, and account for various scenarios, even if the application has been built and is already running.

C

WHAT IS C#?

As you dive into the planning, prototyping, and development of Silverlight applications, you will undoubtedly be immersed in the many facets that compose them. Graphics, audio and video files, and information (such as data from an XML file or database) make up the complex fabric of any application.

The thread that stitches it all together, however, is often the lines of code flowing in your application's code-behind files and other files in your solution folder. Silverlight applications are commonly developed in C#, a programming language that is part of the Microsoft .NET framework and one of the most-utilized object-oriented programming languages in software and web application development.

Blend 3 Can Also Do Code!

Expression Blend includes a robust code-editor window that provides color coding, code hinting via "Intellisense" (found in more intense software-development applications such as Visual Studio), and seamless integration with the design environment.

But, I'm Not A Programmer...

Although the subject of programming languages may sound daunting (and C# more like something a modern classical music composer would use than a designer), an understanding of this crucial concept in Silverlight application development will further your ability to conceive, develop, and plan projects of any scale.

Before cutting to the chase, however, it helps to understand a little background of C# and programming languages in general. If you've worked with client-side scripting languages such as JavaScript, or other programming languages such as Java, you will find many similarities as you read through this chapter. If not, you may be surprised at how intuitive and accessible C# can be, even if you've never worked with a robust programming language before.

WHAT IS C#?

C# is a programming language that is part of the .NET family of languages, and is used to develop applications for the desktop, websites and applications, and Silverlight and WPF applications. You will find C# in the code-behind (.cs) files that are paired with XAML documents in your Silverlight or WPF project, as well as in standalone files in your solution. This code controls the behavior and appearance of objects, as well as the handling of data within your application.

The versatility of C#, as well as the .NET framework itself, provides programmers with the tools necessary to create Rich Internet Applications (RIAs), database-driven websites, and traditional Windows applications (such as WinForms applications).

In the context of Silverlight or WPF applications, C# can play a role as minimal as wiring up buttons and creating basic interactivity, to enabling full-blown communication with databases, web services, and the creation of complex games.

C# is an object-oriented programming (OOP) language and therefore shares many features with other staple programming languages, such as Visual Basic (VB), C++, and Java. However, C# incorporates many unique characteristics that make it versatile enough for the rapid development of applications in a variety of scenarios.

Before going into some of the syntax and features of C#, let's discuss where it comes from, and what it's capable of.

A BIT ABOUT OBJECT-ORIENTED PROGRAMMING (OOP)

The features, concepts, and principles of object-oriented programming are the foundation for how most software and web applications are developed, and transcend any specific language or platform. The goal is versatility, flexibility, and the ability to create and classify objects that become the core building blocks of a program. These objects can ultimately be extended, transformed, and evolved.

A 50-foot view of the flexibility and features of object-oriented programming can go a long way in planning a project that will not just deliver today, but be ready for future expansion and evolution tomorrow. With that being said, the goal of OOP is often to create "plug-and-play" scenarios, where building blocks of an application can be easily reused in a number of situations, as well as upgraded or interchanged without having an adverse effect on the application as a whole.

For example, can we create a photo gallery application that could later be upgraded to include video clips? Is there a way to upgrade the components necessary without having to rewrite the foundation?

It may surprise you to know that these same considerations, concepts, and principles are not too different from how you would approach any planned project, whether it's building a house or designing an online photo gallery for a client.

MEASURE TWICE, CUT ONCE

Because web applications (as well as houses and photo galleries) will often expand or evolve, we always want to answer some key questions before starting any project:

1. What types of building blocks will I need to build my product? Can any/all of these be reused?

2. How do I build my product so I can upgrade/replace some of its parts without having to go back to the drawing board?

3. How do I expand and evolve my product without having to go back to the drawing board?

4. Will I be able to create variations of this product for different uses and scenarios later on without starting from scratch?

The concepts and principles of OOP (as well as the languages that support it) enable us to answer those questions in a number of creative ways. C# and the .NET framework can give us all the tools and foundation for flexibility, portability, and expansion when developing Silverlight applications.

Although the numerous principles and approaches of object-oriented programming are beyond the scope of this book, it's important to note a few key features. Let's get to know those features through something we all know and love: the automobile.

THE CAR PROJECT

Engineers who design and build automobiles have lots of things to consider before putting pen to paper (or mouse to screen). They have to think not only about the basics (drive, park, brake, and so on), but about the increasing number of add-on options that you can pack into that car. They have to also consider if their car will have any commonalities with other cars on the market so they can utilize existing parts and not have to design new ones. More importantly, if they want their car to become a popular model year after year, can they build it in such a way that the existing design can be easily expanded and built upon?

The prototyping phase becomes essential to the present and future success of the automobile, and a good designer/engineer (yes, that's you!) knows the capabilities of the technology involved so he or she can prototype a new car to (and even beyond) its potential.

Some key features of an object-oriented programming language can be best illustrated as follows if you're using the car analogy:

Frameworks and Libraries	Standard tools, materials, and principles that you use to build the foundation of your car. This could include common engine parts, assembly line machinery, and so on.	Standard libraries and utilities for developing your web application (such as those that compose the .NET framework). This could include objects for supporting media files, animation, and connecting to and manipulating data sources.

Classes and Objects	Blueprints that will be the basis for all the cars and parts you will create. A blueprint for a tire could be considered a class, and the tires made from that blueprint are considered objects.	A code blueprint you create to define building blocks of your application. For instance, a class could define a user control that is reused throughout your application to load and display JPEG thumbnail images.
Polymorphism	Imagine if the foundation of your automobile could be easily adapted to produce a truck, SUV, or compact car?	An object in your application is flexible enough to take on many forms—for instance, a media player that handles audio, video, and static images at different times.
Subclasses and Inheritance	A new blueprint based on the original that creates a variation of your car (sport edition, station wagon, luxury model), while inheriting all the base features of the original model.	A class that derives from one which already exists; perhaps a user control that derives from one that displays images, but can now also display video.
Properties	Your cars all share common properties that determine characteristics such as color, interior, and transmission type. The values for these, however, can be unique from car to car.	A user control in a complex game application is used to create many enemies that all have common features. However, each enemy can have unique color, size, and attack speed.
Methods	Behaviors that are common to all of your cars—park, drive, brake, and reverse.	Behavior that is common to several objects in your application—for instance, the ability of all storyboard controls to stop and play their respective animations.
Events	Actions that can occur in your car that yield responses. For instance, the "brake" event stops the car.	Common mouse behavior, such as clicks and mouseovers, are familiar events, and can trigger responses in your application (such as the stopping/playback of an animation).

DIVING DEEPER

With a bit of background on C# and object-oriented programming as a whole, it's time to look at C# in context of a Silverlight application. As you've probably seen, C# code exists in your application in code-behind files, standalone .cs files, and in rarer cases, integrated directly into XAML documents.

The first stop is to take a look at the primary code-behind file created when you generate a new Silverlight project.

THE ANATOMY OF A CODE-BEHIND FILE

Each significant XAML file in your project is created with a companion code-behind file; this file contains C# code that is necessary to set up and support that XAML file, and is also where you add any code necessary to control the appearance and behavior of objects in that XAML file.

You can think of this code-behind file as setting the stage for all of the things your application will need to do its job. You can add code in these files to create interactivity (such as making a button stop and play a timeline when clicked), control media objects such as video and audio, or pull data that your application will use and display.

Let's take a look at a typical code-behind file that supports your Silverlight application's primary XAML file (see Figure C.1).

NAMESPACES (ASSEMBLIES)

At the top of each code-behind file, you'll find several "using" statements, followed by unique paths known as *namespaces*. A namespace points to a code library (assembly) that provides essential tools for building your Silverlight application.

Some of these namespaces provide the very foundation that is necessary for all Silverlight applications, whereas others are required only when using specific types of objects or functionality within your application.

Think of namespaces as the tools and materials your application needs, very much in the same way that you'd need certain essential tools and materials available for a construction project.

Figure C.1 *Looking at a code-behind file in Expression Blend.*

PAGE CLASS

The *class* is the building block of your application, as well as all objects within your application. A class is a code blueprint used to create one or more objects of the same type, much like a blueprint can build one or several houses on a block in your neighborhood. The page class defines and encompasses your Silverlight application as a whole.

The concept of classes is covered in more detail later in this chapter.

CONSTRUCTOR (OR CONSTRUCTOR METHOD)

The *constructor* is a block of code that is run automatically when your application is run. The constructor is easily identifiable because it takes on the same name as your application. You typically add any code to the constructor that you want to run automatically when your application starts up (for instance, starting a storyboard animation).

The constructor is referred to as a *method*, a named block of code that defines some type of behavior inside of your application. As you develop your Silverlight application further, you'll add more methods to this file and others to create new functionality. However, the constructor is a required (and fixed) method that can be added to but not removed.

UNDERSTANDING EVENTS AND EVENT HANDLERS

Each and every day, the actions we carry out are driven by a series of call-and-response-style exchanges. If we receive a call from a co-worker about a project that's due, we react by carrying out a task to complete that project. If we see a car in front of us, we respond by pressing the brakes in our vehicle to avoid a collision.

The flow of your Silverlight application is driven in very much the same way. Users click a mouse button and an animation starts in response, or perhaps they make a selection from a drop-down menu, and information related to their choice is displayed on the screen.

This call-and-response system is defined in C# through the use of events and event handlers.

Events are actions that can trigger responses—these can be user-driven actions such as mouse clicks or key presses, or non-user-driven events such as the loading of data or the end of an animation sequence.

Just about every object in a Silverlight application, from a simple shape to a custom control, is capable of triggering events. You can tell objects to listen for and trigger events using the panels in the Blend design environment, or using C# in the code view.

In Figure C.2, a standard UI button has been added to the main canvas. You can tell that button to expect and react to a click from the Events view of the Properties panel.

Here, we have asked the button to listen for a Click event, and respond by running code in an event handler named myButton_onClick. This event handler will need to be created in the code-behind file.

You can also set up the button using pure code, as shown in Figure C.3.

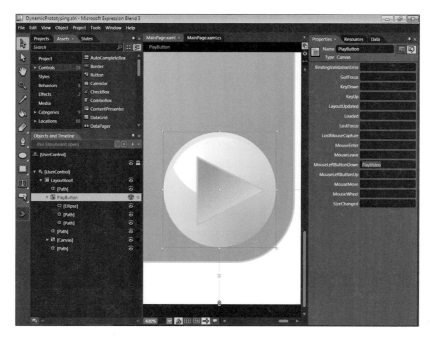

Figure C.2   *Using the Events category in the Properties panel to tell a button what to do after it has been clicked.*

Figure C.3   *Setting up a play video action in pure code.*

This has the identical effect as assigning the event from the panels, except one is created in XAML, and the other in pure C#. As with the first approach, a block of code named myButton_onClick will need to be created in your code-behind file for the whole thing to actually work (and not generate a build error).

Event handlers are pre-defined code responses to specific events that occur in your application. For instance, we can create an event handler that stops a timeline when a specific button is clicked.

An event handler is defined in your code-behind file as a method (a named block of code). You tie an event handler to a specific object and an event using the panels in the Blend design environment, or using C# in your code-behind file.

In the case of the button shown earlier, you can create a myButton_onClick event handler that will tell your application what to do when that button is clicked (see Figure C.4).

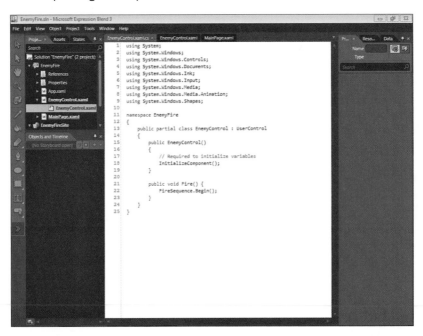

Figure C.4   Looking at the code-behind file we can see how an event handler is enabled.

The event handler will stop a storyboard named MyAnimation when, and if, the button to which it's assigned is clicked.

> TIP:
> When assigning events and event handlers in the design environment, Blend makes your life easy by automatically creating the appropriately named event handler for you in the code-behind file. All you'll need to do is add some code to it to determine what happens when it's fired.

TARGETING OBJECT METHODS AND PROPERTIES

Every object in your Silverlight application, whether it is an ellipse, a button, or a piece of data, has methods and properties—things it can do, and things that describe it.

For example, a storyboard is built with methods such as Begin(), Pause(), and Stop() that control its playback behavior. These are methods that every storyboard has that we can rely on at any time. If we are trying to call any of these methods using C#, we use the storyboard's name, followed by a dot, and the name of the method we want to call, as follows:

```
MyStoryboard.Begin();
```

This "dot" syntax is used religiously in C# (and most other languages), and enables us to target a specific object and, in turn, one or many of its methods and properties.

Similarly, every object has properties, or values that describe the object. These properties can be used to set and describe dimensions, such as width and height, color, transparency, visibility, and more. If you have a canvas within your application that you'd like to toggle on and off, you can use its Visibility property and a bit of C# to do so, as follows:

```
Canvas1.Visibility = Visibility.Collapsed;
```

You are hiding the canvas by assigning a value of "Collapsed" to its Visibility property. As you may have guessed, this not only *describes* but also *controls* its visibility.

At times, methods and properties may seem to do the same thing—but what's important to remember is that methods contain behavior, whereas properties contain values.

To summarize, methods establish an object's abilities and behaviors, while properties contain descriptive values. Storyboards, UI controls, media objects, and even your own custom controls can and do have pre-defined methods and properties. You can even create your own methods and properties to suit a specific purpose in your Silverlight application if an existing one just won't do.

VARIABLES, OBJECTS, AND DATA TYPES

There will undoubtedly be times when it's necessary to store, track, and manipulate information in your Silverlight application. From keeping scores in a game, to tracking the number of photos in a photo gallery and beyond, we will use C# to create and manage pieces of data that we'll rely on.

One of the most basic ways to store data is through the creation of variables, named *containers*, in which we can store simple values. We can easily update variables to compensate for continuously changing conditions in our application. For example, we may need a variable to store a score in a Silverlight shooting game we've created.

Fortunately for us, creating a variable is a one-line affair, as follows:

```
int score = 0;
```

We've created a variable named score, and assigned it a starting value of 0. We preceded the name of the variable with the type of information it's going to store—in this case, *int*, or an integer. This is referred to as data typing, which is essential to memory management as well as error checking to ensure that we don't get a character (or any other unrelated value) where a number is expected.

We can easily update our score later on in the game as we earn points, and doing so is pretty much as simple as creating the variable in the first place:

```
score = 5000; //Set to 5000
score += 5000; //Add 5000 to existing score, whatever it is
score -= 200; //Subtract 200 from the existing score
```

You'll notice that we omitted the data type (int) when referring back to our variable. This is OK, as the data type only needs to be established when the variable is created.

CASTING

Sounds pretty Hollywood, but *casting* is simply referring to the practice of transforming one data type into another for a specific purpose. We may want to give the player a bonus by adding 20% to his or her score—for this, we actually reach outside of standard integers and are playing with decimal points.

To make our score play nicely with the new math, we can do the following:

```
float bonusScore = .20 * (float)score;
```

Here we've created an expression that calculates 20% of our current score for a total bonus amount and assigns it to a new variable called bonusAmount.

There are actually quite a few different ways to convert data types other than the preceding example. You can also use the Convert class to convert between different base data types, as follows:

```
float bonusScore = .20 * (float)score;
int intBonusScore = System.Convert.ToInt32(bonusScore);
```

METHODS

A *method* is a named block of code, which contains some type of functionality that ideally can be called and used as many times as necessary in an application. This could contain the code that calculates a score, stops and plays a timeline, or creates new players in a Silverlight game. Methods are the building blocks of functionality in an application, no matter how simple or complex, and in C#, every line of code is executed in the context of a method.

Once defined, a method can be called once or many times depending on its role; some methods are designed especially as responses to events in an application (event handlers).

If you've worked with other programming languages before such as ActionScript, or even scripting languages such as JavaScript, you may already be familiar with methods (referred to as "functions" in some other languages).

You can define methods in your code-behind files to add functionality to your application; in some cases, methods are defined for you (such as the constructor discussed earlier), or automatically when setting up event/ event handlers in Silverlight.

The following structure defines a method in C#:

```
public void PrintHello() {
      MessageArea.Text = "Hello!";
}
```

However, a method is not called automatically when you create it; you'll need to call it later on somewhere in your code to actually run it, like so:

```
PrintHello();
```

For more versatility, a method can be defined with parameters, which allow values to be passed into a method each time it's run. Because parameters are not values themselves, but rather "placeholders" for values, you can pass in different information each time a method is run to make it as reusable as necessary.

The following method calculates a percentage, and takes two parameters, as follows:

```
public void  GetPercentage(double num1, double num2) {
      double perc = num2/num1;
      MessageArea.Text = perc.toString();
}
```

You can now call this method as needed and pass it any two values, like so:

```
GetPercentage(450.5,12.35);
GetPercentage(12500, 3500.5);
```

> TIP:
> You'll notice that the two parameters you defined in the previous method were preceded by a data type. Parameters also need to

be typed, just like variables. This way, the method knows what type of information each parameter will contain.

TO RETURN OR NOT TO RETURN

Methods not only can run a series of statements, but can also return a value if necessary. Take the second statement in the preceding GetPercentage method, for example:

```
MessageArea.Text = perc.toString();
```

This takes a calculated value and displays it in a text field named MessageArea within your application. However, the value is not stored anywhere that we can reuse it or reassign it, and becomes intangible.

What if we needed that value for multiple purposes: as part of a bigger equation, to assign to a variable, or display in multiple places in the application? We can instead have a method *return* a value so it can be assigned or used somewhere else.

To do this, we make two adjustments to the method: First, we assign a return type that tells C# what type of value the function will return. The return type of void (currently assigned to our method) means that the method returns nothing. Instead, we'll adjust this to say that our method will return a decimal point value, as follows:

```
public double GetPercentage(double num1, double num2) {
        double perc = num2/num1;
        MessageArea.Text = perc.toString();
}
```

Second, we'll need to include a return statement in our method that "pushes" the value back out to whatever needs it:

```
public double GetPercentage(double num1, double num2) {
        double perc = num2/num1;
        return perc;
}
```

Now, we can take the percentage value and use it in a variety of ways with fewer limitations:

```
private double savingsPercentage = GetPercentage(200.00,15.00);
MessageArea.Text = GetPercentage(200.00,15.00).toString();
```

It's important to note that event handlers, methods that respond to events in an application, must always have a return type of void. You can, however, always call one method from inside another, so if you wanted to calculate a percentage on a button click, you could accomplish that like so:

```
private void myButton_onMouseLeftButtonDown(object sender,
	MouseEventArgs args) {

MessageArea.Text = GetPercentage(200.00,15.00).toString();

}
```

To summarize, methods are named blocks of code that perform an action, return a value, or both, and are the foundation for any functionality in an application. All statements within an application exist in the context of methods.

PUTTING IT ALL TOGETHER: UNDERSTANDING CLASSES

In programming, the ability to create reusable chunks of code is the key to creating streamlined and easy-to-manage applications. You've seen a bit of this when exploring the concept of methods; however, we may need to create something that includes several methods, properties, and other characteristics.

The class is the foundation of C# and other programming languages, and is how you create a code "blueprint" that can be used to create one or many objects of the same type.

In a Silverlight, your entire application is a class, as well as the objects you draw and place, custom controls, and the core UI controls. In this context, a class serves as the master container for an application, and will include other classes that define the objects that compose your application. A typical application consists of classes that are part of the .NET framework (such as those that create graphics or storyboards) and those that you create yourself (such as custom controls or utility classes for managing data).

Reverting back to the automobile analogy from earlier in the section, you can think of a specific model as defined by a class, and each of the parts (tires, engine, and drivetrain) as objects created from other classes.

Together, all of these different types of classes come together under one roof to make up the car as a whole (see Figure C.5).

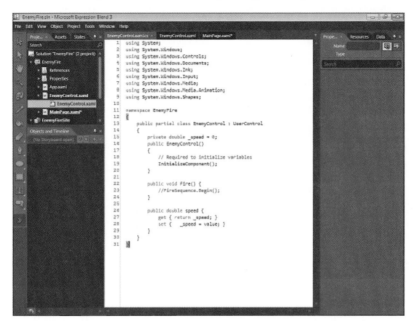

Figure C.5   *Looking at classes and their specific parts (members).*

A ready-to-view example of a class definition is the application class created when you start a new Silverlight application (see Figure C.6).

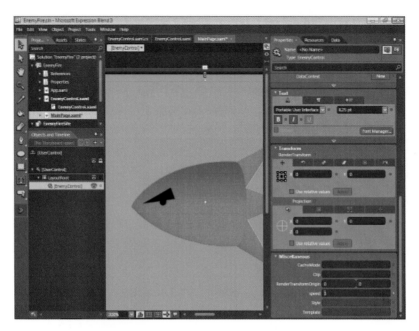

Figure C.6   *Default class definitions for a Silverlight application.*

This contains any namespaces (assemblies) that are necessary to build the application, and an explicit class definition that contains class members such as methods, properties, events, and so on.

PUTTING IT ALL TOGETHER: METHODS

In the context of a class, methods determine the abilities and behavior of a specific type of object. For instance, an EnemyControl() class that is used to create enemies in a game may include methods for motion, firing, attack, and defense.

This behavior will then be common to all objects created from the EnemyControl () class. Regardless of the number, placement, and name of the enemy object, it will have the same methods as determined by the original class definition. In a Silverlight application, these can be created in the design view (through drag and drop), or programmatically using C# (see Figure C.7).

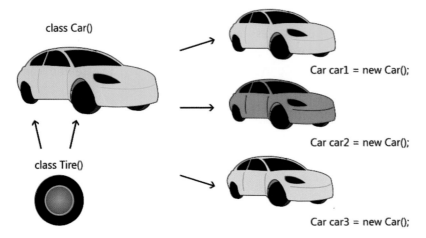

class Car()

Car car1 = new Car();

Car car2 = new Car();

class Tire()

Car car3 = new Car();

Figure C.7   We can create classes programmatically using C# in addition to using the design view.

In addition, every class serves as a type, and we can data type new objects similar to how we do with variables and simple base types like string, double, and int:

```
public EnemyControl enemy = new EnemyControl();
```

Figure C.8 is an example of a custom control named EnemyControl that, as with all custom controls, is nothing more than a new class that your Silverlight application uses.

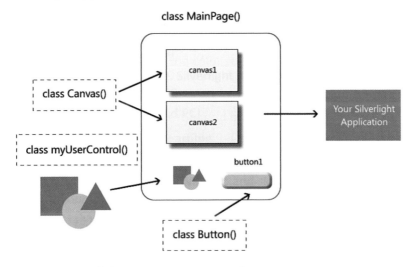

class MainPage()

canvas1

class Canvas()

canvas2

Your Silverlight Application

class myUserControl()

button1

class Button()

Figure C.8   Defining a new custom control.

In addition to the mandatory constructor is a method called Fire(). This method is not just part of the class definition, but will be part of every EnemyControl object created within your application. With that being said, every instance of an EnemyControl, regardless of when it was created, can have a Fire() method called from it, as follows:

```
EnemyControl enemy1 = new EnemyControl;
EnemyControl enemy2 = new EnemyControl;
EnemyControl enemy3 = new EnemyControl;

enemy1.Fire();
enemy2.Fire();
enemy3.Fire();
```

> TIP:
> A method's parameters and their respective data types establish what is known as the method's signature. In certain scenarios, you can create more than one method by the same name, and each can have a unique signature that makes it possible for them to co-exist in the same space. A common C# technique known as overloading enables you to define and switch between methods of the same name in different scenarios where different numbers and types of parameters can be used.

PUTTING IT ALL TOGETHER: PROPERTIES

Much like a class method determines the behavior for a series of objects, properties in a class determine characteristics that are common to a series of objects. Referring back (again) to our car analogy, we could say that color, horsepower, and transmission type all would be classified as properties of the Car class.

Therefore, although all cars feature these three characteristics, the values from car to car may be very different. One car may be tan, 150hp, and have automatic transmission. The other (which you'd more likely leave in the driveway for all neighbors to see) could be fire-engine red, 260hp, and feature a nifty six-speed manual sport transmission.

In the context of a Silverlight application, we can create properties for a custom class, custom control, or even the application itself using what are known as getter/setter methods.

In the EnemyControl() class (custom control) created earlier, you may decide to add a property that determines the attack speed of each enemy. To do so, the syntax would be as follows:

```
public double speed {
      get {}
      set {}
}
```

Here, the get method returns the value when speed is called, and set updates the value when called. Values are often stored in private variables that are accessible only to the getter/setter:

```
private double _speed = 0;
public double speed {
      get { return _speed }
      set {    speed = value }
}
```

Now, to access the speed of any enemy object, you would reference it like so:

```
public EnemyControl enemy1 = new EnemyControl();
MyTextArea.Text = (string)enemy1.speed; //Displays 0
enemy1.speed = 100;
MyTextArea.Text = (string)enemy1.speed; //Displays 100
```

C# knows, when speed is being read, to use the getter to return the value. When it is being assigned a new value, it uses the setter to update the value inside of the object.

The cool thing about defining properties in a Silverlight application is you can easily update those values in the Blend Design environment using the Properties panel on the right. Public properties will reveal themselves as type-in fields under the Miscellaneous panel on the right.

This makes it possible for anyone to customize an instance of a custom control regardless of their code comfort level.

> NOTE:
> This is only available when working with custom control instances created in the Design environment—programmatically created custom control instances can only be updated by C# at runtime (while the application is being viewed in the browser/ desktop).

PUTTING IT ALL TOGETHER: EVENTS AND EVENT HANDLERS

Discussed earlier in this chapter, events and event handlers provide the call-response structure necessary to make things happen in your movie, especially in regards to user-driven activity such as mouse clicks and key presses. As you've seen, you can assign an event and event handler to most objects in your Silverlight application (such as a button) to make it do something.

However, what's more empowering is the ability to assign events and event handlers globally to a specific class of objects. For instance, you may want each of the EnemyControl() instances created in your game to change direction or speed when it's clicked on. Because you may have an unknown number of enemies in your game (many of which will be created programmatically), it makes more sense to assign the event handlers within the EnemyControl() class itself. This way, each EnemyControl() will automatically be "born" knowing how to respond when it receives a mouse click (see Figure C.9).

Figure C.9   Creating new EnemyControl() instances with code.

Here, the event handler is defined as a private method (accessible only from within the class itself) within the class. The event handler is wired up to the Click event from within the class constructor, as follows:

```
this.MouseLeftButtonDown +=new MouseEventHandler(thisEnemy_onClick);
```

Although it's not necessary to delegate the event handler within the constructor, this approach makes sure that the enemy is ready to be clicked as soon as it's created and available. Now each enemy in your game, whether it's dragged and dropped to a canvas in the Design view or added programmatically, will increase speed when clicked (no further work is necessary!).

SUBCLASSES AND INHERITANCE

A powerful and essential approach in class-building is the concept of *subclasses* (sometimes referred to as *derived* or *child* classes)—classes that are derived from an existing (parent) class. This makes it possible to create a new class that inherits all the abilities and characteristics of another class, while still having the flexibility to add unique members to the new class.

It also speeds up development by avoiding the need to "reinvent the wheel" if two classes are similar or rooted in the same code foundation.

Inheritance is used in a Silverlight application before you even draw your first ellipse or add your first canvas. A look at the application's class definition reveals this:

```
public partial class MySilverlightApplication: UserControl {…
```

Here, the class name for your new application is followed by UserControl, which tells C# that this new class is actually based on the core .NET class UserControl. Doing so avoids having to re-program all the base functionality that makes your Silverlight application do what it does.

Inheritance is why most objects in your movie share many of the same abilities right out of the box, such as the following:

- The capability of receiving and responding to events, such as clicks, mouseovers, and so on.

- Core properties such as width, height, visibility, and so on.

- The ability to be displayed on the screen or display and contain other visual objects.

A BETTER ENEMY?

If you wanted to create a different kind of enemy in your game, you could easily create a new custom control. Because all custom controls are based on UserControl, we know that a new enemy class would be able to receive clicks and have the same core properties for width, height, and visibility. However, what happens to all the cool custom methods and properties we defined on our original enemy, such as speed, the ability to fire, or the behavior of speeding up when clicked?

If starting over with a new custom control, we'd likely have to leave those behind; however, inheritance enables us to base a new enemy from our original one. The new enemy can then inherit all the behaviors and characteristics of the original, while leaving room to define some new shiny behavior that is unique to the new enemy.

In Silverlight, you can do this by selecting a base control when you create a new custom control. In code, you can do this by modifying the Base Class type in the class definition, as shown here:

```
public partial class SuperEnemy: Enemy
```

Now, when creating a new SuperEnemyControl(), you can still call the methods and properties of the original, like so:

```
public SuperEnemyControl superEnemy1 = new SuperEnemyControl();
superEnemy1.Fire();
superEnemy1.speed= 200;
```

However, SuperEnemyControl now has a unique method that is not present in the parent EnemyControl class, as follows:

```
superEnemy1.Shields();
```

The best part of all of this is that any improvements to the EnemyControl class will also trickle down to the SuperEnemyControl class and all the objects based on it!

SUMMARY

C# is a powerful object-oriented programming language that is the basis for all functionality in a Silverlight application. Silverlight applications use a subset of Microsoft's established .NET framework, which provides lots of functionality right out of the box. However, the flexibility of C# lets you define new classes and extend existing ones to create code that suits any application in any situation.

Even if you are not a code-head by nature, understanding the basics can allow you to map out and streamline the functionality and structure of a Silverlight application.

D

WHAT IS WPF?

With the rise of Rich Internet Applications and technologies such as Silverlight, it is clear that the robust abilities and flow of desktop applications has heavily influenced web applications, and users expect more than ever in the Web space. However, the reverse has also become true: The slick, highly interactive and animated user interface eye candy often found on Websites and Web applications has raised the bar for desktop software user interface design. In the words of a good friend mine and acclaimed user-experience designer: "I know it's a *calculator*, but does it have to *look* like a calculator?"

Over the last several years, the traditional method of developing Windows applications has been via the Windows Forms API, which sits atop the .NET Framework. However, the Windows Forms (or *WinForms*, for short) environment has some clear limitations in terms of creating slick user interfaces, and relies heavily on the use of the default Windows system controls as opposed to the highly customizable UI we're accustomed to seeing in web applications.

Windows Presentation Foundation (WPF) was introduced to solve the potential limitations of traditional WinForms applications by providing a way to create rich graphical user interfaces for desktop applications that continue to utilize the languages, skills, and overall logic that has been a core part of the .NET Framework and Windows application development as a whole.

INTRODUCING WINDOWS PRESENTATION FOUNDATION (WPF)

Windows Presentation Foundation, referred to more commonly as *WPF*, is a system for rendering graphics and media for the creation of high-end user interfaces. In addition, WPF takes advantage of .NET application development features, such as security, media handling, and data binding. WPF supersedes traditional user interface APIs (such as WinForms) by providing advanced graphics features, such as gradient rendering and transparency, animation, advanced media control, and 3-D graphics rendering.

WPF is designed to take advantage of modern graphics hardware, which provides a broader range of possibilities for creating UI than historically has been possible. Because WPF is built on the .NET Framework, developers can take advantage of WPF's capabilities while utilizing the same tools and languages they are accustomed to when building WinForms and WebForms applications.

Most of all, WPF shares the same presentation framework features as Silverlight, including the ability to develop with XAML. This means you have the same capabilities for creating graphics, including media, storyboard-based animation, and much more.

DEVELOPING WPF APPLICATIONS: TOOLS AND LANGUAGES

WPF shares the same development tools and languages that you've become accustomed to when creating Silverlight applications; this includes the Expression Studio suite of applications: Expression Blend and Visual Studio. Not surprisingly, .NET family languages such as XAML, C#, and VB play the same vital role in WPF application development as they do in Silverlight application development.

There are some key differences in the available features and environment when moving between Silverlight and WPF—therefore, the Expression Blend workspace (and XAML itself) will differ slightly when choosing WPF applications as your project type.

Figure D.1 *Panels specific to WPF features, such as the Triggers panel, are only available when WPF applications is your project type.*

WHO USES WPF?

WPF is quickly becoming the choice way of creating Windows desktop applications, so you'll find many developers who have already created applications on the .NET Framework migrating to WPF in favor of traditional WinForms applications.

Because WPF is part of the .NET Framework and shares skills, tools, and languages with Silverlight and WebForms, it is also potentially within reach for web or RIA developers. It is likely you'll find that more firms and independent developers are extending their projects beyond the browser and implementing them as WPF applications.

Development firms such as Thirteen23 (www.thirteen23.com), Archetype (www.archetype.com), and Cynergy (www.cynergysystems.com) work in both spaces, and WPF applications such as Thirteen23's blu are a great example of how web pizzazz can meet software development savvy.

Thirteen23 leveraged WPF to create a rich, interactive desktop experience showcasing Twitter's web services (see Figure D.2).

Figure D.2   *Thirteen23's blu WPF application supports a number of more innovative features, including automatic URL shortening, in-line "twitpic" integration, and drag-drop photo uploading.*

WPF VERSUS SILVERLIGHT: WHAT'S THE DIFFERENCE?

WPF was built from the ground up to build rich experiences for Windows. WPF takes advantage of the full spectrum of functionally offered by the .NET framework and this allows it the ability to take full advantage of the operating system and hardware beyond what a plug-in-based runtime can do.

Although the features mentioned next are by no means a fully inclusive list, they point out some of the more obvious differences that would be encountered when moving from WPF to Silverlight (or vice versa):

Controls: WPF and Silverlight share a similar control metaphor. Both offer an extensive set of behaviors for rich experiences and business applications. The Visual State Manager, for example, which originally shipped in Silverlight, is now also available in WPF via the WPF Development Toolkit. Even though it is not yet possible to directly reuse it in one or the other platform with the majority of the controls, the trend seems to be maximizing recycling between both platforms.

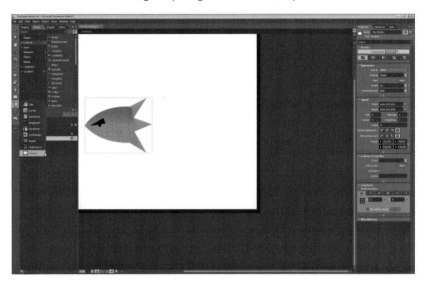

Figure D.3   The WPF workspace Features a number of additional layout containers such as the ViewBox and UniformGrid.

XAML: XAML within WPF and Silverlight applications tends to be the same on many levels. However, you'll notice some structural and elemental differences in WPF XAML. On the most basic level, WPF applications utilize the <Window> element as their root (as opposed to the UserControl found in Silverlight applications); in addition, many elements found in WPF XAML (such as WPF-exclusive controls) are not supported within Silverlight XAML. Inclusion of these elements in a Silverlight project will result in XAML errors.

Venue: Ask most anyone what the big difference between WPF and Silverlight is, and they'll say "WPF runs on the desktop; Silverlight runs in the browser." On a 50-foot level, this is true; however, the introduction of Silverlight 3's "out-of-browser" capabilities blurs these lines a bit. The choice on whether to utilize one or the other depends on your knowledge of your target audience, their environment, and what type of resources and features your application will need.

Platform Independence: Silverlight holds the advantage over its bigger brother here, and can play to a wider audience due to its ability to run across multiple browsers and operating systems. As long as a browser/system has the Silverlight plug-in installed, the user can take advantage of that Silverlight experience. WPF applications, however, are deployed much like a standard WinForms executable (.exe), and therefore are grounded to the Windows OS.

Hardware Acceleration: WPF has long had the ability to leverage a host system's hardware resources (such as graphics cards) for heavy lifting and computation when it comes to interface rendering. Recently, Silverlight 3 introduced hardware acceleration for many of its features too.

Data Binding: Although both WPF and Silverlight make use of data binding (such as XML data to a drop-down control), WPF includes some more advanced data-binding features, such as the inclusion of data sets, direct binding to XML, and xPath binding.

3-D Graphics Support: Silverlight 3 added support for 3-D Perspective transformation, which simulates 3-D by allowing transformation of 2-D objects along three axes. However, WPF still includes full support and manipulation of 3-D objects, including meshes, camera, and lighting transform. These properties can also be animated, opening up virtually unlimited possibilities for the inclusion of 3-D UI elements within an application.

Figure D.4   The Echo streaming music player developed by Thirteen23 (www. thirteen23.com) takes advantage of WPF's 3D capabilities to display album art, as well as WPF's integrated support for Windows Media for audio playback.

The Visual State Manager: Initially exclusive to Silverlight but now also available for WPF via the WPF Toolkit, the Visual State Manager allows for exacting control over states within a control or application. Manage changes in appearance on buttons, checkboxes, or just about any control, and create multiple visual states for applications as a whole. The VSM is accessible via code (for instance, using the VisualStateManager class in C#), or through the intuitive States panel in the Expression Blend workspace.

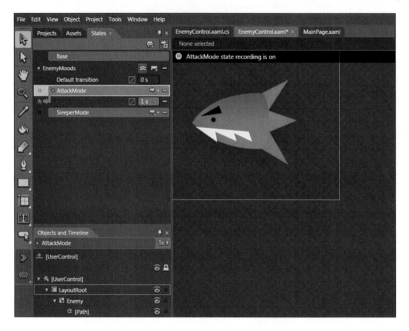

Figure D.5   Silverlight's Visual State Manager, shown in the Expression Blend workspace via the States panel.

DeepZoom: DeepZoom is a Silverlight exclusive, allowing for advanced zoom-in capabilities on images and graphics. Unlike a standard "stretch it as far as you can" approach that uses basic transformation and scaling, DeepZoom can work with high-resolution/high bit-depth images and re-render as necessary to provide crystal-clear fidelity even at high zoom depths.

Although creating DeepZoom experiences is beyond the scope of this book, it's definitely worth learning more about. Visit the official DeepZoom "Getting Started" site at silverlight.net/learn/quickstarts/deepzoom/.

PROTOTYPING WPF APPLICATIONS WITH SKETCHFLOW

You may have noticed that Expression Blend offers an option for creating a WPF SketchFlow Application, which is good news for software developers looking to leverage the powerful prototyping features of SketchFlow to illustrate and design potential desktop applications.

The environment, toolset, and process for prototyping a WPF application is nearly identical to that of a Silverlight application; however, some important considerations need to be made as you work with your team to "sketch" your future application, as follows:

- **Features:** Are there features in a WPF application that you can take advantage of that are normally unavailable within Silverlight or any other web-based application?

- **Venue:** Considering that a WPF application will be running on the desktop versus a browser, how will this affect the flow, appearance, and layout of screens within your prototype? How do you best depict features that include interaction with the OS and desktop?

- **Controls:** There are a number of controls available only to WPF applications; make sure to keep this in mind, as the included "Sketch"-styled controls available within the Assets panel depict a smaller number of controls than is actually available.

E

WHAT IS SILVERLIGHT?

The Web has evolved in such a way that users expect more than ever, and user experience has become the focal point of success or failure for most any Website or Web application. With the exit of static HTML pages, and the prevalence and evolution of technologies such as the Adobe Flash platform and AJAX (Asynchronous JavaScript and XML), the bar has been raised for how an application looks, feels, functions, and responds.

The birth of Rich Internet Applications heralds in an era where web applications and websites function more like desktop applications, and information is no longer a page refresh away, but is presented seamlessly while preserving the state and appearance of the interface. The purpose of RIAs is to integrate attractive user interface, data, functionality, and usefulness into a single destination that breaks the traditional page-click-page model that even the most sophisticated database-driven websites still employ today.

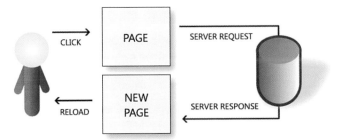

Figure E.1   The traditional page request model means that each request for information reloads the page/interface for a not-so-seamless experience.

For designers and developers, this means having the tools necessary to not only build these types of applications from prototype to product, but in some cases to repurpose products and information that they've already built in the past.

The introduction of the Silverlight platform and the Expression Studio line of applications does exactly that—providing designers, information architects, and user interface developers a platform on which to collaborate and build, and developers a way to utilize their existing skills to build and deploy a final product.

THE SILVERLIGHT PLATFORM AND PLAYER

The Silverlight Player (also referred to as the Silverlight *runtime*) is a cross-browser, cross-platform plug-in that enables users to view Rich Internet Applications created with Expression Blend, Visual Studio, or any application that publishes to the Silverlight platform. Silverlight applications are built upon an optimized, compacted subset of Microsoft's .NET Framework, which provides programmers with coded solutions and libraries for handling common tasks such as media playback, rendering user interface and controls, data handling, and database connectivity.

Similar to other technologies such as Adobe's Flash Player, Silverlight can create slick user interfaces, stream video, and load and manage real-time data and provide the complex interactivity needed for games and full-blown web applications.

Silverlight applications are published as .xap files, which are packages that contain the resource files, compiled code, and markup necessary for the Silverlight plug-in to render and run your application.

The Silverlight Architecture is composed of two primary components: the Silverlight .NET Framework and the Core Presentation Framework. The Silverlight .NET Framework is an optimized subset of Microsoft's .NET Framework, and provides core components and base class libraries, data integration, networking, garbage collection (for memory management), and the Common Language Runtime (CLR).

The Core Presentation Framework includes all UI-centric features, such as user input, vector graphics, text, media handling, and of course, Xtensible Application Markup Language (XAML) for specifying how the user interface will be rendered.

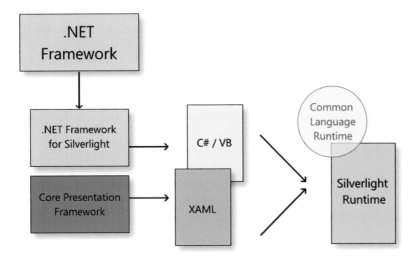

Figure E.2   The Silverlight architecture is composed of the Silverlight .NET Framework and the Core Presentation Framework.

SILVERLIGHT 3

Silverlight 3 is a huge move forward for the Silverlight platform, boasting many new features in the areas of workflow, video, graphics, and performance. These are apparent in Expression Blend 3, where Silverlight designers and developers will notice the addition of new tools and features to take full advantage of the new features available in Silverlight 3.

Some key Silverlight 3 features include the following:

- **Out of Browser Mode.** Silverlight 3 applications can run as desktop applications without the need for any additional plug-ins. And yes, it works on both Mac and PC!

- **Perspective 3D Transformation.** Now you can bring 2D objects into the 3D plane with Perspective 3D Transformation, opening up a world of interface possibilities with flip and skewed-plane style effects (to name a few).

- **Pixel Effects.** Previously only available in WPF applications, now real-time effects such as blurs and drop shadows can be rendered in XAML. Developers can also create their own effects.

- **New Animation Easing Effects.** In addition to the standard easing behavior available with earlier versions of Silverlight, advanced easing behaviors such as elastic and bounce can be added to your animations to provide more realistic motion.

- **Direct Binding Between Element Properties.** You can now bind together property values across objects in your Silverlight application, streamlining the relationship between elements and opening up new possibilities for data integration in your application.

- **Improved Video and Media.** New support for new media types such as H.264 and AAC encoding means increased fidelity of streaming and on-demand video. The addition of RAW audio/video pipeline support opens up Silverlight video to a host of new third-party codecs and encoding outside of the Silverlight runtime.

Figure E.3   The TED player, developed by Thirteen23 (www.thirteen23.com), leverages Silverlight features such as video streaming with full-screen playback, 3D perspective transforms, and an out-of-browser experience.

In addition, Silverlight 4 features were announced in November 2009 and include the following:

- **Printing support.** Comprehensive printing support now enables the creation of a virtual print view, enabling applications to deliver print-friendly documents.

- **More controls.** A full set of controls with more than 60 customizable, skinnable components makes it easy to build forms that can be sorted, resized, and validated. New controls include RichTextArea with hyperlinks, images, and editing.

- **Localization enhancements.** Localization enhancements with bidirectional text, right-to-left support and complex scripts such as Arabic, Hebrew, Thai, and 30 new languages.

- **Managed Extensibility Framework.** Managed Extensibility Framework supports building completely modular applications, allowing for fast startup and download, efficient development and testing, as well as agile customization and servicing.

- **Windows Communication Foundation RIA Services.** Windows Communication Foundation RIA Services introduces enterprise class networking and data access, allowing applications to work with any source of data and any server.

- **Enhanced animation.** Enhanced animation capabilities allow for more dynamic, interactive presentation of data in lists.

- **Webcam and microphone support.** Webcam and microphone support allow sharing of video and audio in applications such as chat and customer service.

- **Audio and video local recording capabilities.** Audio and video local recording capabilities capture RAW video without requiring server interaction, allowing new scenarios such as capturing voice or video to send in e-mail, or allowing the recording to be edited locally before saving.

- **Interaction models.** New features such as right-click and mouse wheel scrolling enable developers to add conventional desktop interaction models.

- **Application performance.** Silverlight 4 applications start quicker and run 200 percent faster than the equivalent Silverlight 3 applications with performance optimizations.

- **Multitouch.** Multitouch support enables a range of gestures and touch interactions to be integrated into user experiences.

- **Multicast networking.** Multicast networking enables enterprises to lower the cost of streaming broadcast events such as company meetings and training, with seamless interoperability with existing Windows Media Services streaming infrastructure.

- **Content protection.** Content protection now available for H.264 media through Silverlight DRM powered by PlayReady. Output protection for audio/video streams allowing content owners or distributors to ensure protected content is only viewed through a secure video connection.

- **Sandboxed applications.** Developers can place HTML within their application, enabling much tighter integration with content from web servers such as e-mail, help, and reports.

- **Notifictions.** Silverlight 4 provides support for desktop pop-up notification windows to easily provide real-time information and feedback to users using a common user interface metaphor.

- **Offline DRM.** Offline DRM extends the existing Silverlight DRM powered by PlayReady technology to work in a disconnected state, enabling users to view content and engage with a Silverlight application where and when they want. Protected content can be delivered with an embedded license so that users can go offline immediately and start enjoying their content.

- **Trusted applications.** Users can read and write files to their My Documents, My Music, My Pictures, and My Videos folders (or equivalent for non-Windows platforms), enabling applications to make local copies of reports and media files. COM automation enables access to devices and other system capabilities such as a Universal Serial Bus security card reader. Users can access other desktop programs such as Microsoft Office Excel to create a report. Group policy objects allow organizations to manage which applications are trusted. Comprehensive keyboard support in full-screen out-of-browser mode enhances kiosk and media applications. Enhancements to networking allow cross-domain access without a security policy file.

TOOLS AND WORKFLOW

When most of us think about the process of creating a new website or application, we can readily assume that we're going to use at least two–three applications for tasks such as graphics creation, writing markup, coding, and publishing (and everything in between).

With Expression Studio, the Silverlight workflow revolves around a tightly integrated suite of applications that handle everything from graphics creation and media encoding to prototyping and programming. Silverlight applications can be built wholly using Expression Design, Expression Encoder, and Expression Blend; however, the process will often be extended to website publishing with Expression Web, or additional development in Visual Studio.

In addition, designers will be glad to know that they can still include standard graphics applications such as Photoshop and Illustrator in the process. Both Expression Design and Expression Blend can directly import Photoshop and Illustrator files and convert each to their necessary XAML equivalent for Silverlight applications.

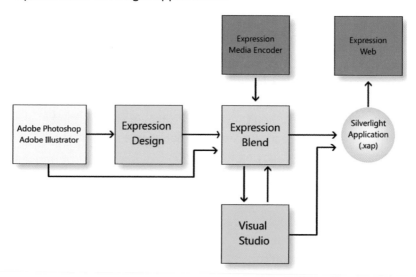

Figure E.4 *The tools and workflow involved in the creation of a Silverlight application.*

EXPRESSION BLEND

With its ability to work as a graphics and animation application, coding environment, and publishing tool. Expression Blend is at the heart of the Silverlight development process. Multiple views allow designers, UI architects, and developers to work in the way that suits them best with tools at hand for nearly every task.

Designers and front-end developers can build, preview, and fine-tune XAML with tools, panels, and menus as they do with common graphics and media applications. An integrated Code Editor is available for "wiring up" interface elements or just about any other coding task.

VISUAL STUDIO

Microsoft's Visual Studio is the pinnacle development tool for desktop, web, and mobile applications built on the .NET Framework and other Microsoft technologies. With extensive tools for writing, debugging, and managing code across several languages (including XAML), Visual Studio is often the preferred choice for high-level coding tasks.

The project and solution files created in Expression Blend. Expression Blend is interchangeable with Visual Studio, so developers can use the more robust coding and software development tools that they are accustomed to without the need to create a new project or convert files.

XAML: A LANGUAGE EVERYONE CAN SPEAK

One of the core building blocks of Silverlight applications is Xtensible Application Markup Language (XAML), which is a structured, XML-based markup language that is used to build and render the user interface in a Silverlight application.

Simply put, XAML elements, or tags, describe how and where graphics are rendered to the screen; this can include bitmaps, vector graphics, media files, and complex UI controls such as grids, checkboxes, and drop-down lists. XAML also provides structure and hierarchy through a number of layout containers and positioning properties for scalable or fixed interfaces.

For example, a button and ellipse positioned within a container could be represented in XAML, as shown in Figure E.5.

```
<Grid x:Name="LayoutRoot" Background="White">
    <Canvas HorizontalAlignment="Left" Margin="84,119,0,197" Width="234">
        <Ellipse Fill="#FF73F4D0" Stroke="Black" Height="92" Width="92"
        Canvas.Left="18" Canvas.Top="19"/>
        <Button Height="32" Width="76" Canvas.Left="150" Canvas.Top="124" Content="Click Me"/>
    </Canvas>
</Grid>
```

Figure E.5   This XAML markup creates a button and ellipse grouped together within a Canvas container.

This results in the following graphics rendered to the screen (see Figure E.6).

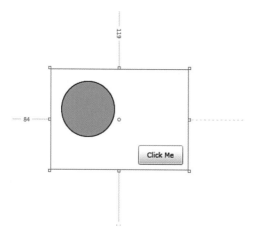

Figure E.6   The resulting graphics rendered to the screen as a result of the XAML code shown in the previous figure.

The relative simplicity and straightforwardness of XAML makes it useful to both designers and developers, and in essence becomes a universal language that both can work with and understand.

EVERYONE CAN WORK TOGETHER

XAML helps to create a symbiotic relationship between the designer and developer, allowing designers and UI developers to construct an application using XAML, and programmers to continue with those same visual elements by adding interactivity, real-time data, and application logic.

See Appendix B, "What Is XAML?" for more detailed information on XAML and examples.

EXTENSIVE MEDIA SUPPORT AND STREAMING

Silverlight 3 has become a choice platform for high-quality video and audio delivery and streaming, with giants such as NBC and NetFlix choosing Silverlight exclusively for its sophisticated streaming capabilities in conjunction with IIS Media Services.

Alongside of the rich tools and graphical capabilities offered on the Silverlight Platform, rich internet applications can integrate streaming or on-demand video that require both high quality and scalability, such as the 2008 and 2010 Olympics which were streamed both live and on demand in the United States using Silverlight technology.

Another example of the integration of the best that Silverlight has to offer is The Webby TV custom video player created by Thirteen23 (www. thirteen23.com) for the 13th Annual Webby Awards. The player combines animation, custom navigation, and rich photo galleries with video streaming and full-screen playback into an out-of-browser, cross-platform experience (see Figure E.7).

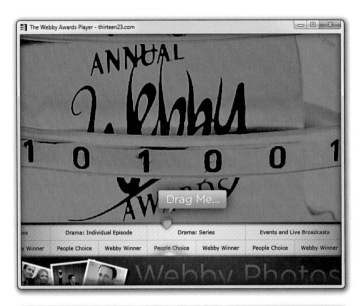

Figure E.7 *The Webby TV Video Player created by Thirteen23 (www.thirteen23. com) especially for the 13th Annual Webby Awards.*

Silverlight 3 offers many extensive video/audio features, including the following:

- Support for WMV, H.264, and AAC audio

- Live and on-request 720p + HD streaming video

- Variable bit rate via smooth streaming, which optimizes the stream rate based on available bandwidth

- GPU hardware acceleration for full-screen, true HD video

- Solid content protection through the Silverlight Digital Rights Management (DRM)

- Extended support for third-party codec's through RAW AV pipeline

F

ADDITIONAL RESOURCES

We hope that *Dynamic Prototyping with SketchFlow in Expression Blend* is the beginning or a continuation of your education on innovation and design and technology.

All good practitioners should have a library that they can reference, and here we make some suggestions on books that we have invested in and have found to be useful. We group them by the following categories:

- Technology
  - Tools
  - Languages

- Design
  - Theory and Inspiration
  - Practice

- Web Links, Training, and Education
  - Tools and Platforms
  - Design and Innovation

TECHNOLOGY

Technology books are always a challenge. Once you write one, they are almost immediately out of date if they are for version-specific tools or languages. Because languages are themselves very technical, it's rare to find books that are accessible for the designer. All the books outlined here will be challenging for designers, but we also think that they are the most accessible and approachable books available.

TOOLS

Many books that focus on Expression Blend are very developer focused and oriented. These books also fall into that realm, but we feel that they are the most accessible and useful.

Foundation Expression Blend with Silverlight by Victor Gaudioso is a great continuation into Expression from dynamic prototyping. In many ways, it's the perfect companion as you leave SketchFlow-based projects and move full-speed into Expression Blend projects. You'll see code and even poke around Visual Studio a bit, but this book is an excellent guide to the more advanced features of Expression Blend. If you are interested in continuing to learn about Expression Blend, this book is the best place to start.

Microsoft Expression Blend Unleashed by Brennon Williams is a more complex dive into Expression Blend. As of this writing, the book focused on Expression Blend 2 concepts, but we feel that Brennon's explanation of concepts and processes make this book worthwhile as a follow-up to Victor's book.

Foundation Silverlight 3 Animation by Jeff Paries focuses exclusively on animation in Silverlight 3 and the capabilities that you would access in both the Expression Blend interface and in code. It's an advanced book and serves as a capable follow-up to Victor's book. It's a deep dive into animation; many of the principles Jeff touches on are very helpful if your goal is to get more advanced with animation in your prototyping work in SketchFlow, as well as to understand the animation models in Expression Blend and how to augment them in code.

LANGUAGES

If you're coming from the world of design and don't have a lot of experience with code or other languages like ActionScript or object-oriented programming, you'll find all of these books to be enlightening but also challenging. You'll be exposing yourself to new cognitive models and ways of thinking. We've listed books here that cover C#, WPF, and Silverlight.

A note about the first four books: They should be considered foundational books for learning and understanding the fundamentals of C# and WPF. For the latest and greatest details on the platform, there will undoubtedly be other books, but what we've tried to do is select books to start with if you are coming to these languages with little experience.

Programming in the Key of C#: A Primer for Aspiring Programmers by Charles Petzold is a beginner's book to C# that was written some time ago. Its writing, style, and fundamental focus make it a great starting point for C#. If you're new to computer programming and C#, start here.

Applications = Code + Markup: A Guide to the Windows Presentation Foundation by Charles Petzold is perhaps the most challenging book on this list, and in developer circles, it's a somewhat controversial tome. However, the style and tone of this book makes it an interesting one for designers. It builds nicely on his earlier book, starting with how WPF applications can be created with C# and then introducing concepts around XAML.

Windows Presentation Foundation Unleashed by Adam Nathan is a nice companion to *Applications = Code + Markup*. In fact, both of these books approach WPF from different but equally valuable directions. If you have some familiarity with coding and are looking for a book with a conventional approach and great content, start here.

Head First C# by Andrew Stellman and Jennifer Green is a part of O'Reilly's visually oriented technology books. It may be a better model for some designers to get introduced to C#. Ensure that you purchase a copy that has been printed on or after September 2008, however—it corrects some errors in examples in the book that appeared in earlier printings.

Pro Silverlight 3 in C# by Matthew MacDonald is an exhaustive book on Silverlight 3. Although the "pro" title can be intimidating, there are excellent overviews in this book from a beginner's perspective as well.

If you have the opportunity, it might be a good idea to visit a local book store and review some of these titles to determine which ones support your learning style best. In our experience, the Head First books are great first titles for understanding a language for many designers.

DESIGN

There's almost an unlimited set of books we could recommend on design. Here are some recommendations to get your design library off to a good start.

THEORY AND INSPIRATION

Theory books give you both a foundation and inspiration into the discipline of design.

Sketching User Experiences by Bill Buxton is in many ways the book that motivated us to write a book about sketching and dynamic prototyping. If you need the ingredients and the narrative for how to influence change in your organization around embracing the power of design, this one is our favorite. If you buy one book from this category, this is the one to start with. Bill also publishes many articles and updates at www.billbuxton.com

The Design of Business by Roger Martin delves deeper into some of the concepts that we explore in Chapter 3, "Patterns and Practices for Innovation," regarding reliability and validity and how they relate to the design process. This is a fantastic companion to Bill Buxton's book and serves as nice business companion to the other design oriented titles. Roger also maintains a great blog and site at ogerlmartin.com/.

Universal Principles of Design by William Lidwell, Kritina Holden, and Jill Butler is a great reference primer of 100 ways to enhance usability, influence perception, increase appeal, and make better design sessions.

Creative Whack Pack and *Innovative Whack Pack* by Roger von Oech are decks of cards that walk you through different exercises and scenarios that allow you to apply creativity and lateral thinking to your projects.

Designing Interactions by Bill Moggridge is sort of a greatest hits of product design and innovation. You can learn a great deal from this book, but mostly this book and its brilliant DVD serve as inspiration for us when we're stuck.

Understanding Comics by Scott McCloud served as a foundation for Chapter 3, and gets to the essence of why sketching is a critical part of the design process that helps us do better work.

The Essential Drucker by Peter F. Drucker is a compilation of some of Mr. Drucker's more popular writings. If you're unfamiliar with Peter Drucker, he is considered one of the top management thinkers of our modern age—in some ways, he was one of the first design thinkers who inhabited the world of business. This book doesn't do justice to his entire body of work, but it does serve as an adequate starting point. There are many business authors we could continue to recommend, but Drucker is the giant with whom all designers should have some familiarity.

PRACTICE

These books all illustrate, capture, and document the professional practice of interactive design, with a focus on innovation in products, services, and interfaces. Some books are overviews and collections of technique and process, and some go into great depth on not just the "why" but also the tactics of execution. Because most of these books are agnostic of technology, they tend to have a longer lifespan than books that focus on technology. We've provided our largest recommendations of books in this section because we feel there's considerable value and knowledge in these books that can enable a better use of the technology and tools covered in *Dynamic Prototyping with SketchFlow in Expression Blend*.

About Face: The Essentials of Interaction Design by Alan Cooper is a bit of a canonical book on interaction design. Its timeless definitions and insights haven't changed and still are relevant today.

Mental Models by Indi Young is a book that covers processes for integrating a user's intent into your design process. As a founder of Adaptive Path and one of the first design leaders outside of academia to capture and collect these processes, Indi's book can serve as a valuable overview for design teams.

Paper Prototyping by Carolyn Snyder offers a deeper dive into physical processes associated with prototyping that serves as a great foundation for working effectively with tools like SketchFlow in Expression Blend.

Grid Systems by Kimberly Elam is a design classic when it comes to teaching foundation principles of design. Much as grids are a foundation of graphics and communication design, this is perhaps even more true of software and application design.

Don't Make Me Think! by Steve Krug is a classic book on guerilla usability testing. Steve provides practical knowledge and insights that can help you validate your designers and determine the types of feedback that you should look for.

Designing for the Digital Age by Kim Goodwin provides the most comprehensive analysis of contemporary thinking around creating products, services, and software in professional practice. If you need to start with one book in your practice library or are making your first addition to your practice library, this is the book to start with.

Designing for Interaction: Creating Smart Applications and Clever Devices by Dan Saffer is a compendium of professional practice for interactive design that provides a good purview of methods available to designers and developers.

Prototyping by Todd Zaki Warfel is a compendium of techniques and technology that enable prototyping. It's a nice companion to *Dynamic Prototyping* because it examines other tools that support the prototyping process as well.

The Back of the Napkin by Dan Roam is an excellent addition and companion to the theories that are presented in *Sketching for User Experience*. It's a great resource for understanding and getting ideas on how to use SketchFlow for the sketching process. Where *Designing for the Digital Age* is exhaustive, Dan tells you exactly what you need to know to get to work right away. This is another critical book we recommend for your library. Dan recently released a follow-up book called *Unfolding the Napkin* that provides in-depth and hands-on instruction across a wide variety of design and business scenarios.

Web Form Design by Luke Wroblewski is a great reference and analysis of how great interaction design works in something that every application possesses—even those that don't appear on the Web, the form. This book is a great introduction that leverages the fundamentals of design and applies them to the complex interactions that we must create, and endure, every day.

Designing Interfaces by Jennifer Tidwell is a book that is similar to Luke's but delves into more detail in topics beyond form design. The book covers application design and a majority of the scenarios that can be encountered in that process.

Designing Gestural Interfaces by Dan Saffer is a compendium of techniques to cover an emerging field known as natural user interfaces. As touch and gestures increasingly become a part of our daily lives, these new principles and techniques will be factors that greatly influence our work.

A Project Guide to UX Design: For User Experience Designers in the Field or in the Making by Russ Unger and Carolyn Chandler is a book of fundamentals for UX design, from practice to tactics. If you're new to the discipline or practice, there are no books that are more thorough or concise.

Communicating Design: Developing Web Site Documentation for Design and Planning by Dan Brown is a compendium of techniques that are useful in the UX process. The book provides an in-depth analysis of the advantages and disadvantages of common techniques used in professional practice.

Rapid Problem Solving with Post-it Notes by David Straker is a timeless book that does a great job of providing guidance on how to use a simple item, the Post-it note, that's in every office and that can help design teams with complex decision making.

WEB LINKS, TRAINING, AND EDUCATION

In this section, we list a number of online resources that we find to be useful.

TOOLS AND PLATFORMS

The Expression Studio Website and Expression Community Site

www.microsoft.com/expression

This site is the official product site for Expression Studio. It is a great jumping-off point for blogs from the engineering product team and an active Expression community that provides a variety of free training. Be sure to also check out the official Expression blog at blogs.msdn.com/expression/.

Silverlight

www.silverlight.net

This is the Silverlight community site, and it contains a wealth of information on how to get started on Silverlight.

Channel 9

channel9.msdn.com/

Channel 9 is somewhat akin to a network or YouTube channel that is all about Microsoft. Often, information and training about new tools and technology will appear here first or at the same time that it shows up on the Expression Studio website.

CodePlex

www.codeplex.org/

CodePlex is an open source collection of resources for Microsoft technology. Many people who create behaviors that can be used in Expression Blend post them here.

MSDN

www.msdn.com/

Microsoft Software Development Network (MSDN) is the definitive resource for all public information published on Microsoft technology. It's a very detailed site and a great resource for going very deep on technology subjects and capabilities; it's also a great launching point for other channels and training.

Scott Guthrie Blog

weblogs.asp.net/scottgu/

If Steve Jobs has an equivalent in the technology world, it may be Scott Guthrie. Scott Guthrie heads up the teams that develop WPF and Silverlight and was the key person behind the creation of .NET. He's an active blogger who still writes all his own tutorials, and his blog is the best place to learn about the details around new announcements with technology.

Electric Beach

electricbeach.org/

Electric Beach is the blog of Christian Schormann, one of the many talented folks responsible for product planning and definition for Expression Blend and SketchFlow. Christian focuses on Expression Tools but also product design and user experience.

Kirupa.com

www.kirupa.com/

Kirupa.com, in their own words, is a site that aims to make designers better developers and vice versa. They accomplish that with wonderful articles on a variety of UX technology. Although the site has many curators, the individual behind the great articles on Expression Blend is Kirupa Chinnathambi, a member of the Expression team.

House of Mirrors

www.blois.us/blog/

House of Mirrors is the blog of a Pete Blois, another member of the Expression team. He explores advanced concepts in many of his posts, but his tutorials are expertly written and teach you how to extend and push Expression Blend. Pete is frequently one of the first to write about new features and provide detailed write-ups on how to take advantage of these features.

Nerd + Art

blog.nerdplusart.com/

Nerd + Art is the blog of Robby Ingebretsen, a former Microsoft employee that worked on WPF. Robby is one of the leaders in helping designers and developers make the most of Expression, Silverlight, and WPF.

Nibbles Tutorials

nibblestutorials.net/

Nibbles Tutorials is a blog that provides advanced Expression tutorials that include all the source projects and detailed steps for each project. It's a great site to learn more about behaviors, simulating 3D, and developing more advanced interactions.

Project Rosetta

channel9.msdn.com/shows/Continuum/ProjectRosetta/

Project Rosetta is a special site designed to help folks that are familiar with Flash transition to the world of Silverlight. If you know Flash, this site is a great jumping-off point.

DESIGN AND INNOVATION

MIX Online 2.0

www.visitmix.com/

MIX Online 2.0 is a Microsoft site dedicated to technology, the design, and the Web. Some of the leading voices in the world of the Web and interaction design are contributors to this site. This site is also a jumping-off point to Microsoft's annual MIX conference, which focuses on design and technology. There are many videotaped sessions available from this site on design topics, Expression, Silverlight, and WPF.

Microsoft Design

www.microsoft.com/design

This site is maintained by Microsoft's UX team, and it's a great resource to learn more about the design processes that take place in Microsoft and around how we apply design principles to our own practice. It also serves as a channel for training on Microsoft tools and technology from time to time with designer-focused training.

UX Array

www.uxarray.com/

UX Array is the official blog of Sara Summers. In addition to writing about SketchFlow, Sara is an active voice and commenter on a wide variety of design topics.

Dynamic Prototyping

www.dynamic-prototyping.com/

This is the support site for this book. In addition to supporting this book with sample work projects, we'll also use the site to post updates to changes in SketchFlow and from time to time make folks aware of special offers that are available to our readers.

Design Thinking Digest

www.designthinkingdigest.com/

Design Thinking Digest is the official blog of Chris Bernard, and it's where he blogs about the intersection of design, technology, and business.

Adaptive Path

www.adaptivepath.com/

Adaptive Path is one of the leading interaction design firms in the world. We are particularly fond of two conferences they hold annually. One is called UX Intensive, and it's the next best thing to going back to design school. The other conference is called UX Week, and it's an annual gathering of some of the best design and technology minds in business.

Institute of Design

www.id.iit.edu/

This is the official site of the Institute of Design, one of the world's leading institutions in teaching advanced design concepts. ID runs a series of annual conferences and workshops that can help you better integrate design processes into your organization.

Interaction Design Association

www.ixda.org

This is the official site of the Interaction Design Association. In addition to having local IxDA chapters all over the world, the site can point you to information about IxDA's annual conference and its excellent mailing list with thousands of active members.

INDEX

Zoom control (SneakerSpot project), 327-330

Bounce Out and Bounciness properties, 343-344

DragAndReturnAction, 341-343

final refinements, 344-345

HideAction, 340-341

ShowAction, 339

Behaviors category (Assets panel), 189

Bernard, Chris, 478

binding data, 160-163, 260-264, 458

BodyCenter-Sketch asset, 90

Bodyright-Sketch asset, 90

Bois, Pete, 477

Bolt, Nate, 52

books

developer tool books, 470

interactive design books, 473-475

language books, 470-471

theory books, 472-473

Border container, 415-416

Border object, 184

Bounce Out property, 343-344

BounceEase function, 232

Bounciness property, 343-344

brainstorming, 43-45

Brooks, Frederick, 50

Brown, Dan, 475

Brush Transform tool, 181

Brushes category (Properties panel), 201

Build Project command (Project menu), 317

Butler, Jill, 472

Button-Sketch asset, 90, 166

buttons, adding states to, 237-243

Buxton, Bill, 1, 472

C

C#

casting, 431

classes, 423, 434-436

code-behind files

constructors, 425-426

namespaces, 424

page class, 425

data types, 430

event handlers, 426-429, 440-441

events, 423-429, 440-441

explained, 419-420

frameworks, 422

inheritance, 423, 441-442

libraries, 422

methods, 423, 429

calling, 432

defining, 432

explained, 431-432, 436-438

overloading, 438

return values, 433-434

objects, 423

NavigateToScreenAction
behavior, 253

navigation

via component screens, 307-310

enabling in projects, 127-133

navigation flow, adding
content to, 83

navigation screens, accessing
through Assets panel, 214

in SketchFlow Player, 96-100,
282-287

NavigationButtonStyles

creating, 367-370

template modifications, 370-373

navigation_component.png
file, 310

navigation_component_v2.png
file, 326

Navigation panel, 283

Navigation Screens category
(Assets panel), 214

Nerd + Art, 477

.NET Compact Framework, 399

.NET framework

applications

desktop applications, 396

mobile applications, 399

*Silverlight RIAs (Rich Internet
Applications), 397-398*

websites/web applications, 397

Common Language Runtime
(CLR), 394-395

development tools, 392-393

explained, 391-392

.NET Compact Framework, 399

and Silverlight, 392

Nibbles Tutorials, 477

notifications (Silverlight), 461

O

Object menu, 208

object-oriented programming
(OOP), 420-422

objects

Border, 184

Canvas, 184

DockPanel, 184

explained, 190-192, 423

Grid, 184

naming, 408-410

objects in Blend, 183

properties, 423, 429-430, 438-439

ScrollViewer, 184

StackPanel, 184

Uniform Grid, 185

ViewBox, 185

WrapPanel, 184

Objects and Timeline panel,
114-118

objects, 190-192

timelines, 193-195, 244-245

Oech, Roger von, 472

offline DRM (Silverlight), 461

FREE Online Edition

Your purchase of **Dynamic Prototyping with SketchFlow in Expression Blend** includes access to a free online edition for 45 days through the Safari Books Online subscription service. Nearly every Que book is available online through Safari Books Online, along with more than 5,000 other technical books and videos from publishers such as Addison-Wesley Professional, Cisco Press, Exam Cram, IBM Press, O'Reilly, Prentice Hall, and Sams.

SAFARI BOOKS ONLINE allows you to search for a specific answer, cut and paste code, download chapters, and stay current with emerging technologies.

Activate your FREE Online Edition at
www.informit.com/safarifree

> **STEP 1:** Enter the coupon code: YNGSSZG.

> **STEP 2:** New Safari users, complete the brief registration form.
> Safari subscribers, just log in.

If you have difficulty registering on Safari or accessing the online edition, please e-mail customer-service@safaribooksonline.com